MW00333313

Praise for *On the Sanctity and Monastic State:*

"His *De la Sainteté* is unquestionably one of the most important works of post-medieval Cistercian writing and occupies a major place in the history of spirituality."
> DAVID N. BELL, medievalist, theologian, professor at the Memorial University of Newfoundland, author of *Everyday Life at La Trappe Under Armand-Jean Rancé, Understanding Rancé, etc.*

"No book within the memory of man has won for itself greater esteem at court, amongst the people, in the upper circles of society. But that would be little, if it had not at the same time produced inestimable fruits of virtue whereof I am myself a witness."
> OLIVIER LEFÈVRE D'ORMESSON: (b.1616-d.1686) French magistrate, friend of Bossuet, Madame de Sévigné, Racine, Boileau, La Fontaine.

"This work, treating of the sanctity and the duties of the monastic life, contains a doctrine accurately derived from Holy Scripture and the tradition of saints. The reading of it will discover to monks the obligations and the perfection of the angelic state to which they have been called. It will prove not less profitable to people in the world by making them understand, from the austerities and the humiliations practiced in the cloister, how great is the corruption in which we live, how deeply the poison has penetrated our hearts, and how violent and incessant must be our efforts against ourselves if we hope not merely to prevent the growth of vicious habits but to pluck them up by the roots."
> JACQUES-BÉNIGNE LIGNEL BOSSUET, disciple of St. Vincent de Paul, theologian, Bishop of Meaux (1681-1704), thought to be one of the greatest orators of all time, "the Eagle of Meaux"

As to the results of its publication Bossuet wrote to de Rancé, "The book has produced all the good effects I had anticipated. It has done great good everywhere. You ought to give thanks to God for giving you so happy an inspiration."

"What is this new work which the Eagle of Meaux has covered under his wings? Its language has all the harmonies of the organ, rich and majestic. One moves through its pages as through a basilica whose rose-windows are ablaze with the shimmering light of the sun. Oh, what a wealth of imagination in a work wherein, from its character, one would least expect to find it! . . . Its first appearance was followed by an interval of profound silence, the silence of astonishment and admiration."

CHATEAUBRIAND, preeminent French literary figure in the early 19th c.

"It used to be said formerly that one should have lived like St. John Climacus so as to be able to compose his divine *Ladder of Perfection*. The same can be said of the author of this book. Five years ago I had the consolation both to hear from his lips and to see put in practice the grand and holy maxims which are contained in his volume, so that what is written in these pages is but the expression of his thoughts and actions. I have read the work attentively. Everything in it, as far as I can judge, is calculated to edify, and full of the Spirit of God. The sentiments are noble and elevated, and on the whole, gives one a sublime conception of the religious life."

ETIENNE LE CAMUS, The Bishop of Grenoble (1681-1707) and Cardinal

Saint Bernard of Clairvaux (1090-1153), the patron, exemplar and rule of Abbé Armand-Jean de Rancé (1626-1700).

BACK TO ASCETICISM: THE TRAPPIST OPTION

A Translation with Introduction and Notes of Armand-Jean de Rancé's *De la sainteté et des devoirs de la vie monastique*

Volume 1

Vincent Ryan, Translator

Lee Gilbert, Editor

"Haec est voluntas Dei, sanctificatio vestra" I Thess 4:3
"This is the will of God, your sanctification."

ARTHUR M. GILBERT AND SON, 2019

De la sainteté et des devoirs de la vie monastique by the Abbé Armand-Jean de Rancé was originally published in Paris by Francois Muguet in 1683. In 1830 it was translated and titled *On the Sanctity and the Duties of the Monastic State* by Abbot Vincent Ryan, founding abbot of Mount Melleray in Cappoquin, Ireland, and published in Dublin by Richard Grace. This derivative edition in two volumes has been re-typeset, re-titled, edited, updated, annotated, and its many citations corrected and amplified. In addition, it has been supplied with 52 illustrations from the public domain together with an Image Index and an Index of Scriptural Citations. For the public domain provenance of images in this volume see page 323.

www.auldsnu.com

12051 SE 31st Place, Ste 15
Milwaukie, Oregon 97222

ISBN 978-0-578-55366-5
Library of Congress Control Number:2019910904

PRINTED IN THE UNITED STATES OF AMERICA

Cover image: *God appearing to Isaac;. 1515–27. Marco Dente.*

Note 18, from *The Cistercians* used by permission of the monks of St. Joseph's Abbey, Spencer, MA; note 37, from *The Modern Catholic Encyclopedia* copyright © Liturgical Press, Collegeville, MN. Used by permission. All rights reserved; note 45, *The Ladder of Divine Ascent* copyright © Holy Transfiguration Monastery, Brookline, MA, used by permission. All rights reserved; note 349, from *The Life of Venerable Anne of Jesus,* copyright © Mediatrix Press, Post Falls, ID. Used by permission; note 352, from *God is Love,* copyright © ICS Publications. Used by permission; note 419, the excerpts from The Sayings Of The Desert Fathers: The Apophthegmata Patrum: The Alphabetic Collection by Benedicta Ward, SLG, trans, CS 59 (Collegeville, MN: Cistercian Publications, 1975). Used by permission of Liturgical Press. All rights reserved.

Contents of Volume I

Introduction

In the mid 17th c. Armand Jean de Rancé, Greek scholar, well-to-do gentleman, doctor of Theology of the Sorbonne and priest, underwent a thorough-going conversion.[1] From being a devotee of both the chase and the salons well into his thirties, he became over the course of remarkably few years the reigning abbot of Our Lady of La Trappe Cistercian Abbey.[2] The story is extraordinary in itself, but also for the consequences that he sent cascading down the years. Without him, the Cistercians of the Strict Observance would have been extinguished long ago, as were the Vallombrosians, the Grandmontines, the Celestines, etc.

From Cistercian life as recovered by him at La Trappe came what might fairly be called the Trappist charism, a way of life or *conversatio* that all the Cistercian abbeys of the Strict Observance that sprang from his reform–all in effect daughter houses of La Trappe–lived for many years. Rancé's goal was to recover Cistercian life as lived at Citeaux, that is, monasticism at its saint-producing epitome.

In endeavoring to return to the charism of the founders of the order, he anticipated the decree on Religious Life of Vatican II by three hundred years. It may fairly be said, too, that he did recover it. One has only to compare the descriptions of life at Citeaux in the 12th c. with accounts given by visitors to La Trappe five centuries later to see that they breathed a similar spirit, that they created both the same sort of saintly monk and

---

[1] For an account of his life see especially *Rancé and the Trappist Legacy* by A.J. Krailsheimer and *Understanding Rancé: The Spirituality of the Abbot of La Trappe in Context* by David N. Bell. A more extensive, popular biography is *The Real De Rancé* by Ailbe Luddy, a monk of Mt. Melleray. The latter was written as a corrective to *The Thundering Abbot* by Henri Bremond, also a popular work but representative of the take on de Rancé by his detractors.

[2] This monastery is located 84 miles southwest of Paris. Founded in 1122, it was erected into an abbey in 1140, and from 1147 has been Cistercian. Edmond Abreact, "La Trappe." *The Catholic Encyclopedia.* Vol. 9. New York: Robert Appleton Company, 1910.

the same sort of Heaven on earth. In other words, de Rancé was successful in what he undertook to do.

Somehow a series of talks he gave to his monks found their way to a publisher and were published in 1683 under the title of *De la sainteté et des devoirs de la vie monastique*. This was a literary and spiritual event at the time, for it found a tremendously receptive readership among the Catholics of France. All but unknown in the English-speaking world, "His *De la Sainteté* is unquestionably one of the most important works of post-medieval Cistercian writing and occupies a major place in the history of spirituality." [3]

Rancé died a holy death in 1700, but his usages and spirituality remained in force at La Trappe–to wonderful effect–throughout most of the 18th c. By 1791, however, the depredations of the French Revolution were taking hold and, "When it became evident that everything had been lost in France, the only organized effort to salvage a viable Cistercian nucleus for the future came from La Trappe." [4] The novice master at La Trappe, Augustin de Lestrange, received permission in 1791 to emigrate with twenty-one monks to Switzerland, to Valsainte, formerly a Carthusian monastery. In 1815, as the political situation began to be more propitious, he sent out foundations of three and four monks here and there.

Concerning these men Fr. Louis Lekai writes in his history of the Cistercians:

> The fact that all were avowed followers of Abbot Rancé, the great reformer of LaTrappe, was of capital importance, bearing heavily on the future history of the order. Before the Revolution, the particular observance of La Trappe was restricted to a few communities; after 1815, the influence of Rancé became the dominant force of Cistercian revival throughout France and beyond, wherever the vigor of expansion had carried the "Trappists," the popular name that in these countries became synonymous with "Cistercians." [5]

From these foundations came all the Trappist monasteries of the present day, every other Cistercian monastery of the Strict Observance

---

[3] David N. Bell, *Understanding Rancé* (Kalamazoo: Cistercian, 2005), 246.

[4] Louis J. Lekai, O. Cist. *The Cistercians: Ideals and Reality* (Kent, Ohio: The Kent State University Press, 1977), 180.

[5] Lekai, *Cistercians*, 181.

having been suppressed. The lineage of every present-day O.C.S.O. monastery in the world traces to La Trappe.

In the early 19th c. French monasticism was driven to English-speaking shores, and in 1830 the Irish abbot, Vincent Ryan, undertook the translation and the publishing of de Rancé's work under the title of *Treatise on the Sanctity and on the Duties of the Monastic State*.[6]

Incredibly then, although every Cistercian Abbey of the Strict Observance in the English speaking world yet enjoys what *cachet* the name Trappist confers as indicating heroic monastic life, de Rancé himself is now *persona non grata* in the order he preserved, and his writings are similarly unwelcome.[7] He seems to be the disgraceful ancestor about whom the less said the better. One only has to tour Cistercian websites to discover how deep is the antipathy both to de Rancé and his spirituality. It is not subtle. It is an hostility that de Rancé scholars have noted. From the history page of one such website:

"Trappist" came into common usage for houses of both monks and nuns perhaps because it trips off the tongue a little easier than "Cistercians of the Strict Observance". Admittedly, the adjective "Trappist" also carries connotations of rigor, unbalanced asceticism, anti-intellectualism, even fanaticism.[8]

From the Q&A page of another:

The form of life known as Trappist represents an overly severe interpretation of Cistercian life with a heavy accent on penance, mortification and

---

[6] In his biography, *Dom Vincent of Mount Melleray*, by Kilian Walsh, O.C.S.O. (Dublin: Gill, 1962), we find a saintly abbot, arch-typically Trappist, from whose faith, penance and persistence sprang Mt. Melleray Abbey in Capoquinn, Ireland. Ironically, my understanding is, though, that the Irish Cistercians have been particularly avid to throw off the Trappist mantle. Nevertheless, though they are in much reduced circumstances, as of October 2017 the guest master of Mt. Melleray could write, "11 monks and growing. The show goes on."

[7] In response to this, a Cistercian abbot previewing this introduction commented, "In my experience Rancé is not a persona ingrata so much as a persona ignorata, but already as a young monk Bell and Krailsheimer both passed through my monastery with their substantial rehabilitation efforts."

[8] https://www.virginiatrappists.org/history/cistercians-order/ accessed July 6, 2018

austerity. Most of the Trappist forms have been replaced since Vatican II by a more genuine interpretation of traditional Cistercian life. [9]

As David N. Bell, medievalist, friend of the Cistercians and de Rancé scholar says, they should know better.[10] Perhaps Bell had in mind this or a similar passage from the life of Saint Bernard by William of St. Thierry:

> "In his own days as a novice . . .he had spared himself nothing, but insisted on mortifying, not only the concupiscence of the flesh (Rom 6:12; 1 John 2:6; Gal. 5:24), as actualized through the bodily senses, but even the very senses through which the actualizing occurred. [11]

Given the current Cistercian insistence on contemplation as the goal of monastic life, the very next sentence of that passage from that first biography of Saint Bernard is very suggestive:

> He thus insisted because, with his own inner senses enlightened by love, he had begun, often and most enjoyably, to experience the sweetness that breathed down to him from above.

It would seem, then, that Saint Bernard, quintessential Cistercian, himself had "a heavy accent on penance, mortification and austerity" as the *sine qua non* of contemplation.

However, most regrettably, the order and its monks have long decided that they are Cistercians now and not Trappists. This identity crisis has been unfolding for a very long time, and by now it is superabundantly clear that the order has utterly abandoned the specifically Trappist notes.[12] Among these are strict enclosure, strict silence, taking the Friday morning discipline, the chapter of faults and libraries largely restricted to Scripture and the Fathers of the Church. To illustrate how mitigated is this last desideratum of de Rancé, at least one monastery of the order boasts,

---

[9] https://newmelleray.org/Q-&-A , accessed July 13, 2018

[10] David N. Bell, "A Holy Familiarity: Prayer and Praying According to Armand Jean de Rancé." *Cistercian Studies Quarterly* 51.3 (2016), 343.

[11] *William of St. Thierry, Geoffrey of Auxerre, et al. Bernard of Clairvaux, Early Biographies* (Carlton, Oregon: Guadalupe, 2012), 20.

[12] "An emphasis on strict discipline and mortification in the areas of fasting, enclosure, silence, and poverty was more observable in Cistercian monasteries until modifications were introduced by the General Chapter of 1969." https://newmelleray.org/Trappist, accessed July 7, 2018.

Our library has about 28,000 books including a couple thousand works of the finest fiction, classical and current, about 75 periodicals and two daily newspapers, three Catholic weekly newspapers. We may go to the local public library for other books, or obtain them through inter-library loan. The community library is like the living room of the Abbey where monks read together in an atmosphere of silence and beauty."[13]

Year by year the logic of mitigation eviscerates the Trappist ethos. Here as in an auto-immune disease, one wonders what could have precipitated this on-going self-annihilation, not only the gradual abandonment of corporate identity and hence existence, but a determined hostility to what one could reasonably call the soul of the order.

In an especially prescient passage, prescient because he taught this before 1965, Merton speaking to novices about the chapter of faults encourages them to accept it as it is with all its imperfections, for the "Lord will bless this attitude much more than the attitude of those who are so eager to change everything that soon they will leave nothing whatever of Cistercian life intact." [14] He notes, moreover, that together with silence the chapter of faults is a characteristically Trappist observance.

With a heavy-hitter such as Merton putting de Rancé in a bad light in *The Waters of Siloe*,[15] however, and Lekai in his history of the Cistercians doing the same, it is no wonder that the order has been in flight from its re-founder. Lekai, for example, writes, "To some extent, the heroic spirit of the first Cistercians had resurged at La Trappe, but for the wonderful vibrancy of Saint Bernard's contemplative spirit, Rancé substituted the gloom of contemporary rigorism."[16] Merton is far more generous, and ends

---

[13] https://newmelleray.org/Trappist, accessed August 17th, 2017.

[14] Thomas Merton, *Monastic Observances* (Patrick F. O'Connell, ed.; Collegeville, Minn: Liturgical, 2010), 239.

[15] Thomas Merton, *The Waters of Siloe* (Garden City, NY: Garden City Books, 1951) , 32-49.

[16] Louis J. Lekai, *The Cistercians: Ideals and Reality* (Kent State University Press, 1977), 151. Of this passage A.J. Krailsheimer writes, "The word 'gloom' and indeed the implications of the clearly pejorative word 'rigors,' here clearly defined as contrary to Bernard, do not command my assent. His [Rancé's] constant and enthusiastic reference to Bernard, his insistence that his monks should look to Clairvaux under the saint as their model, and his exhortation to other monks and nuns of the order to do the same, sufficiently witness to his fidelity to the saint. . . . It is hard to think of any abbot or community in the order by whom Bernard was more honored, studied, and, according to their lights, followed than by Rancé and la Trappe–even after Rancé's death." *Bernardus Magister*, John R. Sommerfeldt, ed. (Kalamazoo, Cistercian, 1992) 555.

his assessment by saying, "So, La Trappe made many saints. It re-established in a clear light the full claims of penance in Christian spirituality. It gave great glory to God. . . . De Rancé left a group of well-established and fervent monasteries that were living the Strict Observance to the highest degree and were the edification of Christian Europe."[17] However, these encomia come after several pages that would have already greatly prejudiced the reader against Trappist spirituality as being too dark, too penitential, too extreme and entirely beside the point in achieving the goal that Merton posits as the end of Cistercian life: becoming a contemplative. This is a view that simply permeates all his writings.

This raises the vital question of when exactly did "becoming a contemplative" became the stated goal of Cistercian life? Was it perhaps at the general Chapter of 1969?[18] This is very germane to the entire situation of the order at the moment, for if one lowers the goal from "pleasing God" or "living a penitential life" or "becoming a saint" to merely "becoming a contemplative," then, of course, this affects the means one takes, the life one leads, the usages adjusted to the goal. If after so many centuries the order has discovered that "becoming a contemplative" is the very quintessence of the Cistercian vocation, then what is standing in the way of sloughing off the chapter of faults, strict enclosure, strong abbatial governance, taking the discipline, strict silence? Why, nothing at all. And this has been done.

However, if this is the policy that is leading to the diminution and ever more likely imminent disappearance of the order through the rejection of a Cistercian charism that was ordered to a higher goal and used more stringent means, then it would seem that Divine Providence, Reality, is indicating that "becoming a contemplative" is an inadequate goal for Cistercian monks. It does seem fair to wonder, does it not, whether in defect of fidelity to the Cistercian charism the blessing of God is off the order.

Lamentably, Merton, Lekai and others in the order rehearse the view that had such wide currency in France in de Rancé's time. A few abbots and authors in particular were in high dudgeon about the putative gloom and doom at La Trappe *until they visited.* One visitor, the Abbot of Tamié, Jean-Antoine de la Forest de Saumon, had been particularly outspoken, but when he came and saw the spirit of the place, the love of every man

---

[17] Merton, *Waters*, 49.

[18] "A sense of the divine transcendence and the Lordship of Christ not only pervades the whole of this Rule (RB) but also permeates our life, totally orientated towards an experience of the Living God." Cistercian General Chapter, Declaration of the General Chapter of 1969 on the Cistercian Life,' quoted in Basil Pennington, *The Cistercians* (Collegeville.: Liturgical, 1992) 129-130.

for Abbe Rancé, and of the monks for each other, the beauty of the liturgy, the good order and fervor obtaining throughout the monastery, he not only changed his mind, but he fell at de Rancé's feet to beg forgiveness.[19] Similarly, the canonical visitor of 1676, Dom Hervé du Tertre, the Abbot of Priéres, came with the intention of putting a stop to de Rancé's excesses. However, the visitation card reads:

> "Despite the great differences of country and condition, we have found them so closely united in the bonds of fraternal charity, so uniform in all things, so consistently zealous in the discharge of their duties, so universally solicitous to maintain regular observance, and enjoying a peace so profound, that during a secret scrutiny which lasted three whole days, we heard not a single world of complaint from inferiors against superiors, or from superiors against inferiors. And not only have we discovered or remarked no discontent, murmuring, disunion, coldness, partiality, aversion or dislike amongst the religious, but not even the least appearance or shadow of such things. For which both they and ourselves ought to render fervent and unceasing thanks to God. [20]

This is the monastery that Lekai paints with "the gloom of contemporary rigors," and the men of which Merton from a distance of 275 years can confidently assert, " The one who fasted the most, took the most disciplines, slept the least, was thought to have the most merit. He was the best monk. And the whole atmosphere of a Trappist monastery was one of athletic activity rather than of contemplative detachment and peace."[21] The abbots of Tamié and Priéres, contemporary witnesses, say nothing of the sort.

There is no doubt about it, on paper de Rancé looks very bad, and can easily be made to look worse, but the fruit of his writings and administration was by many accounts a heaven on earth. The obverse is also true. If de Rancé "left a group of fervent monasteries that were living the Strict Observance to the highest degree and were the edification of Europe," those who dismiss and ignore him are rapidly emptying the

---

[19] Ailbe Luddy, O. Cist., *The Real de Rancé* (Dublin: Talbot, 1931), 183.

[20] Luddy, *Real,* 182.

[21] Merton later qualified his remarks about Rancé and La Trappe in correspondence with Jean Leclercq saying that he felt that his own treatment of him in the Waters of Siloe had "something in it of caricature. It is certainly true that Abbé de Lestrange was much more austere than Rance." Patrick Hart, ed. Survival Or Prophecy?: The Letters of Thomas Merton and Jean Leclercq (NY: Farrar, Straus and Giroux, 2002), 23..

monasteries of the Strict Observance, which while they have not been a scandal, are hardly in their collapse the edification of Christendom.

Now, in discussing just how Cistercian, much less Trappist, is their manner of life in the early 21st century, one does not want to incur guilt by subjecting consecrated persons to sarcasm or irony. They have given up so much in order to follow the Lord and are fulfilling their vows according to their best lights. They are clearly living some sort of monastic life, but it is fair to ask—is it not— just how Cistercian or even Benedictine is this life proving to be? As the logic of mitigation unfolds, it is also fair to ask as well at what point does the order even calling itself Cistercian become a form of stolen valor as calling themselves Trappists already is?

One would have to say that keeping Rancé's *On the Sanctity and Duties of the Monastic State* out of the hands of both monks and prospective monks is the decided policy of the order, at least of the English speaking abbots, for it was last published in English 1830. Moreover, of all his many works in French, until recently it was the only work to be translated into English for the benefit of his anglophone sons in the order or for the many devout Catholics who would likely have been interested in them, as were their French counterparts of the 17th c. It seems a species of *damnatio memoriae*. Although he sought penance and humiliations in his lifetime, Rancé would be surely be justified in wondering now, "If I am a father, where is the honor due me?" (Mal 1:6). Abbots long dead and those now passing from the scene cannot say with Saint Paul, "I handed on to you what I myself received" (1 Cor 11:23), for they clearly did not do so, and moreover were determined not to pass on the Trappist usages that they had received.

With the General Chapter of the order having recently been concluded in Fall of 2017, and with a blog having been temporarily set up to cover it, it was possible to get a glimpse of the order's present concerns and mood. One thing very striking was a comment the designated blogger made about the youthful looks of a nun who presided at one session, youthful although she was born in 1967. In other words, she is all of fifty years old. This certainly gives the impression that the leadership of the order is itself very young and that very likely many of them never would have had a taste of the Trappist usages that formed the abbots and novice masters they encountered on first entering the order, for they were done away with at the General Chapter of 1969. That makes the blogger's comments all the more poignant:

A theme that has come up several times in our work in the aula is a concern for handing on the Cistercian charism to the next generation. We have received such a rich tradition. It has been handed down through the centuries, and we are now its custodians. The decisions we make will affect this passing on of the baton. When we look around, we see a lot of diminishment in our Order. Will there even be a next generation? In a great number of places, vocations aren't exactly booming. [22]

How can they pass on what they themselves have not received? For that matter, what have they received? What, after all, is the "rich tradition" left to them? [23]

In a survey of Cistercian websites one thing comes vividly to the fore. Whereas there is an endlessly repeated mantra of "contemplation" in modern Cistercian writing as the goal of monastic life, for de Rancé, as for Saint Bernard, Saint Stephen Harding and Saint Alberic before him, sanctity above everything else was the goal, sanctity as expressed in a crucified life that was, till very recently, the well-worn monastic path to contemplation here below and to ensuant contemplation of God forever in the Beatific Vision. The goal was to become as Christlike as possible, and particularly with de Rancé to offer one's body as a living sacrifice of praise, to arrive especially at humility by being humbled to the dust–in other words, death to self, body and soul: the spirituality of Saint Bernard of Clairvaux.

Given the number of deaths at La Trappe between 1662 and 1695, it is fair to say that de Rancé had this down to a highly refined, effective system that launched hundreds of men into contemplation of God forever—and quickly, too, for the most part. It is hard to imagine God being displeased. If from the human standpoint this is blameworthy, it should be noted that a good bit of the blame should be laid at the feet of natural circumstances rather than Trappist spirituality.

For one thing, many of the men arriving at La Trappe were already middle-aged or beyond. Secondly, hundreds of years earlier, in 1122, the monastery itself had in all likelihood been deliberately located in its very

---

[22] http://cgen-ocso.blogspot.it/2017/09/day-14-of-general-chapter.html

[23] This General Chapter also formally suppressed Holy Trinity Monastery in Utah, founded in 1947 from Gethsemane Abbey. *The Salt Lake Tribune* of August 26, 2017 reports, " By the end of this month, the last of the monastery's eight monks will have left for their new home at St. Joseph Villa Catholic nursing home in Salt Lake City." The website for the monastery says only, "On August 27th, 2017, the final Mass was celebrated at Holy Trinity Monastery."

damp, unhealthy location, so propitious for pulmonary infections and meditation on death. [24] Thirdly, not only was little known of nutrition, but Rancé and his monks were sacrificing their own sustenance and well-being to satisfy the hunger of the many poor who came begging at their gates.

So death, a welcome guest at La Trappe, visited often indeed. As repugnant as this may be to modern sensibilities, it is vain to raise against it the accusation that such a spirituality violates the Divine prohibition of suicide. This Thomas Merton implicitly does in *The Waters of Siloe* when he refers to the monks of La Trappe as a "suicide squad," a phrase that undoubtedly went a long way toward sabotaging the Trappist tradition and rendering the wisdom of Rancé unwelcome in his own order.[25]

In our time, and probably in every time, there is a well-entrenched myth to the effect that we should not overdo penitential practices for fear of injuring our health—that this would be against the Fifth Commandment. Lambertini [Benedict XIV] demurs and cites many authorities:

> The...question is, whether, without any intention of shortening his life or hastening his death, a man may lawfully embrace a hard manner of living for a supernatural end, namely, that he may restrain concupiscence and serve God, and this although he foresees that it will, as a matter of fact, accelerate his death. And to this the true answer is given by theologians, that he may not only do so lawfully, but meritoriously. So, Azores, De Lugo, Filliucci, Theophilus Raynaud, and the author of the Theologia Claustralis, who cites examples of saints and religious orders approved by the Holy See [For these sources Lambertini supplies abundant citations]. To these may be added what we find in the Life of Saint Hilary, Bishop of Arles, that by abstinence from food, by hard work, and long journeys on foot, he had so reduced, exhausted, and worn out his frame, that he scarcely fulfilled his forty-eighth year.[26]

---

[24] De Rancé writes, "Bernard tells us that monks formerly built their monasteries in unwholesome places, in order that being frequently sick, they might be induced to meditate continually on death." Cf. PL 182:706B (1854): "Sancti enim patres, majores nostri, valles humidas et declives monasteriis exstruendis indagabant, ut saepe infirmi monachi, et mortem ante oculos habentes, securi non viverent'"

[25] Merton, *Siloe*, 47.

[26] Prospero Lambertini, *Heroic Virtue: A Portion of the Treatise of Benedict XIV on the Beatification and Canonization of the Servants of God* (London: Richardson, 1850; repr: Miami: Hardpress), 1:366.

Saint Hilary, then, is held to be an example of heroic virtue not in spite of this self-imposed holocaust, but because of it. Of course, if one were to do the same thing with the intention of ending his life more quickly, that would be suicidal and in violation of the Fifth Commandment.

However, given that self-preservation is the first instinct (both of one's body and one's *amour-propre*), it is not surprising that the order has repeatedly, resolutely and effectively imposed silence on de Rancé, and in the most scholarly and reasonable terms. For that matter, one could say too that in rejecting de Rancé they have placed him in heavenly company, for they have also rejected Saint Bernard as penitent all the while–in an incredibly successful rhetorical sleight of hand–exalting him as a contemplative. One would have thought that Saint Bernard would be in his penitence as well as in his prayer life the heroic exemplar of every Cistercian as he was for Rancé. In his excellent *Understanding Rancé*, David Bell summarizes the section on penance from the one sermon we have on Saint Bernard from the founder of La Trappe:

> His mortification of the spirit was matched by his mortification of the flesh. Witness the joy he found in afflicting his body. Witness his vigils and fasts and abstinence. The ruin of his own health was of no consequence, and he treated his ailments not with medicinal care but with rustic brutality. And if he was ill and recovered? He simply returned to his austerities and mortifications. Indeed, if God had preserved his life, it was only that he might offer it back to God as a living sacrifice. Rancé calls him a martyr, a victim of penitence who ate his bread in the water of his tears. He lived only to crucify his body, to walk in hard ways, and 'the penitence of this incomparable man condemns our own laxity and laziness and covers us with confusion.'[27]

Were it not so tragic, it would be amusing that the Abbot General (and presumably the whole order with him) is concerned about the waning vigor of the order.[28] There has been a dramatic fall off in numbers that promises to be much more dramatic in short order.[29] It is not first of all,

---

[27] Bell, *Understanding*, 135.

[28] Eamon Fitzgerald, "The Waning Vigor of the Order," *American Benedictine Review.* Sep 2016, Vol. 67 Issue 3, 236-245.

[29] Referring to the Cistercian monastery from which he was dismissed on the eve of first vows, a former Trappist writes, "Those years back it was on the verge of being a nursing home. It is now not far from being a half inhabited hospice, albeit with a maze

though, a waning of personnel, but looks to be rather a waning of fidelity to the Cistercian charism, and a consequent waning of Divine interest in the perpetuation of the order. If it will not bring forth fruit, why should it clutter up the ground (Luke 13:7)?

The chapter of faults, the taking of the discipline and other Trappist distinctives were suppressed in the early seventies as something utterly foreign to the spirituality of our times.[30] However bringing the monastic ethos into line with our times necessarily dooms monasticism. Strict enclosure also is a thing of the past. One can go home to bury his father, but that being the case, what is standing in the way of a Cistercian priest flying across country to officiate at the wedding of a niece? These things having been done, it would be absurd not to allow a monk to pop down to the public library. And on and on. The logic of mitigation continues to unfold.

Meanwhile, almost incredibly, the Abbot General wonders what can be done to stem the waning vigor of the order. To at least one layman who had a ringside seat on this spectacle, scholar of Cistercian history A.J. Krailsheimer, the answer seemed obvious enough: de-mitigate. In his *Rancé and the Trappist Legacy,* A.J. Krailsheimer pointedly quotes the author of *De la sainteté et des devoirs de la vie monastique*: "The number of Monks has never increased more than through the greatness of their austerity . . . The Spirit of Christ calls people to strict congregations, the spirit of man to lax ones."[31] Under that view, abandoning the designedly radical, self-sacrificial Trappist charism necessarily involves the implosion of the order, and so it is proving to be.

This also was the view of Julien Paris, abbot of Foucarmont, whose book, *Du Premier Esprit De L'ordre De Citeaux,* had a profound influence on de Rancé. Bell writes, "Paris's logic is . . . inexorable: if the decline of the order was due to a failure to keep the rule in its entirety, the Order may accordingly be restored and re-formed by re-establishing *'l'entière Observance de la Règle de S. Benoit.'*"[32]

---

and a garden and a gift shop and a retreat house . . .lay staff and volunteers abound. Where are the monks? Where is the new blood? Nowhere to be found. Why?"

[30] Merton could see this coming in the late fifties, for in his instructions to novices he describes the chapter of faults as characteristic of the order and urges his charges not to change it or get rid of it. cf. Thomas Merton, *Monastic Observances,* (Patrick F. O'Connell, ed; Collegeville: Liturgical, 2010) 238.

[31] Alban J. Krailsheimer, *Rancé and the Trappist Legacy* (Cistercian: Kalamazoo, 1985), 101.

[32] Bell, *Understanding,* 130.

Now, however, one wonders at what point Cistercian life becomes so attenuated that each of the order's monasteries may more justly be called Saint Benedict's Home for Devout Catholic Gentlemen. It is coming to that when New Melleray offers the possibility of five and half hours of lectio per day and in such a library as that. [33] As the numbers dwindle it is useless to recall the other times in the history of that monastery and others when it seemed that the flame was about to go out, but then at the last moment sufficient new candidates appeared.

That dynamic is certainly common in the history of the order and was true of Citeaux, for that matter. Saint Stephen Harding was apprehensive about the future of that abbey–the eventual fountainhead of the order– when Saint Bernard and his thirty companions showed up at the door, but Saint Stephen and his monks were living an ardently self-sacrificial life that brought down unusual graces, graces that a severely mitigated conversatio likely does not warrant. If the Cistercians of today were living the charism of their Trappist forbears, they could expect replenishment, but now . . .? It seems unlikely. If things continue to follow this course– the course of mitigation–nothing would be less surprising than that the Department of Corrections of the State of Iowa buys New Melleray for a minimum security prison within the next thirty years.

Reading through the English version of De La Sainteté it seems–does it not–that Rancé richly deserves to be a doctor of the Church. His argument is ineluctable. After all, he grounds it with hundreds of citations, more than half of them Scriptural, and the balance from the Fathers and Doctors of the Church. The rapid implosion of the order after dismissing him and his argument seems like nothing so much as corollary support for him and for it.

There is, moreover, the present-day internal witness offered by Cistercians themselves, if not by the Holy Spirit speaking through them. In February of 2017 the abbot of one monastery summarized reports that had been given to him on formal conversations that took place within the abbey:

"Some expressed disappointment in the loss of the lay brother vocation. Some expressed disappointment with what looks like a loss of the ascetical

---

[33] "Our monastic cells are rooms where we may pray, read, study, and sleep in solitude. We have about five and a half hours a day to spend in personal prayer and reading which may be done alone in one's cell, or in the Church, or in the library, or outside when weather permits. Part of this time may also be used for physical exercise." https://newmelleray.org/Q-&-A, accessed July 13, 2018.

character of the Order. Some were disappointed in the loss of common work, common lectio, and other features that in an earlier era bolstered the common life; some disagreed with a more participatory style of leadership in the Order."

Here do we not see longing expressed by men with a Cistercian charism for a return to Cistercian life? It is a life they aspired to, were implicitly promised, but which they have been denied by their superiors. Are they then obliged by the vow of obedience to keep pace with the mitigation? Neither Saint Bernard nor de Rancé think so. Rancé discusses this in Chapter VIII, Question 9, citing Saint Bernard.

Saint Bernard addresses this in *De Praecepto et Dispensatione Liber,* a work that while it did find its way into English in 1970 has rapidly achieved rare book status, being out of print and unavailable, presumably because in it we find a somewhat juridical Bernard out of sync with his much preferred contemplative self. Could it be that the preservation of the Cistercian order depends on bringing the contemplative Bernard, the penitential Bernard, and the juridical Bernard into focus as one man, the archetypical Cistercian, with a word in season for every excess and defect of the order?

This work of spiritual re-integration de Rancé attempted and largely achieved both in *De La Sainteté* and in his administration of La Trappe. Can his daughter houses and spiritual heirs continue to dismiss him and to jettison their own patrimony without enormous loss to themselves and to the Church: the utter loss of Cistercian life? It seems unlikely.

The consequences both for the Church and Western Civilization, for that matter, can hardly be overstated. It is scarcely a subject of inquiry in which statistical analysis will yield wisdom, but one would have to be entirely innocent of history not to notice that the Age of Faith's emergence in Europe is coterminous with the incredible spread of the Cistercian reform, and later monastic decadence with the dimming of faith, scandal-causing clerical debauchery, the Reformation and all its consequences, not excluding World War I and II, the utter secularization of the West and the current apostasy.

Of course, laying all this at the feet of monastic infidelity to the sanctity and duties of the monastic state leaves the Black Death, the rapacity of kings, the commendam system and much else besides unreasonably guiltless. Nevertheless, Our Lady at Fatima and elsewhere has called for prayer and penance to bring down graces on our time, graces without which many persons will suffer eternal perdition. It is dangerous, then, to speak–as the New Melleray website dismissively does–of "severity for its own sake." As Saint Thomas Aquinas notes, God is not interested in pain, but in justice, in penance that offsets sin.[34] If the world were not saturated in judgment-inviting sin, then it would be reasonable to speak of "severity for its own sake." If there were nothing for which to do penance, then, yes, it would be most reasonable systematically to lay it aside.

Yet, since this is not the case, who better to set the pace for the Church, to show forth the fruits of a self-sacrificial life than the orders historically penitential, and especially the Cistercians? From the re-appearance of Trappists and the Cistercian charism, both the Church and the world would have a great deal to gain. Not by reading excellent fiction in a well-stocked library did Saint Bernard, archetypal Cistercian, bring down the grace to found 160 monasteries[35] and to light up European civilization, but by a life of extreme penance, self-abnegation and, yes, prayer and contemplation. Yet, given the hedonistic trends in the world and the momentum of mitigation in the cloister, one would be justified in wondering whether a return to the Cistercian interpretation of the Rule of Saint Benedict, the interpretation of Citeaux and Saint Bernard, is remotely possible. Of course, if we collect the data and plot the trends, if we are "realistic," the answer is clearly negative; but Catholics and Christians subscribe to Biblical realism, whose principal tenet is the Resurrection of the Dead.

Given this perspective, it is actually heartening, is it not, that we find ourselves in a situation somewhat analogous to that of the monastic world in which the founders of Citeaux and Saint Bernard found themselves in the 10th century, and Armand-Jean de Rancé in the 16th. In both eras these founders looked upon the monastic surround and found it wanting in its fervor, usages and fruit. In both instances the remedy they took was to intensify the rule of Saint Benedict with the wisdom of the Desert Fathers. Especially is this the manifest case with de Rancé with his heavy reliance on the works and wisdom of Saint John Climacus, Saint Basil and Saint John Cassian.

In contemporary Cistercian thought this has been specifically adduced as a reason for abandoning Trappist usage and returning to the putative "spirit of Citeaux." The fact is, however, that the founder of Citeaux explicitly relied on the tutelage of the desert fathers, as did Saint Benedict

---

[34] Aquinas, ST Supplement, Q. 15, Art. 1, ad. 1.

[35] "He founded one hundred and sixty-three monasteries in different parts of Europe; at his death they numbered three hundred and forty-three." Gildas, Marie. "St. Bernard of Clairvaux." *The Catholic Encyclopedia.* Vol. 2. (New York: Appleton 1907).

himself, who in the beginning of his rule sets out, not to create a school of contemplation, but a school of the Lord's service, and who ends by pointing to the early fathers and specifically the rule of Saint Basil for additional schooling in virtue. Before founding Citeaux, Saint Robert of Molesme exhorted his monks, *"Legite gesta sanctorum, Antonii, Macarii, Pacomii"* Read the deeds of the saints, Anthony, Macarius, Pacomius. [36] In his time de Rancé set before his monks the wisdom of the desert, of Saint Benedict, of Saint Bernard: the wisdom of the founders of monasticism and of its specific Cistercian iteration. Here for the first time since 1830 is that wisdom in English translation, living waters sprung from the saintly abbot of la Trappe, the only possible font for the re-flourishing of the Trappists and the simultaneous re-appearance of Cistercians, the penitential monks of Citeaux.

*   *   *   *

Of course, the attenuation of devout life has set in not only among the Cistercians, but also among the Benedictines, and for that matter across the entire Catholic world, at least in the West. [37] Did we not in the same period that the Cistercians were throwing off their Trappist usages also throw off those demanding Lenten disciplines of fast and abstinence, strict abstinence on Fridays, the family rosary, and many devotions? De Rancé surely points the way now, as he did in France of 1683, to conversion of life for religious and lay alike. Certainly all that he says is addressed to monks, but laymen can take heart from learning that anyone ever lived so devoutly, but more importantly *how* they so lived.

We cannot all retire to monasteries, of course, but a digital fast and an entertainment/ distraction fast inspired by such retirement is very much needed by many of us. We in the world can hardly meditate on death all the

---

[36] Quoted by Ordericus Vitalis in his *Historia Ecclesiastica*, PL 188:637A.

[37] What could more clearly indicate that the Benedictine monasteries of today follow a mitigated Rule of St. Benedict– a rule whose celebrated virtue already was that it moderated the monasticism found in the rules of St. Basil, St. Columban et al–than this avowal by the abbot primate in 1995? : "RB is still used today in many monasteries and convents around the world. The monastics of today do not follow it literally but still find in it much wisdom to live the common life. It still protects the individual and the community from arbitrariness on the part of the abbot or others; it still provides a way of living the Christian life. Monastic communities accept it as their basic inspiration even as they mitigate it, supplement it, or adapt it to the living conditions of today." +Abbot Primate Jerome Theisen, O.S.B, S.T.D in *The Modern Catholic Encyclopedia,*(Collegeville:Liturgical,1995),78-79. Online: http://www.osb.org/gen/rule.html.

day long, but now and then when we pick up de Rancé, it is a worthwhile exercise. If we do not weep for our sins, as they do–or should–we can, as de Rancé suggests, weep that we do not weep. If we have mitigated our observance of the commandments and of our religious practices, here is someone to call us back forcefully to a safer path. If we cannot all be Trappists, we can at least be fervent Catholics and conduct ourselves in a far less worldly way than we commonly do. To that end Rancé is an enormous help, a refreshing and bracing breeze from another age.

*   *   *   *

When first published in 1683, Abbe Armand-Jean de Rancé's *Le traité de la sainteté et des devoirs de la vie monastique* drew a great deal of notice both in the monastic world and among the French public. The only English version, *A Treatise on The Sanctity and the Duties of the Monastic State,* was published in 1830 never to be re-issued until now, 189 years later.

The translation is evidently by Abbot Vincent Ryan, the saintly founder of Mt. Melleray Abbey near Cappoquin in Ireland. In Ailbe Luddy's history of this abbey[38]–more than half of which is the biography of Abbot Ryan–he notes, "He translated into English a number of ascetical treatises, mostly the works of the illustrious John de Rancé . . ." Luddy mentions, too, that Abbot Vincent spoke French with the fluency of a native. David Bell also observed that the translation is almost certainly by Abbot Ryan.[39]

In re-issuing the English version we faced a basic editorial choice, whether to re-present the book as a cultural artifact of 1830, or to relaunch de Rancé's argument. We have chosen the latter path, but that necessitated bringing the grammar, punctuation, usage and spelling up to date.

Since de Rancé was careful to place his argument in the context of the entire monastic tradition and to show that he was doing so by citing his sources abundantly, it seemed incumbent to follow his lead by thoroughly sourcing the same passages. This we have done, but we hope to so more thoroughly in a scholarly, hardcover version of this book, suitable for monastic and scholarly libraries, for one thing because very many of these references are in Latin. Also, Abbot Ryan's preface, more germane to his era, will be included in that version However, we have embedded all his plentiful scriptural references in the text of this volume. While Abbot Ryan

---

[38] Ailbe Luddy, *The Story of Mount Melleray* (Dublin: Gill, 1946).

[39] Bell, *Understanding*, 232.

gave the Latin Vulgate translation of every Scripture verse cited, we have simply retained the reference.

Both in Rancé's original and in Ryan's translation, the citations are often cryptic or incorrect. In readying this re-issue for publication it became evident early on that both Rancé and Ryan were working on the fly and very likely by candlelight. For example, Psalm 39 was cited as Psalm 93, and there were hundreds of such errors. Whereas as they were brief to the point of being cryptic, with the citations I have endeavored to be explicit, and in the eventual hardcover version of this work could reasonably be accused of being prolix. Here, however, I have made an effort—albeit often unsuccessful—to keep the footnotes to one line and the Latin to a minimum. There are several citations I was not able to decipher and have left them in their cryptic (to me) form.

Rancé cites many works that are no longer readily available except as they have been subsumed into the *Patrologia Latina* or *Patrologia Graeca,* and there they are found in Latin. When I cite them, PL stands for *Patrologia Latina*. In the citation "PL 32:894", for example, 32 is the volume number and 894 is the *column* number. As I write this in 2019, the entire *Patrologia Latina* and *Patrologia Graeca* are available online, incredibly, as are several other works Rancé cites.

Since relatively few people have Latin, my original intention was to find an English translation of every passage cited by Rancé/Ryan, but realized eventually that this would involve great delay in publication. However, I did find many English translations and most of these are cited in this form: NPNF1 or NPNF2 which stands for *A Select Library of Nicene and Post-Nicene Fathers of the Christian Church.* Edited by Philip Schaff and Henry Wace, these represent twenty eight volumes in two series of fourteen volumes each. These, too, are presently available online.

Some months into preparing these volumes for re-issue, I discovered that David N. Bell has been working on an original English translation of *De la sainteté et des devoirs de la vie monastique* since 2005. He indicates that it will be more complete and more accurate than Ryan's. In fact, concerning Ryan's translation Dr. Bell writes,

> The book admirably succeeds in conveying the spirit of Rance's work, but as a translation it is seriously flawed. The translator had no hesitation in adding words and phrases (occasionally whole sentences) omitting words

or sentences, and re-phrasing or paraphrasing the actual text, and sometimes his translation is just plain wrong.[40]

Perhaps, then, it would have been more accurate to list Vincent Ryan as a co-author rather than merely a translator, but if we have here what amounts to a joint work by two saintly Cistercian abbots, that seems gain rather than loss.

With such a scholarly edition about to appear I felt all the freer to bolster Rancé's argument in footnotes with texts that he did not or could not have had to hand, together with occasional comment. While Bell's translation will be of perennial value, there is yet room for a version addressed to the people and issues of our time. Such notes and comments are relatively few.

In addition, the two volumes contain a total of some ninety-six illustrations supportive or evocative of the de Rancé/Ryan ethos, none of which were in the original nor in Ryan's translation. The Cistercian ethos and usage has no place for images, but this version is not primarily addressed to monks, but to the faithful generally, hence the abundant illustration.

For the Scripture he renders in English, Abbot Ryan used the Douay-Rhiems version. In that version, the book known as Sirach in modern translations is titled Ecclesiasticus and cited as "Ecclesiastic." Also, in the Douay-Rhiems version instead of 1 and 2 Samuel and 1 and 2 Kings, as in modern versions, there are four books of Kings, with 1 Samuel being 1 Kings. Where he has not followed the DR, we simply give the Scripture as Abbot Ryan rendered it.

Lee M. Gilbert

---

[40] Bell, *Understanding*, 232

The Dedicatory Prayer

TO THE MOST GLORIOUS AND EVER BLESSED VIRGIN MARY, MOTHER OF GOD, AND CHIEF PATRONESS OF THE CISTERCIAN ORDER

It was under your protection, O most glorious Virgin, Mother of God! That I undertook this translation; and I felt confident that you would not fail to obtain for me the necessary assistance for accomplishing it. The truths it contains, the perfection to which it exhorts, are those sublime principles on which the holy state of religion stands, wherein the sacred counsels of thy adorable Son are exemplified, and made the standing rule of thy devoted children.

Animated with that confidence which impelled me in the beginning, encouraged me in the progress, and finally supported me in the conclusion of the work, I now present it to you, O Queen of heaven, and our glorious advocate, most humbly beseeching your maternal goodness, to accept the offering, and the desires of the offered; to diffuse your powerful influence through its pages, and bless the endeavours of your unworthy servant.

Obtain for those who shall read it, or hear it read, the gift of understanding,–the light of the Holy Ghost, that precious grace, which, giving a convincing force to the words, shall at the same time inflame and strengthen the will in practicing what they inculcate.

And as the glory of God, your honour, my own and my brethren's salvation, were the ends I proposed in this undertaking, may we so attend to its lessons, as to finally succeed in producing the blessed fruits of sanctity and perfection which it inculcates, and in laying up treasures, which will endure for eternity.

—Vincent Ryan, O.C.S.O.

BACK TO ASCETICISM:
THE TRAPPIST OPTION

1| THE OBLIGATIONS OF RELIGIOUS LIFE IN GENERAL—CONTENTS:

1

THE OBLIGATIONS OF RELIGIOUS LIFE IN GENERAL

Question 1. —What is a true religious man?
Answer. —He is a man who, having renounced the world and all visible and perishable things by a solemn vow, lives only for God, and is occupied only in such things as are eternal.

Q. 2.—What do you understand by these words, having renounced the world by a solemn vow?

A. —I understand that a true religious has renounced the world, together with all its affairs, occupations, goods, honors and pleasures, by a public protestation, authorized by the Church, and that he has made the use of them unlawful to himself by the engagement he has contracted with God, who alone should henceforth become the object of his thoughts, of all his affections, and of all his desires, in such a manner, that he cannot use even such things as nature indispensably requires, but in reference to God, and with the intention of pleasing Him.

Q. 3.—In what, therefore, does the obligation of a religious differ from that of a Christian, who hath also renounced the world by his baptismal vows?

A.—It is true that a Christian has been buried with Jesus Christ by baptism, and has received a new life by this sacrament, the principal and soul of which new life is the spirit of the same Jesus Christ. It is true, I say, that such a person ought to be dead to the world, to its goods, to its honors, to its affairs, and to its pleasures; and in order to satisfy this duty, it suffices that he renounce them in the dispositions of his heart. Though he may lawfully keep possession of and use them, yet he ought to be so disengaged from them in his interior dispositions that he may be poor in affluence, chaste in marriage, temperate in good living, and united to God in the communications which he must necessarily have with men.

But all this is too little for a religious. He should not confine himself to these general obligations. He must live in an actual disengagement from all things. And as eternity is his only inheritance, so it should be the only object of all the actions of his mind, and of all the motions of his heart. The counsels which Jesus Christ gives men in general, by his vocation are become indispensable precepts to him. Therefore, if his disengagement be not entire, his abnegations true and effective, and if these sentiments do not flow from his heart into his actions, and influence them, he fails essentially in the discharge of the duties of his state.

This is a truth that can be contested by those only who are unacquainted with the essence of the monastic state, who have never penetrated its substance, or who have not read what the Holy Fathers have taught us concerning it. As vessels which are destined for the divine service cannot be employed in any other use without profanation, so should the religious soul who by his special consecration is become the temple of the Holy Spirit, and the sanctuary of the divinity- (1 Cor 6:19) keep himself continually in the divine presence; nor can he withdraw himself from that divine object willingly to occupy himself with visible and perishable things without committing a sort of sacrilege.[41]

Saint Basil says:

> The purity and sanctity which is so essential to the religious life consists in attaching ourselves to God in all things, and in inviolably uniting our-selves to Him at all times, as the author of all sanctity, which is done by having an ardent zeal and fervent desire to do everything that may be pleasing to Him; and we see that such things as are presented in the tem-ple of the Lord to be consecrated to Him are rejected as unworthy of Him when they are defiled with the least stain; and it is equally certain, that to employ anything once given to God, in profane use, is an insupportable impiety and presumption.[42]

Q. 4. —On what is this great disengagement founded, which you require in religious persons?

A. —The consecration to God by vow, is, to speak properly, the immolation of an holocaust, which permits neither restriction nor reserve.

---

[41] John Cassian, *Conferences* 23.3.8 (NPNF2/11:524)

[42] S. Basilius, *Regulae Brevius Tractatae*, Interrogatio LIII, PG 31:1118c (1857).

The saints were not afraid of speaking too strongly when they taught us that a religious who lost the presence of God willfully for a moment committed a spiritual fornication.[43] Though the Fathers have differently spoken on this subject, yet they all agree in the same thought, and when they called the monastic state the life of immaterial substances,[44] a continual meditation of the judgments of God,[45] a crucifixion, [46]a state of apostolical perfection, [47]an angelical conversation,[48] they desired to inculcate nothing more than that a religious person should be insensible to all human affections and live separated from all things mortal; that his conversation should be all in heaven, and that the monastic state being raised above nature, as Saint Basil remarks, elevates man to the purity of angels.[49]

Q. 5.— *Are we not therefore to conclude, that the religious who do not preserve the purity of their state, are very far from serving God in a manner agreeable to Him?*

A. —Such religious persons who do not live according to the purity of their state fall thereby not only into a soft, effeminate, and relaxed mode of conduct quite opposite to the sanctity of their profession, and consequently do not serve God in a manner agreeable to Him, but moreover, as they have forsaken the way in which He would have them to walk, and as they no longer co-operate with Him in His designs, they produce no other effect than to diffuse the poison of scandal throughout

---

[43] Editor's note: With this the Prior General of the Carthusians, Dom Innocent Le Masson, disagreed strongly, saying, "This is not true and not practicable . . . . There is no saint who has not lost God from his mind for a single moment, save perhaps the Blessed Virgin. And to describe this single moment's lack of attention as spiritual fornication is to exaggerate greatly." Quoted in Henri Bremond, *The Thundering Abbot* (London, Sheed, 1930), 237.

[44] Rancé only cites "S. Greg."

[45] "Monasticism is an angelic order and state achieved in an earthly and soiled body. A monk is one who holds only to the commands of God in every time and place and matter. A monk is one who constantly constrains his nature and unceasingly watches over his senses. A monk is he who keeps his body in chastity, his mouth pure, and his mind illumined. A monk is a mourning soul that both asleep and awake is unceasingly occupied with the remembrance of death." St. John Climacus, *The Ladder of Divine Ascent* (Boston: Transfiguration, 2012), 54.4.

[46] John Cassian, *The Institutes* 1.4 (NPBF2 11:203)

[47] St. Bernard, *Monastic Sermons* (trans. Daniel Griggs; Collegeville: Liturgical, 2016), 153.

[48] Serapion Episcopus, *Epistola ad Monachos*, PG 40:931 (1858).

[49] St. Basil *Serm. de Inst Mon.*

the Church, obscure the splendor of her glory by their bad example, and give occasion to her enemies to blaspheme the holy name of God, and thus provoke our Lord Jesus Christ to reproach them as Saint Paul did the Jews on a former occasion: — By you the name of God is blasphemed among the Gentiles (Rom 2:24).

2 | THE MONASTIC STATE—CONTENTS:

2

OF THE INSTITUTION OF THE MONASTIC STATE

QUESTION 1. — *Were men the Founders and Institutors of the monastic state?*

Answer.— No: it was Jesus Christ Himself who founded it; and those who were raised by Him to establish it in the world, at the different periods which were marked out by His eternal foreknowledge, were only the ministers of His orders, and the executors of His holy will.

Q. 2. — *From what passage of the Gospel does it appear that Jesus Christ instituted the monastic state?*

A. — It may be seen in Saint Luke, where our Lord says: Sell what thou hast, give it to the poor, and thou shalt have a treasure in heaven, and then come and follow me (Luke 18:22). Again He says in another place: If any man comes to me and hates not his father and mother, his wife and children, his brothers and sister, yea, even his own life also, he cannot be my disciple (Luke 14:26). The same thing may be seen in Saint Matthew: "Whosoever leaves house or land, father or mother, sister or brother, wife or children, for my sake shall receive a hundred fold, and hereafter life eternal" (Matt 19:29).

Hence we may easily infer that our Lord Jesus formed the design of instituting a holy state in His Church, in which men might serve Him in an entire separation from all worldly things, in an invariable application to His divine majesty, and in a literal observance of all His counsels. This, in effect, has been exactly accomplished in the monastic state—while its vigor was nourished, its purity preserved unsullied, and while the constancy and fidelity of those who professed it was unconquered by the envy, malice, and violence of the devil.

Q. 3. — *The rules of religious institutions are not, therefore, to be considered as human inventions?*

A. — They are not, but, on the contrary, as laws written by the finger of God; and this was evidently demonstrated when Saint Pachomius received—by the ministry of an angel—the rule which he established for the government of his brethren. Moreover, this has been done invisibly as many times as it has pleased God to institute religious orders by the ministry of His saints.

Q. 4. —*Who were they who first embraced the religious state?*

A. — Some think that Elias, Eliseus, and the Rechabites were the first who professed it. However, it is more probable that they were only the figures of it, and that God, who was pleased to give continual marks in the Old Testament of the considerable events which were to take place in the New, raised up these incomparable men—of whom the world was not worthy—to prefigure that multitude of holy solitaries, who would be, in after times, the glory, the strength, and the sanctification of His Church. Such was the opinion of Saint John Chrysostom and of Saint Jerome, who, speaking of the origin of the monastic state, trace it back to the time of the prophets.[50]

Those who, with Cassian, seek its beginning in the life of the great Saint John the Baptist in the desert, and in the lives and manners of the Apostles, were of the opinion that these truly divine men transmitted their disengagement, their poverty, their penance, their sanctity and perfection to the monks, that these precious qualities became their inheritance, and thus they were the descendants of those great men, their children, successors, and disciples.[51]

There were others who wrote that they who assembled in the vicinity of the city of Alexandria (when the Church was yet in her infancy), who lived in poverty, who had all things in common, and who divided their time between certain pious exercises and manual labor, were they who began the monastic life. However, we shall not dwell any longer on those who had the more qualities, practices and austerities which are common to monks, but rather on the reality of their condition.

It is generally admitted that Saint Paul, the hermit, was the first, after the preaching or promulgation of the Gospel, who embraced the solitary life, and who concealed himself in the lower Thebaide, in order to follow

---

[50] *St. Jerome: Letters and Select Works* (NPNF2/ 6:299).

[51] Cassian, *Conferences* 3.18. 6 (NPNF2/11:481).

and find Jesus Christ in an entire separation from men, and in a perfect nakedness of all things.[52] Saint Anthony, to whom God revealed the existence of Saint Paul, practiced the same kind of life in Egypt, though he lived in a solitude less remote, and more accessible to those who came to seek Him, either for the cure of their infirmities, or for the sanctification of their souls.

This saint being sanctified in the desert by the long continued labor of many years, was forced to leave it and to become the guide of many persons who chose him as their Superior and Father, and from him Egypt soon abounded with cells and monasteries.[53]

Saint Pachomius appeared soon afterward in the upper Thebaide, and assembled there a great number of solitaries and received from God, by the ministry of an angel, as we have already remarked, the rule by which he was to direct them. [54]

Saint Macarius retired almost at the same time into the desert of Skete,[55] Saint Ammon into that of Nitria,[56] Saint Serapion repaired to the deserts of Arsinoe and Memphis, [57]and Saint Hilarion withdrew to Palestine. [58]This was as it were the source of that innumerable multitude of solitaries and monks, who in a few years spread all over Africa and Asia, and which since flowed into all parts of the west.

Behold what the origin and the beginning of the monastic state was; behold whom they were whom God was pleased to make its founders and its institutors. All that was done in preceding ages can be considered only as plans and figures which received their accomplishment, their true effect and real perfection, by the labors and ministry of these great men.

---

[52] *St. Jerome: Letters and Select Works* (NPNF2/6:299).

[53] St. Athanasius, Ernest A. Wallis Budge, ed. *The Paradise or Garden of the Holy Fathers* (Vol. 1; London: Chatto, 1907), 3.

[54] Budge, *Paradise*, 144.

[55] Cassian, *Conferences* 2.15.3 (NPNF2 11:446).

[56] Budge, *Paradise*, 50.

[57] Alban Butler, *The Lives of the Fathers, Martyrs and Other Principal Saints* (Vol. I; New York: Kenedy, 1903), 639.

[58] St. Jerome, *Letters,* (NPNF2/ 6:303).

3

OF THE ORIGIN OF THE SOLITARY STATE

QUESTION.—Would it not be profitable to us, were you to inform us more in detail what the origin of the solitary life was, and what the designs of God were in establishing it?

ANSWER.—As I have proposed to myself nothing more than your edification, and as this is one of my principal duties, I will tell you with all simplicity, my brethren, all that I could gather from the writings of the Holy Fathers on this subject, that thereby I may satisfy your request.

It is to be remembered that the principal design which Almighty God proposed to Himself in the new covenant which He made with men was to establish in the world a religion worthy of His Divine Majesty, and to form therein true adorers, who might adore Him in spirit and in truth, as our Lord Jesus Christ says, "The hour cometh and now is, when the true adorers shall adore the Father in spirit and in truth" (John 4:23); that is to say, in that purity which can be the effect only of the plenitude of His spirit and of the abundance of His grace.

God was known in Judea, His name was great in Israel (Ps 75:2), according to the words of the prophet, but He was not adored there in a manner proportionate to His infinite greatness. The homage and acknowledgment which were there offered to Him were low and imperfect, for the law was itself incapable to raise men to perfection (Heb 7:19). In effect, the greatest and most profitable things which the Jews proposed to themselves at that time was to live under the shade of their vines and fig trees, to feed and nourish themselves with the fruits of the earth, and to enjoy the sweetness thereof in peace and tranquility. Children thought that nothing could be better than to pass their lives in their fathers' houses and under the caressing protection of their mothers, and they considered the enjoyment of their possessions after their deaths as their greatest happiness. In that all their views and desires were centered. We can except only a few privileged souls, who, assisted by a special favor of God, raised themselves above the letter of the law, lived in a separation from present things, animated with the hope of future goods; and thus appeared in the Old Testament as living types and figures of what was to be accomplished only in the New.

Finally, the time which had been decreed in the eternal councils being accomplished, Almighty God, in order that He might construct that new house, which, according to the prediction of the prophet (Hag 2:10), should be more resplendent in glory and holiness than that which preceded it, laid the foundations thereof on the ruins of the former. He formed a new law for Christians, the excellence and perfection of which consists, in a principal manner, in the contempt and renunciation of the goods, pleasures, and all other things which the Jew considered as the greatest recompense they could desire for their fidelity in the observance of the law, and the only object of their hopes.

God, therefore, raised up men according His heart. He called them to His service and gave them at the same time both the will and strength to execute His orders. They, therefore, having renounced all things, and without attending to what nature might propose as an opposition to this immediate and complete separation, forsook their goods, their occupations, their fathers, their mothers, and followed Jesus Christ, who called them, without delaying one instant (Matt 4:22).

The Apostles were these true adorers who first embraced this state so pure and perfect, and who ascending—according to the language of the Holy Scripture—to the summit of this evangelical tower, transmitted the same spirit to almost all those whom they converted to the faith of Jesus Christ. The martyrs possessed it in an eminent degree, since they not only renounced their goods, their parents, their children, their brethren, but even their own lives; and they preferred the glory and the happiness of losing them for the sake of Jesus Christ, to all worldly honor and advantage.

But Christians being multiplied, the Church, like a too fruitful mother, began to be weakened and languished by reason of the great number of her children. The fury of persecutions being appeased, the faith and fervor of Christians diminished in repose; and the examples as well as the instructions which they had received from the Apostles were soon effaced from their hearts as well as from their memories.

Nevertheless, God, who was pleased to maintain this perfect purity in His Church, preserved some of its members from the general relaxation, filling them with the spirit of His Apostles, by which being animated, they, like a new train of martyrs, forsook their parents, their wives and children, by a sort of death, which seemed not less real, less holy, nor less miraculous, than that which the first martyrs endured.

They retired into the most distant solitudes, exposed themselves to nakedness, to cold, to thunder, and to all the injuries of the most rigorous seasons, to the fury of wild beasts, and, in a word, to the rage and envy of devils, and that in order to praise God, and to contemplate His infinite perfections, in the silence of the passions, and in a separation from everything that might distract them from the meditation of eternal truths.

This spirit diffused itself on both hermits and Monks. They soon filled deserts and monasteries. The Anthonies, Hilarions and Pachomiuses, having been commissioned by the Lord, assembled men, who joined them in the practice of the same perfection, and in the exercises of the same disengaged and unencumbered life; and that this new institution should not be considered as a human invention, God justified the part He Himself had in it, by prodigies equal to those which He had operated by the ministry of the Apostles; for these apostolical founders of the monastic state put the devils to flight, cured the sick, raised the dead to life, commanded the elements, and made the savage beasts obey them.

All the monks who followed them, and of whom these great men have been truly fathers and masters, have been formed according to the views of God in the same holiness and separation from created things. This purity was remarkable, not only in the persons of the founders, in whom it shown with peculiar splendor, but also those who were instructed by them. Moreover, the sanctity as well as the penance of those religious men who founded the different monastic orders in every succeeding age of the Church, has been but little, or rather nothing at all, inferior to those who founded them in primitive times.

If the present disposition of things produce a contrary opinion, it is to be accounted for only by the ruin and corruption of the times, but the monastic state, in itself, is now what it was at every other period. God, whose designs are immutable, and who has not revoked His orders, does not require, at present, a less perfection, nor a more inferior disengagement in those whom He calls to the religious state, than He did seventeen hundred years ago. Nor did Saint Bernard fear any exaggeration when he assured his brethren, that they had promised God to live in the perfection of the Apostles.[59]

Thus, that the greatest part of monks have at present but little of this primitive sanctity; that they have entirely degenerated from the spirit of their fathers; that there is scarcely any mark or character of this profound abnegation to be found in their lives—to which they are essentially obliged— and that they are as deeply immersed in human affairs and worldly concerns as they should be distant from them will be no difficult matter to discover if we trace things to their source, and judge of them, not by abuses and customs, but according to truth.

Nor will it be difficult to decide—having discovered its Source—that the monastic state is a life of sovereign and universal mortification, that it requires its professors to be continually employed in such things as relate to God, without distraction of mind or division of heart; that it prohibits the most innocent worldly connections; that a true religious man, as Saint John Climacus says:

> Has no longer any love which captivates him, no cares which occupy him, no anxieties which trouble him, neither for his relations nor for his friends, nor for the riches and glory of the world; and that having cast away all care, all affection, and all attachment, and above all things hating himself, he follows Jesus Christ in a perfect disengagement, with a fervor always new, having nothing more frequently in his heart and mouth than the words of the Royal Prophet: What can I desire in heaven or earth, but thee, O Lord? (Ps 72:25) [60]

God, who has discharged this religious soul from all the duties of charity and justice which are incompatible with those of the holy state to which He has called him; who has broken even the smallest bond which might still keep him bound to creatures; who no longer requires that he should assist the poor, comfort the afflicted, visit the sick, instruct the ignorant, nor even bury him to whom he is indebted for existence, God, I say, who calls him to Himself, puts Himself in the place of all the other things from which He has called him. He discharges him from the solicitude of Martha to engage him in the contemplation of Mary, and proposes His Divine Majesty to him as the only object of his future cares and love.

It is therefore evident that religious persons have the happiness to fill

---

[59] *Monastic Sermons*, 153.

[60] *Ladder*, 60.1.

the place of martyrs in the Church of God, that they imitate the perfection of the Apostles, that they succeed them in the practice of that perfect abnegation in which those holy companions and followers of a God-man lived, and that their state obliges them to nothing less than to exemplify in their lives the eminent sanctity of the ancient solitaries and recluses. They cannot, therefore, reject these qualities which are absolutely essential to their state without straying from the order established by God, without ruining His designs, without opposing the end which He proposed to Himself in their regard, without withdrawing themselves from the number of those who adore the Father in spirit and in truth, and consequently, without injuring their profession in the most delicate part; and thus, in making their hopes vain, they unhappily would deprive themselves of the entire fruit of their conversion.

4 | OF THE DIFFERENT FORMS OF RELIGIOUS LIFE—CONTENTS:

4

OF THE DIFFERENT FORMS OF LIFE WHICH WERE ESTABLISHED AMONG THE ANCIENT SOLITARIES

Although it be true that those who have treated this subject have spoken of it in a manner which differed in the terms they employed, yet it is a thing no less certain that they all agreed to the substance, and that they divided the entire monastic profession between those who lived in monasteries, and those who were hermits or recluses.

Cassian in his Conferences remarks four different sorts of monk. [61]He places those who live in monasteries in the first rank, because he believed that they began in the time of the Apostles, and that the hermits issued from them, as fruits are produced from flowers, or rather as disciples are formed by their masters.

The anchorites or hermits, therefore, hold the second place, according to his opinion. He then speaks of certain irregular monks, whom he calls sarabites; and lastly, treats of a fourth kind of solitaries, who began to appear in his time, and who, leaving their monasteries, through the impulse of a spirit of libertinism and independence, attributed to themselves the name and quality of anchorites.

Saint Jerome says there were in Egypt three sorts of solitaries; that some lived in monasteries, others lived alone; and the third sort consisted of only three persons, who lived together.[62]

Saint Benedict nearly follows Cassian's opinion, since he divides the solitary life between the anchorites, the cenobites, the sarabites, and the girovagues.

Saint John Climacus speaks only of the anchorites, the cenobites, and of some solitaries who lived, two or three together, under the direction of a Superior.

Hence we may conclude, that these divisions demonstrate the different ways of life established among the ancient solitaries; that those who lived in monasteries under the direction of a superior, and who observed the common rule, were the cenobites; that they who lived separate in solitude should be called anchorites; and that others who had only the appearance of these two professions, without having anything of the sanctity and reality peculiar to them, were monks, who, living in disorder and corruption, were unworthy to be placed among true solitaries, or even to bear the name.

QUESTION 1. — *Who were they that, among the ancient solitaries, were first called anchorites?*

ANSWER. —The anchorites have always held the first rank in the monastic state, on account of the perfection of their virtue and the eminence of their sanctity. They agree with the cenobites in this, that like these latter they propose to themselves the same end, which is to serve God, to be closely united to Him, and to possess Him by a total renunciation of

---

[61] *Conferences* 3.18.4 (NPNF2/11:480)

[62] Jerome, *Letters*, 6:22.

all earthly things. The cenobites proceed in the ways of God, by crucifying their own will, by the labors and exercises of an exact and regulated conversatio,[63] in the society of their brethren, assisted by their prayers, and under the command and direction of a superior. The others tend to the same end, by separating themselves from all creatures, by an entire abnegation of themselves, by a total disengagement from everything that is not God, and by immediately and continually applying themselves to that infinite and divine object, fortified and assisted by the grace of Jesus Christ alone, and the charitable interposition of the holy angels; thus literally observing these words of the Holy Scripture: "Be not solicitous what ye shall eat —Behold the fowls of the air . . ." (Matt 6:25). They give up the care of their bodies, as well as that of their souls, to the will of Divine Providence.

But that I may explain more amply what I think of this angelical state, I will tell you, my brethren, that the anchorites are those admirable men, who, being led into the most profound solitudes by the same divine spirit who before conducted Jesus Christ into the desert, have no other guide or rule of life but the same divine spirit, nor spectators of their combats but the holy angels. These are the chaste doves of whom the prophet speaks, who being borne upon the wings of a lively faith and constant hope, fly from the midst of the world in order to seek and to find a new earth, a new heaven, and a new sun which never changes, but which may enlighten and console them with an invariable light (Ps. 54:7).

Having consumed all the inclinations of corrupt nature in the fire of an ardent charity, they have concealed their loves so perfectly in Jesus Christ— according to the words of the holy Apostle—that if their actions were examined, there could be nothing discovered in them which is not pleasing to that Divine Master, because He Himself produced these actions in them, and by them, by the fullness of His Holy Spirit, which He had communicated to them. Or rather, there could be only one action discovered in them, for having, as it were, lost all remembrance of things visible, they are employed only in sighing after the full possession of that infinite majesty whom they already enjoy by their anticipated contemplations of His ineffable beauty, looking forward to the dawning of that glorious day in which God will, according to His promises, inebriate them with His delights, and establish His everlasting dwelling in them (Ps 5:12).

The saints sometimes considered them as angels incarnate, who, by their continual prayers to God, protected whole states and empires; sometimes

---

[63] By *conversatio* is meant "monastic way of life."

as pillars who supported the Church by the purity of their faith; at other times, as penitents, who, with torrents of tears, appeased the anger of God irritated against sinners; now as martyrs, who, by their voluntary sufferings, confessed the name of Jesus Christ, and gave public testimony of the sanctity of His holy religion, and of the almighty power of His grace; and again, as brilliant stars, who, diffusing their lights all over the world, dissipated its darkness, and prevented men from languishing in the night and sleep of sin. [64]

This is what we learn from Saint Gregory Nazianzen, who says:

> These holy solitaries were closely united to God, by being separated from the rest of men and from themselves; they were in the holes of rocks and in heaven at the same time; by their tears they brought down a happy deluge which washed away a part of the sins of the world; by raising their hands to God in prayer, they extinguished the flames of temptation, resisted the devils, overcame the persecutions of men, tamed wild beasts, vanquished the most violent passions, and put the enemies of God to flight. [65]

Rufinus confirms the same thing in his Ecclesiastical History, in which he tells us:

> I have seen, in truth, the treasure of Jesus Christ shut up in the frail vessels of human bodies, and having found it, I would not conceal it, as if I were determined that others should not be made partakers of it. . . . I have seen many fathers among them who led a heavenly life on earth, and new prophets raised up to shine in the world, as well by their eminent piety as by their predictions of future events. We have seen men the greatness of whose merits was proclaimed by the number of prodigies and illustrious miracles which God wrought by their hands; and indeed it is just that they who renounce both the possession and the love of temporal things, should be invested with a divine power and authority. I have seen some among them whose souls were so purified from all malicious suspicions with regard to their neighbor, that they had even quite forgotten the ill that is

---

[64] "Freed from all earthly cares, they emulated the holiness of the Angels while still living in this mortal flesh. They scaled the heights of virtue, their brilliance was beyond belief, they were manifestly in no way inferior to the Fathers of antiquity." Prologue from "The Life of Saint Pachomius, Abbot of Tabennisi" by an unknown Greek author. In Heribertus Rosweyde, *Vitae Patrum* (Antwerp: Officina Plantniana, 1615; from translation by Benedict Baker at http://www.vitae-patrum.org.uk) / Budge, *Paradise*, 1:XV.

[65] Oration 12.

committed in the world: their souls were so calm, and their hearts so re-plenished with good and tender dispositions, that it might be said of them with justice—'Those who seek thy law, O Lord, enjoy a profound peace.'

Moreover they live in the desert in cells far separated from one anoth-er, but closely united in charity; and they choose to have their dwellings thus removed from one another so that as they seek only God, so their silent repose and their fervent inflamed meditations may not be disturbed by the noise of visitors or their useless conversations. Thus having their souls in heaven, and each individual remaining in his grotto, they await the coming of Jesus Christ, as children do the coming of their father, or as soldiers prepared for battle expect the arrival of their general; or, in fine, as servants the return of their master who is to give them both liberty and reward. There is no uneasiness among them concerning their food or their clothes, knowing that such anxiety is the fruit of unbelief; but as they ardently seek the kingdom of God and His justice, so all these things are given them over and above, according to our Savior's promise (Matt 6:32).

If they sometimes want anything necessary for the body, they ad-dress themselves to God, and not to men, and having asked it of Him as their father, they immediately obtain it. So great is their faith, that they remove mountains from one place to another; and many of them, by their prayers, stemmed the inundations of floods which destroyed the neigh-boring countries; they entered barefoot into the midst of rivers, and going into the deepest parts, killed the most enormous monsters; in a word, they have performed as many and as great miracles, even in our days, as the Prophets and Apostles have formerly done; so that we may say without rashness that the world subsists at present only by the merits of these great saints.

That which is most extraordinary is that though excellent things usu-ally being very rare, nevertheless it is a fact that the number of these Sol-itaries is as great as their virtue is incomparable. They are dispersed in places near to cities and in the country; but the greatest and most consid-erable part live secluded in the deserts where they form a celestial army al-ways prepared for battle, where they await the arrival of their king whose order they are ready to obey. Under Him they propose to themselves the conquest of the immortal kingdom above, for they are an army of con-querors who fight with the arms of prayer and defend themselves from the attacks of their enemies with the shield of faith. They live in a perfect purity of manners; they are always in peace, in sweetness, and repose: the bond of charity does not unite them less closely than flesh and blood could have done. A holy and a divine emulation is continually excited among them. Everyone endeavors to be the most mild, the most patient, and the most humble. If anyone be found among them who excels in prudence and wisdom, he humbles himself so profoundly, and makes himself so familiar with the rest that it seems as if— according to the command of God— he was the last among them, and the servant of all his brethren.[66]

But nothing can equal the account Saint Ephrem gives us of the penance, sanctity, mortification, and other circumstances of the life and death of these holy solitaries. "They have no dwelling," says this great saint:

But caves and rocks. They shut themselves up between mountains, as between inaccessible walls and ramparts; the ground is their table, the wild herbs which the earth produces spontaneously is their ordinary food, and the water which flows in brooks, or falls from the holes or openings of the rocks, serves to allay their thirst. Every place where they meet serves them as a church. Their prayer is continual, and they pass whole days in that holy exercise. The praises of God with which they make the concavities of the mountains resound are the sacrifices which they offer Him. They themselves are both the priests and victims of their sacrifices. They heal our infirmities by the efficacy of their prayers; and these holy intercessors are always present before God, from whom they are never separated. They know not what it is to aspire after honors and seek after elevated places. All their glory consists in the sentiments of their own nothingness, by which they endeavor to become faithful imitators of Him, who, being rich, became poor for the love of us.

They give themselves no rest in this world, because they are replenished with spiritual delight. They wander about in deserts, and live with the wild beasts whom they meet. They sometimes stand on tops of mountains like burning torches, which enlighten all those who approach them, animated with sentiments of true piety. They are in solitudes like unshaken walls in which they enjoy a constant and undisturbed peace. They repose on hills like doves, and dwell on the tops of the highest rocks like eagles. If sometimes they are wearied with their continual labors, they find a sort of delight in taking a little rest on the bare ground; but they soon awake, start up, and with new fervor make the adjacent parts resound with the praises of God. They are protected from their enemies by their Lord and King Jesus Christ, who never forsakes them, and by armies of holy angels, who continually surround them. The earth no sooner receives

---

[66] Rufinus, *Historia Monachorum seu Liber de Vitis Patrum*, PL 21:387 (1849).

the impression of their knees, but it finds itself watered with their tears; and when their prayers are ended, the Lord Himself disdains not to wait on his faithful servants.

Their death is not less holy nor less admirable than their life, according to what the same saint relates. They have no care about building monuments, for they are crucified to the world; and the fervor of their love for Jesus Christ is such, that it has long since deprived them of life. It frequently happens that the place where they stop to conclude their fasts, becomes that of their grave. Many of them, in the fervor of their prayer, fall into a sweet and gentle sleep, from which they never awake. Others being, as it were, fastened to the points of sharp rocks, freely gave up their souls into the hands of their creator. Some, while they were walking according to their usual simplicity, died on the mountains which became their tombs. Others, knowing that their time was at hand, being confirmed in the grace of Jesus Christ, arming themselves with the sign of the cross, placed themselves, without any assistance, in their own graves. Some of them slept in the Lord, while they were eating a few herbs which the hand of Providence had sent them. Others were found who expired while they were singing the praises of God—death alone putting an end to their prayers and closing their mouths. In fine, these incomparable men incessantly await the moment in which the voice of the archangel shall awake them from sleep, and in which the earth, by the command of God, shall restore the bodies which are deposited in its bosom, when they shall spring and flourish again with a new and never-ending beauty and strength, and shall be clothed like the lilies with infinite glory and beauty; when, in fine, Jesus Christ will place a diadem of eternal splendor on their heads, as a reward of the labors they have endured for His service and glory.[67]

I am convinced, my brethren, that the above relation has already produced the most ardent desires in your hearts, by which you feel animated to walk in the footsteps of these blessed solitaries, and being inflamed with a holy ardor, you may say to yourself what the two disciples said heretofore: "Were not our hearts burning within us while He spoke" (Luke 24:32). I am convinced, I say, that you are violently borne on the wings of thought to the desert, and that each individual cries out within himself, in the words of the Prophet: "Who will give me, as it were, the wings of a dove, and I will fly away and be at rest" (Ps 54:7). But you must restrain your sentiments, moderate your zeal, and refuse your assent to all it inspires and suggests;

---

[67] St. Ephrem. Serm. 1. in sanctis Pat. Defunct.

for those happy times are no more—the entrance of those once sanctified deserts is no longer accessible—the doors of those hallowed solitudes are now closed; and Thebaide is no longer free as it formerly was.

Q. 2. — *Who were they among the solitaries who were called cenobites?*

A. — It is true, my brethren, that God considers the desert no more in the same manner as He did formerly in the first ages of the Church; that He has withdrawn His Holy Spirit from it, and that He no longer pours down His benedictions on that once favored place; but it is no less true, that he has not shut up the entire excellence of the monastic state in the eremetical life.

The graces which Jesus Christ has communicated to the cenobitical state have not been much inferior to those who bestowed on the former. He has not showed Himself less wonderful in many of His saints who served Him in monasteries than in those whom He led to the desert. The Church did not find much less assistance and ornament in the one than in the other. Though the eremetical state, when considered in itself separately, is superior to the cenobitical, it has nevertheless frequently happened that the cenobites attained to the same degree of sanctity as the anchorites. And one feels convinced that though the spirit of God—who breathes where He pleases—withdrew the Pauls, the Anthonies, and Hilarions from the midst of the world, yet we must acknowledge that judging things impartially, and according to general rules, the cloister was the nursery in which the anchorites were usually formed. It was in the labors, in the fatigues, in the combats, in the mortifications, in the obedience—and in the other painful exercises which are there practiced—that the dispositions essentially necessary for living well in the desert were acquired.

Monasteries are, in effect, the fields of admirable fecundity, where these divine plants were formed, in which they were cultivated, and in which they acquired their growth and perfection before they were transplanted in the desert. In a word, if you can no longer conceal yourself in the depth of wild and desert with the Palemons, the Paphnutiuses, and Macariusses, you can, and you ought to imitate the Pacomiuses, the Theoderets, the Benedicts, and the Bernards, since your state—as we have said many times—obliges you to nothing less than to practice and tend continually to the accomplishment of all that Jesus Christ has recommended as most holy and perfect.

Is it not to you cenobites that the following words of Saint Bernard are addressed ? :

Your profession is most high; it transcends the heavens; it is equal to the

angels; its purity is nothing inferior to that of those pure spirits; for you have vowed not only the acquisition of sanctity, but also the perfection of all holiness, and the perfection of perfection itself. The duty of others consist in serving God, but your duty obliges you to be always perfectly united to Him; it suffices for others to believe in God, to know Him, to love Him, to adore Him; but all this is too little for you. You are obliged to penetrate the splendors of His wisdom, in order that you may know Him as He is in Himself, and thus to enjoy him by fruition.[68]

Saint John Climacus, speaking of the religious of a certain monastery of Egypt, confirms the same truths. He says:

I saw things among these saints which were truly useful and admirable. I saw a society of brethren united together by the society of God, and who possessed in a wonderful degree all that may be considered most perfect in the active and contemplative life. They exercised themselves in every kind of virtue, and in contemplation, in such a manner, that they had scarcely any want of their superior's advice: so much did they animate one another to a holy vigilance . . . . There was another thing seen amongst them which produced in the beholders a reverential awe; for it seemed to be something more angelical than human, and it was this: there were several ancients among them, on whose venerable countenances shone such resplendent majesty, that it was admirable to behold them; and yet they ran like little children to hear the superior's commands, and place all their glory and happiness in their submission and profound humility. I saw men there who had passed fifty years in the practice of obedience, and having requested them to tell me what advantages they had derived from the painful exercises of that virtue, some of them told me, that being led into the depths of a profound humility, they were entirely delivered from all intestine wars and combats; and others, that they had acquired a perfect insensibility of injuries and affronts.[69]

I saw others among those men worthy of eternal memory, who snowy locks announced a venerable old age, and whose angelical faces proclaimed their consummate virtue. These had, by their continual labors, and by the assistance of divine graces, obtained the gifts of most perfect innocence, and of a wise simplicity, which savored in no manner of that enervated reason and childish levity which makes old men in the world be

---

[68] In PL 184:307 this is attributed to Guigo, Prior general of the Carthusians

[69] *Ladder*, 72.15.

so frequently despised. Nothing could be seen in their exterior but an extreme sweetness, a wonderful kindness, and an agreeable cheerfulness; all which announced sincerity, candor and justice, both in their words and actions, which are not frequently found in others; and as to their intention, they sighed only after God and their superior, like innocent, simple little children, who lovingly view their father; and yet they were no less bold and courageous in turning the eyes of their souls, and all their strength to consider and oppose the devil, and all their spiritual adversaries.[70]

These sentiments are not less confirmed by what we read in the life of Saint Mary of Egypt, concerning the monastery situated on the banks of the Jordan into which holy Zosimus retired by the appointment of God:

There might be seen in that house fathers with venerable looks who were admirable in their actions, fervent in spirit, and who served God without interruption. They sang psalms every hour in the night, and made them their delicious entertainment during the whole day while they were unceasingly occupied in manual labor. Unprofitable conversations were there quite unknown; they never entertained the least thought of temporal things, nor did they so much as even know the names of such affairs; but they employed all their time in meditating on the nothingness of this life, which is only a passage full of sorrow and misery. There was but one thing that seemed to them important, and that was to consider themselves dead to the world—which by forsaking they had renounced—and in general to all other things which are not God. This they endeavored to acquire with all possible ardor and attention. Living thus as if they did not live, they nourished their souls with never failing food, which is the word of God, and sustained their emaciated bodies with only bread and water, that they might more securely hope in the mercies of their Divine Master.

These solitaries labored so powerfully to advance in virtue, that they exhibited a sort of paradise on earth. The solitude in which they lived was so profound, that though their monastery was so holy, yet it was not visited, nor even scarcely known to those who lived near it; and the principal gate was never opened unless some solitary came there on necessary business.

On the first Sunday of Lent, the sacred mysteries were celebrated according to custom, and every individual received the precious body and blood of our Lord, which gives life to the soul; then, after taking a lit-

---

[70] *Ladder*, 74. 21.

tle corporal food as usual, they all assembled in the oratory, where, after praying on their knees for some time, they gave one another the kiss of peace; then kneeling down a second time, the embraced their abbot, and asked his benediction, that they may be thus fortified to begin and go through the combat in which they were about to engage; the gates to the monastery were then thrown open, and they all with one voice sang this psalm: 'The Lord is my light and my salvation, whom shall I fear? The Lord is my protector, of whom shall I be in dread?" (Ps 26:1) They then departed, leaving only one or two brethren in the house, not to watch it, since they had nothing that thieves could steal, but in order that the praises of the Lord might still resound in their oratory.

Each individual took food with him according to his will and desire; some took figs, others legumes steeped in water. There were some who took only their habits, contenting themselves with the herbs they found in the desert, which they eat when they were forced by hunger. Everyone was permitted to live according to the dictates of his own fervor and zeal, however uncommon and extraordinary that might be; and it was an inviolable rule among them not to seek any information how they lived, or what manner of fasting they had practiced during the time. They then immediately passed over the river Jordan, separated far from one another, and met together no more; for solitude was more pleasing to them than the most agreeable companies of towns or cities; so that if they saw anyone, even of their own brethren, coming towards them, though at a great distance, they immediately took another course; thus living to God alone, and to themselves, very frequently singing the divine praise, and eating only to sustain life. Having fasted in that manner the greater part of Lent, they returned to the monastery before Easter Sunday, the day on which Jesus Christ, who is the life of our souls, arose glorious and immortal from the dead; and they met altogether there on Palm Sunday. Every one was accompanied by the testimony of his conscience, which proved with what utility he had spent his time in his retreat, what seeds of virtue he had sown in his heart, and how he had animated himself to undertake new labors for the service of God.

Behold what manner of rule was perfectly observed in that house! Behold how those holy men united themselves to God in the desert, and how they fought against themselves, that they might please Him alone; for they were well persuaded that everything that is done for any other end than that of pleasing God, instead of being profitable to those who do it, is rather hurtful to them.[71]

Saint John Chrysostom gives us the same elevated idea of this holy state, when he tells us in his time:

> If anyone took the pains to visit the solitudes of Egypt, they would find them more beautiful than any earthly paradise; innumerable companies of angels, under the figure and appearance of men, lived there. There were entire tribes of martyrs and whole companies of virgins assembled there together. The tyranny of the devil was there destroyed, and the empire of the Son of God flourished there in all its splendor. In these vast countries the camps of Jesus Christ, His celestial armies, His heavenly shepherds, might be seen distributed in every part; the sanctity of women was not less resplendent than that of men. . . . The heavens did not shine more brilliantly, with all their variety of stars and planets, than the deserts of Egypt did with the great number of solitaries' grots and cells, who, being divested of all things present, and crucified to the world, raised themselves continually to the summit of evangelical perfection. For they spent whole nights in watching and in singing the divine praises, and the days in fasting, praying, and working with their hands, faithfully imitating the zeal and virtue of the Apostles.[72]

Saint Gregory Nazianzen, speaking of the monasteries of Egypt, gives us an exalted idea of the perfection of the monastic state; he calls them sacred and divine schools, and continues thus:

> These holy Solitaries, separating themselves entirely from the world, and being retired in the desert, live only for God, but in a manner so perfect, that none of those who as yet live in mortal bodies can ascend the summit to which they have attained. Some of them have chosen an entire solitary life for their inheritance; living and conversing only with God and themselves, they have no intercourse with men, and know no more of the world than what the desert in which they live can communicate to them concerning it. Others live in society, and they, by fulfilling the duties to which they are obliged by the laws of fraternal charity, are both solitaries and cenobites; and though they are dead to the rest of men, and to all the

---

[71] Sophronius, *Vita Sanctae Mariae Aegypticae Meretricis*, PL 73:675 (1849)

[72] *Saint Chrysostom: Homilies on the Gospel of Saint Matthew* (NPNF1/10:53).

affairs which trouble and agitate our lives and sport as it were with our existence, they are nevertheless, as it were, an entire world to one another by exciting and animating themselves mutually to the love and practice of every virtue.

They pass their lives speaking of the solitaries of Pontus, in watching, fasting, prayers and tears. Their continual prayer makes their knees become as hard as the camel's skin; their breasts are bruised and they become black and blue by the repeated blows.

Their prayers are interrupted by the sighs and groans which burst from their hearts, which pierce the souls of those who hear them, and fill them with compunction. They spend whole nights in singing their Creator's praise, and unite themselves to Him by raising themselves above all earthly things. They employ days and nights in singing psalms and canticles to the praises of the Lord, in meditating on His holy law. In a word, His praise is always in their mouths . . . and though they observe a rigorous silence, yet they are the heralds of His glory.

But that which is most great and admirable is, that their poverty is all their treasure—their glory is in ignominy—their strength in weakness, and their delight consists in a total privation of pleasure. They embrace a poor and abject life in order that they may one day deserve to enjoy the glory of heaven. They possess nothing in this world, because they are elevated above it; and though they live in the flesh, they are far from living according to the flesh. God alone is the portion of the inheritance which they hope to possess. They make themselves poor in time, that they may become rich in eternity; and this, their poverty, is so effective that it makes them kings even in this life . . . . They are pillars which support the Church, the first fruits of the saints, the pearls and precious stones of the temple of which Jesus Christ is the foundation and cornerstone.[73]

What Saint Augustine relates of the monks of his time, is not less edifying nor less admirable. He represents them as the glory and the ornament of the world—as a resplendent proof of the truth and sanctity of the Church—as a manifest conviction of the false wisdom of heretics; and in fine, as a finished model of the most consummate perfection. "I will not speak," says this great saint:

Of things concerning which you have no information; I will tell you only

---

[73] Oration 12.

of those which you dissimulate, and of which you pretend to be ignorant: for who knows not that a great multitude of Christians, perfectly chaste, daily spread themselves more and more over all the earth, particularly in the East, and in Egypt? You know it as well as we.

I will not speak of those whom I have first named, who have concealed themselves from the sight of men, who eat only the bread which is brought them from time to time, and who drink the pure water of the spring; who, dwelling in the desert, enjoy the company and the conversation of God, to whom they are united by the purity of their thoughts, and who enjoy the delights of a sovereign beatitude, in contemplating that infinite beauty, which can only be seen with the eyes of the soul, and then only when the soul is in a state of grace and love.

It would be superfluous to extend my discourse on this subject, it being almost impossible that they who do not spontaneously revere a state so excellent, so sublime and holy, can be excited to it by my words. It is sufficient that I demonstrate to those who boast of their false purity that the temperance and virtue of the great saints who are in the Catholic Church are now risen to such an elevated degree of perfection, that, according to the opinion of some, their austerities should be restrained within the bounds of nature, so very wonderful do their lives seem even to those who disapprove of them.

But if that sort of life appears under a form too repugnant for our sloth, who can help admiring and praising those of another class, who, having renounced all worldly pleasures, live in society, leading a chaste and holy life—who employ all their time in reading, praying, and manual labor—who never converse together but on such matters as are connected with the great affair of their eternal salvation, or to excite one another to a more ardent love of our Lord Jesus Christ—who are never puffed up with pride, nor agitated with troubles, nor chilled with envy, but are always humble, always modest, always in peace; they live in perfect harmony, in a perpetual contemplation of the divine perfections, and offer up to God all the gifts and graces they have received from His paternal goodness and liberality, as a sacrifice which is infinitely agreeable to Him.

No one among them possesses anything in particular—no one is a burden to any person: they employ themselves in such things as may furnish them with necessary subsistence, and which are no impediment to their recollection in God. They deliver their work when finished to those who are called deans, and who are so called because they preside over ten: thus they are exempt from the care of providing their food, clothing or other necessities, in health or in sickness. The deans provide all things for them. They watch over the brethren, and regulate everything that is connected with the economy of the house. These subaltern superiors are commissioned to administer such things are indispensably necessary to human weakness, but yet they give an account of all to him whom they call their father.

As to these fathers, they are most holy in their manners, are very learned in divine knowledge. All their actions and manner of conduct are noble and elevated. They govern others whom they call their children without sentiments of pride or insolence. They command with great authority, and are obeyed with great affection.

All these religious come out of their cells at the end of the day, and meet together to hear the instructions of their father, at which time they are not yet fasting. There are not less than three thousand under each father, and sometimes there is a much greater number. They listen to his discourse with an incredible zeal and a wonderful silence, and their sighs, tears, and motions, announce the effect his words produce in their hearts; but this is done with such modesty, and tranquility, that the least noise is not heard.

The exhortation being ended, they go to the repast, at which they content themselves with that which is necessary for the preservation of life and health, repressing every irregular desire, lest they should commit any excess in things the most simple, in such a manner, that they not only abstain from flesh and wine, in order to remove every incitement from the passions, but they also refuse themselves the use of many other sorts of food, which are so much the more agreeable, as they seem to some persons to be pure; for many relaxed members of the cloister authorize the desire of delicate food, but by a mode of reasoning not only weak, but extravagant; for, according to their opinion, it is sufficient to abstain from flesh meat, and with this exception every other sort of food may be lawfully used.

If anything remain after their refection, which is frequently the case, by reason of their hard labor and frugal repasts, it is distributed to the poor with much more care than it had been collected; for they do not labor in order that they may have an abundance of ordinary food; on the contrary, they never allow anything to be kept but what is indispensably necessary; so much so, that they send ships loaded with corn to those parts where the inhabitants are poor. But I have been sufficiently diffuse in what is notorious to everyone. In effect, were I to undertake the design of extolling the customs, the life, the order, the institute of those holy men, I could not do it in a manner suitable to the subject; and were I to add florid magnificence to this simple narrative, I would fear lest some should imagine that the things

I relate wanted to be recommended by additional ornaments, whereas they contain sufficient beauty when presented in their own natural simplicity.[74]

But, my brethren, the description Saint Basil gives of this holy state contains something so great and sublime, that I would deprive you of an instruction equally important and consoling, did I refuse to relate it in detail: I call that living in perfect community, says that great bishop and eminent solitary:

> When all possession of goods is personally banished; when all contradictory sentiments are cut off; when all disputes and oppositions are destroyed; when all things are in common: minds, thoughts, bodies, and everything necessary for their food and preservation; when all members of a community, by united exercises of piety, enjoy God in common; when they mutually sustain the same labors and combats, and hope to obtain the same eternal crowns; in a word, when many persons form but one, and when one is only found in many.
>
> Can anything be compared to such a society—anything be more complete or happy than this intimate unity and affinity? What can be more agreeable than this concord of minds and hearts? People of different nations are there so perfectly united in the bonds of holy conformity that there seems to be only one soul in so many bodies, and many bodies seem to be only the organs of one soul. When anyone among them is attacked with any corporal infirmity, his state becomes the state of many by the interest they take in the evil he suffers. If any other is unfortunately wounded in the more noble part by falling into sin, he is immediately assisted to rise from his fall by a great number, who unite in applying a remedy to the wound.
>
> Equally the masters and servants of each other, and always maintaining an inviolable unity, they give constant proofs of an exact servitude, which is not effected by misfortune, nor by violence, such as overwhelm those who suffer with pain and sorrow, but is the effect of a free spontaneous choice— charity making those who are free to become subject to one another, and to preserve their liberty by the free choice they have made of their state.
>
> These men are perfect imitators of our Lord, and fulfill in all things the example He gave to the world during His mortal life, for when He formed the society of His disciples who were His immediate followers, He made all things become common. And as He gave Himself in common to them, so

---

[74] *St. Augustin: The Writings against the Manichaeans.*(NPNF1/ 4:59).

the solitaries, in submitting themselves to the will of their superior, and in observance of their rule, demonstrate in a perfect manner the holy model drawn up by Jesus Christ and His Apostles. The care with which they maintain this perfect community of things among themselves, renders them zealous imitators of the life of the angelical spirits above. For as there are neither contentions nor disputes among the angels, as each individual in the celestial court possesses the happiness of all in general; and as they all universally enjoy their particular advantages in full; as their riches are not these material goods that may be limited or divided, in order to relieve the wants of many; as their possessions have nothing of the lower world, but are purely spiritual treasures, hence each one preserves his particular advantage without diminution, and they are equally rich in communicating them to one another without pain or anxiety. And in effect, as all the riches of the angels consists in the contemplation of the sovereign good, and in perfect knowledge of all the virtues, they can all attain to that acquisition, ascend to the possession of, and individually enjoy that heavenly treasure. This is what the solitaries realize among themselves. As they are entirely disengaged from the things of the earth and attentive to acquire only those of heaven, they possess altogether, and each individually, a common good—by a communication which is exempt from every species of separation or division.

Let no one imagine that I have entered into this detail in order to exaggerate the life and merit of the members of the monastic state; for my words, so far from enhancing its dignity by their power or strength, are rather calculated to enervate its real worth by their insufficiency. In the mean time, I had no other design than that of describing as much as possible the greatness and excellence of a profession so sublime. What can be compared to it in this world? There a father is seen who imitates our heavenly Father, and children who endeavor give their Superior the testimony of their tender affection. Children, I say, who have but one heart, who mutually attend to receive from the father the rule of conduct in the practice of virtue, and who, not considering nature as the principle of this union, make it depend on a basis more solid and sublime, which is the grace and operation of the Holy Spirit.

What similitude can be found here below to explain their eminent virtue? Certainly there is nothing on earth adequate to the purpose; it can be found only in heaven. The Father whom we have there is impassible; He governs men without passion, and by His wisdom alone. The children of this Father, being produced from incorruption, are consequently incorruptible. Charity binds all who are in heaven, and the same virtue unites those who are on earth. The devil is intimidated, and dares not attack an army so formidable. He finds that his forces are insufficient to oppose enemies who are so well disciplined and so vigorously prepared for combat, particularly as he beholds them strong and united by the spirit of charity, which serves as a shield to defend and secure them, so that he cannot perceive by what way or by what means he may attack them.

Consider how great the union of the Maccabees was in the time of combat, and you shall find that, however great it had been, that of the Solitaries is still greater. The Royal Prophet spoke of it when he exclaimed in one of his inspired psalms, 'O, how good and how pleasant a thing it is to see brethren dwell together in unity' (Ps 132:1): signifying by the word good, the life that is led in monasteries, and by agreeable or pleasant, the joy that springs from the union of minds and hearts. Those who embrace this kind of life worthily seem to be in pursuit of heavenly and divine virtue.[75]

But, my brethren, we need not go to Palestine or to Thebaide, nor go back to those ancient times in order to seek for examples, since we have them at home present with ourselves. If we consider the *Rule of Saint Benedict*, what it prescribes to those who profess it and the duties it enjoins, we shall find therein faithful copy and a real delineation of all that hath been practiced in the monasteries of the East. This great saint addresses his rule to men whose chief employment should be to fight against their vices and passions, under the standard of Jesus Christ, with the arms of a faithful and exact obedience. He requires that they should keep the judgments of God continually before their eyes; that they should consider the pains with which He will punish the crimes of the wicked, and the crowns with which He will reward the fidelity of the just. He requires that they should watch over themselves with such exactitude, and regulate their most indifferent thoughts, the motions of their hearts, of their hands, of their eyes, of their tongues so correctly that nothing unworthy of the perfection of their state may ever surprise them, but that the whole body of their actions may be irreprehensible.

He commands the brethren to live in such a perfect union, that there may be no division nor dispute among them; but that in their society may be found a holy emulation, which will animate them to render each other mutual testimonies of respect, charity and tenderness. He commands them to love their superior with a cordial love; to execute his orders with the same exactitude as they would the will and commands of God Himself; that they imitate Jesus Christ in His humiliations, abnegations and sufferings; that

---

[75] S. Basilius, *Constitutiones*, PG 31:582c

they place themselves beneath all men by the sentiments of sincere humility; that they become entire strangers to the maxims and conduct of the world; and that they aspire to eternal things with all the ardor and affections of their souls.

In fine, he requires that they endeavor to raise themselves by the exercises of a steady piety to that perfect charity, which, banishing all fear, makes men serve God on earth as the angels serve Him in heaven—that is, without being influenced by any motives of interest or fear, but purely animated by the love of justice alone, by disinterested love for Jesus Christ, and by the consolations they enjoy in doing His will.[76]

These are the divine maxims, my brethren, which formed the different institutions that sprung from this great rule, as so many rivers from a source, or rather from an inexhaustible treasure of graces. Those of the Carthusians, of the Cameldulians, of the Valombrosians, of the Celestines, and, among many others, of the Cistercians, who made it a principal duty to observe the spirit of this great saint in all things, and thereby held forth the example of a life so perfect and accomplished in every respect, that it may be said with truth, that the ancient solitaries had no other advantage over them than that which they derived from the precedency of time.

The Cistercians appeared at a time when the monastic state was reduced to a degree of universal debility. Like so many luminaries in the midst of profound darkness, they filled the world with the splendor of an unexpected light. They adorned the Church with new beauty—they sanctified it—and the Lord, through the merit of their virtue and sanctity, diffused His graces and benedictions over countries both distant and barbarous.

I will here lay before you a monument of the eminent virtue of these admirable monks, taken from the account given us by William, Abbot of Thierry:

> I remained during some days with the saint (says he, speaking of Saint Bernard), though I was very unworthy of such an honor, and wherever I turned my eyes, I beheld objects of admiration, as if I saw a new heaven and a new earth, for I saw the wonderful life of our primitive fathers, the ancient monks of Egypt, perfectly exemplified in these men of our times. The image of the golden age was then perfectly delineated in Clairvaux, for there men might be seen who were formerly rich and honorable in the world, but who, at that time, place all their glory and happiness in being poor for Jesus Christ, and who planted a church by their blood, by their

---

[76] *Rule of St. Benedict* [henceforth RB], Prologue, chapters 5, 7, 73.

labors, by their pains, by hunger, thirst, cold and nakedness, acquiring for that house the peace and tranquility which they now enjoy by the injuries and necessities they endured. They did not so much endeavor to live for themselves as for Jesus Christ, and for the brethren who were to serve God in that abbey. They were not anxious about what they wanted, on condition they could establish the house in such a manner as to be able to maintain itself; but yet so, as the voluntary poverty which was vowed there for love of Jesus Christ, might be faithfully observed.

In descending the mountain and approaching the monastery of Clairvaux, it is easy to see that everything about it announces God; the humility of the poor of Jesus Christ is proclaimed aloud in that silent valley, by the simplicity of its buildings; and, in a word, those who came into it, found there a silence like that of midnight, though at midday, and though the valley was full of men, all laboring, for none are permitted to be idle, all are occupied in the work which had been enjoined them. The only noise which was heard there was the sound of the different instruments they used, or that of the voice of the brethren who sang the praises of God. The fame of this great silence, and the order they observed to keep it, impressed such awe on the minds of even the seculars who came there, that they were afraid not only to speak bad things, but even such as were not sufficiently grave and serious.

The solitude of this desert— in which those servants of God remained hidden and which was surrounded by a thick shady forest closed in on all sides by the neighboring mountains— represented in some manner the cave of our Holy Father Saint Benedict, in which he was found by the shepherds, as if they intended to preserve some form of the dwelling of the saint whose life they desired to imitate. For though they were so numerous, they were not less solitary, and the order in which charity was regulated was such that though there were many in the place, yet each individual was as if alone. For, as a man whose life is disorderly and irregular becomes a tumultuous company to himself, here on the contrary, unity of mind and silent regularity make it so happen that so great a number of persons are individually as if alone, and the interior solitude of their hearts was conserved by the exact order and discipline which regulated all their words and actions.

If their house and other buildings were simple, their manner of life was no less so. The bread they used seemed rather made of earth than flour. It was made of the corn which that barren desert with difficulty produced— after much labor and fatigue—the brethren having endeavored to cultivate it with every attention and application. The other sorts of food which they served up had no taste but what hunger and love of God could give them, and yet the novices were so simple in their fervor, that they found these things too delicate; and considering as so much poison everything which gratified the taste, they refused these gifts of God, on account of the pleasure they experienced in eating. [77]

It is by such testimonies as these, my brethren, that you ought to judge of the cenobitical state. It is by the words and the character of the saints that you are to discover the true character of a state so holy. I flatter myself that I have said sufficient on the subject to inform your minds, and to give you every reasonable satisfaction. For if you can live in these deserts here, you can, as I have already said, acquire the perfection of those who have dwelt in them heretofore, by imitating those holy monks, of whom we have related such extraordinary and wonderful things.

---

[77] Guliel. Abb. Lib. 1, *de vita St. Bernardi*, ch. 7. / See also, *Bernard of Clairvaux: Early Biographies* (Carleton, Oregon: Guadalupe Translations, 2012), 35.

5 | OF THE CENOBITICAL STATE— CONTENTS:

5

OF THE ESSENCE AND PERFECTION OF THE CENOBITICAL STATE

QUESTION 1.— *In what does this perfection consist, and what are its essential parts?*

ANSWER.— As the designs of Almighty God, my brethren, in forming the monastic state in His Church, were to place men therein who might serve Him in spirit and in truth, and who by being disengaged from all created things might serve His adorable Majesty in all purity and holiness: it must be allowed that the first and principal duty of a religious man is to unite himself to God in the silence and repose of his heart, to meditate continually on His holy law, and to keep himself perfectly free from everything that might turn his thoughts from that holy occupation, and thus to raise himself by a constant application to that perfection to which he is called, and which consists in the faithful accomplishment of the will and counsels of Almighty God.

As this has been the end which God proposed to Himself in the institution of this state, so it is that which is most essential to it. And it is no less true that all our practices of piety and penitential exercises should have no other end. In effect, if we have embraced the practice of fasting, watching, manual labor, silence, separation from the world, continency, poverty, and obedience, it was for no other purpose but that we might thereby obtain of God that sanctity which is the essence, the foundation and the end of the religious state.

This was the reason why the cenobites of the East expressed nothing at the time they made profession but an entire renunciation of all temporal affairs and created things, and from every object that might prevent them from attaining to that intimate union in which they were obliged to live continually with God.[78]

Cassian had no other opinion. He tells us in the person of the holy Abbot Moses that the end of a solitary is purity of heart, to which he ought to advance by all the exercises of his profession, and in which he ought to preserve his heart from the least dissipation and anxiety, so that he might offer it to God as a sacrifice of perfect sanctity.[79]

Saint Basil teaches us in his writings that a religious has embraced a state which surpasses human nature; that there is nothing corporal or sensible in it; that he has chosen the state and condition of angels; that he should be continually employed in contemplating the majesty of God, and that the consideration of no other beauty should be able to withdraw him from it. He says that the religious life is the state of such persons who live only for Jesus Christ; that the sanctification of a religious man consists in being united to God at all times, with all his strength in an inviolable manner, and in seeking to fulfill His holy will with all possible care and attention.[80]

Saint Jerome says that the monks who sing the praises of God day and night, should fulfill that duty with the same sanctity as the martyrs who praise Him in the land of the living, since they themselves are martyrs, and because they perform on earth what the angels do in heaven.[81]

This is what Saint Benedict had before his eyes when he prescribed rules for the sanctification of his disciples, in which he leads them by different degrees of humility to that perfect charity which—banishing all fear—makes that be accomplished without pain, as it were naturally and through a holy custom, which before was not performed without fear and apprehension of punishment.[82]

Saint Bernard enumerating the different employments which the religious may occupy in the monastery, includes none but such as center in God, of which He is the only and true object. For whether they live in sighs and shed tears like Lazarus, or imitate the charity and solicitude of Martha, or in fine, whether they have chosen the contemplation of Mary for their inheritance, they may say with the prophet, "My eyes are always

---

[78] S. Dionysii Areopagitae, PG 3:531.

[79] "What is all this except ever to offer to God a perfect and clean heart, and to keep it free from all disturbances?" *Conferences* 1.1.6 (NPNF2 / 11:297).

[80] *Brevius,* Interrogatio LIII, PG 31:1118.

[81] Epis. In Ps 125 / S. Eusebii Hieronymi Stridonensis Presbyteri, PL 26:1183D.

[82] "When, therefore, a monk shall have ascended these various grades of humility, he shall presently attain to that perfect love of God which casteth out fear" *RB* 7.

turned to the Lord" (Ps 24:15). They can affirm that they behold only Jesus Christ, that their eyes are only open for Him, that although they serve Him in different employments, yet they are always in His presence, and that nothing is able to divert their thoughts from Him. For, in effect, Lazarus is occupied in meditating on His judgments, Martha in providing for His necessities, and Mary inflamed with holy love sighs continually after the enjoyment of His infinite perfections.

These are truths so evident my brethren that they require no authorities to prove them. Every religious person ought to be convinced that his state is entirely spiritual, and that its ultimate end is nothing else but the sanctification of those who are called to it (1 Thess. 4:3).

This is a conviction which is established in every soul whom the spirit of God enlightens. He separates them from the world in order to conceal the world from them. He makes them dwell in the secret of His face, covering both the persons and the things from which He separates them, as it were with a veil, so that they may attend to Himself alone, so that the world not being less crucified to them than they are to the world, they now live only for God, and have neither thoughts, words, nor actions but to say to Him with the Apostle: "My God, thou art my life, and death is my happiness" (Phil 1:21). Thus, you see, my brethren, that the state and the profession of those monks whom we call cenobites consist in a constant application to God. In that the entire essence and perfection of their state are found, and all their other duties tend to it, as to their ultimate term.

Q. 2— Is it not a common opinion, that the essence of the religious state consists in the practice of the three vows of poverty, chastity and obedience?

A.— It is certain, my brethren, that if the vows of poverty, chastity and obedience, are taken in all the extent in which the saints present them to our view, there is nothing in the religious life but is found comprised within their sphere; but, not, however, if they are only considered in a merely literal manner, if by chastity nothing more than purity of the senses is understood, by poverty a simple disengagement from exterior goods, and by obedience a common and ordinary submission, which is usually reduced to non-rebellion against superiors, and to seeking some permission from them in the different circumstances and necessities of life. Though these vows are the necessary means to acquire the essence and the sanctity of religious profession, and though they are the three pillars on which the spiritual temple must be raised, nevertheless they tend to something more excellent and perfect. They require more disengaged, more sublime dispositions. This is an angelical state that cannot be shut up within such narrow limits;

and to pretend to confine it to the bounds of this triple renunciation, is to desire to reduce a building of rare beauty and magnificence to its simple foundation.

Q. 3.—Tell us in what manner we ought to understand the three vows, beginning first by the vow of chastity?

A. We cannot doubt, my brethren, that Jesus Christ requires a purity in such persons as He calls to His service, and are consecrated to Him by the sacred vows of religion, proportionate to the sublimity of that affinity. Chastity of body may be sufficient, if you please, in the marriages which are contracted among men. However, He who is beautiful above the children of men in an infinite degree, expects to find a purity in the souls whom He receives into the number of His spouses which may be proportionally worthy of His own purity. It is to them more particularly than to others, that these words of the prophet seem to be addressed: Let your sanctity be such that my sanctity may be its rule and measure ("Be holy for I am holy," Lev 11:44 and 1 Pet. 1:16). In effect, you find the spouse in the Canticles requires that the beauty of his spouse should be so accomplished—his heart is so sensible to everything she does—that an indifferent look, a little disorder in her hair wounds him in a deep and sensible manner (Cant 4:9) so much so that He cannot endure the least spot or defect in her (Cant 4:7). He calls her beautiful twice, to give us to understand that she ought to possess a twofold beauty, and that she should not possess the perfect chastity of her soul in a less degree than that of her body (Cant 4:1).

There is no reason to think that our Lord could be satisfied with a mere exterior chastity in such persons with whom He contracts a union so direct and intimate, as is that which He effects by the religious vows, or even that of the soul when only confined to exemption from exterior disorders. On the contrary, He requires a perfect chastity, that is to say, a purity which banishes all vice and passions from the soul, and in a word, everything that might displease Him. Can it be imagined that the soul which is exempt only from the more gross impurities can be more pleasing to Him, if at the same time she is filled with pride, vainglory, anger or envy? And do we not find that the foolish virgins—though they preserved their chastity without blemish—were nevertheless excluded from the nuptial chamber, and treated as if they were impure fornicators.

Hence, my brethren, the chastity to which a religious is obliged signifies much more than a well regulated mode of conduct. It comprises the whole body of his actions, and admits nothing that might tarnish their beauty. For he has given himself to Jesus Christ, and consequently all his thoughts, words and actions, and even the smallest moments of his life, belong to that divine Lord and Master. This is the object which should exclusively fill the entire capacity of his heart.

Therefore, everything that he admits therein which is not Jesus Christ, or dignified with His name, authority or love, should be considered as belonging to the number of those things which should be constantly and irrevocably excluded from his affections. Nor can a religious man entertain anything of such a character without offending that perfect charity in the practice of which he should always live.

But in order that you may not think that all I have said here is nothing but the fruit of my own imagination or particular opinion, I will now relate those of Saint Basil, and give you a detailed idea of his sentiments on this subject. This great saint tells us:

> The gift of virginity does not consist in abstaining from marriage, but it is moreover necessary to be a virgin in all the conduct of life and in every particular action. The chastity of men called to this state of life should appear in everything they do, and every one of these motions should be exempt from the least corruption and impurity. In effect, fornication is frequently committed by conversation, adultery by looks (Matt 5:28). Corruption enters into the heart by other senses, as the bounds of temperance are exceeded by intemperance in eating and drinking.
>
> Therefore, if we have formed the design of retracing the marks of the divine perfections in our souls by keeping ourselves from the contagion of all irregular passions and affections in order that we may deserve the enjoyments of eternal life, let us be studious to do nothing that might be unworthy of this holy profession, or might expose us to the judgment of our enemy. For Ananias was first at liberty not to offer his goods to God, nor to bind himself by any vow, but since he had consecrated them to God, and suffered his sacrifice to be defiled with the motives of vainglory, seeking thereby the praise and the admiration of men, by an action so very remarkable; and having afterwards detained a great part of the price for which he had sold them, he drew down on himself such a weight of divine indignation, of which Saint Peter was the minister, that he found no time to repent (Acts 5:1-11).
>
> Hence, before we make profession, and engage ourselves in the religious life, we are at liberty to choose that of marriage, and to settle in the common way, according to the law of God, and the permission granted by Him for that purpose. But as soon as a man has freely made choice of this kind of life, which is so very extraordinary, and engaged himself therein by a vow, he must preserve himself for God from all impurity, with

the same care as we keep the sacred vessels from every defilement, lest he should draw down on himself the guilt of a horrible sacrilege, by defiling a body consecrated to God by the vows of religion, by returning again to the ways of a soft and effeminate life.

When I speak in this manner, I do not pretend to confine myself to the precept by which we are obliged to avoid one species of sin and disorder, as they who limit the perfection of virginity to the chastity of the body alone, are willing to persuade themselves. But my design is to demonstrate that those who desire to live to God alone should not suffer their affections to be corrupted with any created thing, and that they should carefully avoid every object that might produce such an effect. For anger, envy, the remembrance of injuries, pride, lies, dissipation, inconsiderate and irregular conversation, sloth in the time of prayer, the desire of insignificant things, indifference in observing the commandments of God, luxury in dress, affected looks, discourses and entertainments which decency and necessity do not allow, all these things, I say, are so contrary to the sanctity of the religious state, that he who is consecrated to God by the vow of chastity, cannot use too much circumspection in avoiding them. For it is almost as dangerous for a religious person to fall into any of these, as to commit the more enormous sins, and to do actions which are expressly prohibited.

Therefore it is necessary that a Christian who has renounced the world should consider these things attentively, so that being consecrated to God, he may not suffer himself to be defiled with any irregular passion. Rather, he ought to reflect in particular that having undertaken to go beyond the bounds of human nature, he has embraced a kind of life in which there is nothing sensible or corporal, because he has chosen an angelical life for his inheritance, the exemption from marriage being an inseparable property of the angelic nature, for which reason he should not be attracted by any other object, however beautiful and excellent it may be, but should be employed continually in contemplating the divine perfections of his God.

Hence, if a Christian, who is raised to the dignity of angels by the religious state, defiles himself again with the passions and vices of the flesh, nothing more can be said of such a one, but he is like the leopard's skin, the hair of which is neither white nor black, but spotted with various colors. Such is everyone who has embraced a life of celibacy. [83]

Cassian inculcates the same truth, when he tells us:

---

[83] Inst. Monast. Serm. 1

The first and principal care of a religious, and the continual effort and intention of his heart, should be to unite himself inviolably to God. His mind should be ever fixed on spiritual things, and everything which does not tend that way, however great it may be, should be considered only as a secondary object. [84]He is bound to offer a perfect heart to God, a heart purified and disengaged from all the confusion and irregularity of the passions. When he strays away from God by any distraction, he should recall his wandering heart as soon as he perceives it, be sorry for it, and lament it with sighs and tears. He should remember that every time he disengages himself from the thought of that divine object, he separates himself from his sovereign good, and that he commits a spiritual fornication when he willfully ceases to contemplate his Divine Savior for a single moment.[85]

Saint Ephrem speaks in the same manner. He tells us:

God is jealous; He is holy, and without blemish; He dwells in souls who fear Him, and He does the will of those who love Him. Do you wish to become a chaste and incorruptible temple of God, that His image is perpetually engraven on your heart? I do not say an image that is drawn on wood, or on any other material object, and delineated by a certain arrangement of colors, but such an image as is imprinted in the midst of the soul in a manner no less wonderful than spiritual, by watchings, fastings, continency, prayer and other holy actions. Endeavor, therefore, my brethren, to imitate the Holy Fathers in the conduct of your lives, and by the practice of their virtues. Like them exercise yourself in continency, cultivate it by the spirit, cultivate it by the heart, cultivate it by the senses, by the composure of your persons, by your habit, by your food, by your tongue, by your looks, by your thoughts, so that you may prove yourselves to be perfect and accomplished champions in all things.[86]

Saint John Chrysostom, who was replenished with truth, said:

A virgin who is anxious about the things of this world, deserves not to be ranked among the virgins, since the renunciation of the state of marriage alone is not sufficient to purchase a title so glorious, but the chastity of the soul is also required.

---

[84] *Conferences* 1.1.8 (NPNF2 /11:298).

[85] *Conferences* 1.1.13 (NPNF2 / 11:300).

[86] De Virg. 4

By chastity of soul, I mean not only having no impure thoughts, nor wicked desires, being exempt from pride and ostentation in dress; but leading a life entirely pure and free from all anxiety concerning the affairs of the world. Just as there is nothing more shameful than to behold a soldier lay down his arms in order to spend his time in alehouses and debauchery, so there is nothing so unbecoming as to see virgins willingly embarrassing themselves in worldly affairs. . . . Besides, one of the greatest advantages of the state of virginity consists in cutting off all the occasions of superfluous cares, as well as all the inutilities of life, and that it consecrates the soul inseparably to the exercises of piety. Without this, it would be less excellent than marriage, because it would produce nothing but thorns in the soul, and would terminate in choking the pure seed of sanctity which should flourish in it . . . .

The five virgins whose lamps were extinguished were virgins as to the body, but they were not pure in spirit. Though they were not corrupted by any criminal connections, they were, nevertheless, defiled by the love of riches. Their bodies were indeed pure, but their souls were filled with adulteries. They were filled with a multitude of evil thoughts, with a continual revolution of covetousness, hard-heartedness to the poor, envy, pride, sloth, forgetfulness; in a word, with all the interior spiritual vices which never fail to destroy the venerable state of christian virginity. For to what purpose does virginity serve, when joined to the hardness of an unmerciful heart?[87]

Saint Augustine inculcated the same doctrine, when he said:

A chaste virgin consecrated to God should possess everything that might adorn her virginity, otherwise her virginity would only serve to her confusion, for to what purpose is the integrity of body without that of the soul? What advantage could she derive from having no carnal connection with any man, if at the same time she was proud, sensual, talkative, quarrelsome . . . .since the Lord abhors such dispositions.[88]

Saint Syncletica, of whom Saint Athanasius speaks with so much encomium, and who according to his opinion did not deserve a less inferior rank among the virgins of Christ than Saint Anthony among the ancient

---

[87] Joannes Chrysostom, *de Virginitate*, PG 48:589 /*John Chrysostom, On virginity; Against remarriage*; Sally Rieger Shore, Elizabeth Ann Clark, trans (New York: Mellenen,1983), 116.

[88] Augustine. *Saint Augustine: Expositions on the Book of Psalms* (NPNF1/8:359).

solitaries, teaches us in few but enlightened words, that the contract which they who are consecrated to God by the vows of religion form with him contains two essential clauses. If they do not fulfill these, He considers them with horror, and rejects their promises with indignation: these are, to give themselves but little anxiety concerning their bodies, and to be very solicitous about their souls. Behold, says this great saint, the articles of the marriage contract, which are drawn up between virgins and their heavenly spouse.[89]

Saint Bernard tells us in the same manner:

> There is nothing more beautiful nor adorned than the heavens; but even they have nothing that can be compared with the beauty of the spouse. For being corporeal and sensible, they shall lose both their being and form, and thus consequently must yield to her whose beauty is spiritual and imperceptible to the sense; her ornaments as well as her form are all of a superior order, and she herself is as eternal as eternity itself, of which she is the image. Her splendor is charity, and charity you know never fails (1 Cor 13:8). It is justice, and justice remains forever and ever (Ps 111:9). It is patience, and the patience of the poor will be crowned in the end (Matt 5:3). What is voluntary poverty? What is humility? Does not the one deserve an eternal kingdom, and the other an exaltation that shall have no end? May not the same thing be said of the fear of the Lord, which remains forever and ever? Prudence, temperance, fortitude, and all the other virtues, are they not so many pearls of great price, which adorn the spouse, and shine with an immortal brightness, because they are as it were the basis and foundation of immortality. Do not imagine that the holy zeal with which the bridegroom loves His heavenly bride, can be satisfied with any other heaven, but that in which this well-beloved already dwells.[90]

Here you see what the saints thought of religious chastity; here you find what the sublime ideas they had of the majesty of God made them say. They could not imagine that a creature raised by his vocation and holy grace to a degree of honor so sublime and excellent as is that of being united to Jesus Christ, as a spouse, could contract an obligation by this sacred engagement

---

[89] S. Athanasius, *Vita et Gesta Sanctae Beataeque Magistrae Synclecticae*, PG 28:1487-1558 / Richard Challoner, *The Wonders of God in the Wilderness* (London, Needham, 1755), 271.

[90] S. Bernardus, Sermo XXVII in *Sermones in Cantica*, PL 183:914d (1854) / St.Bernard, *St. Bernard's Sermons on the Canticle of Canticles.* (trans. a priest of Mount Melleray; Dublin: Browne, 1920), 1:305-306.

less than that of being pure in body and mind. Nor could they imagine that a vowed religious should fail to acquire—as much as possible in a nature subject to so many infirmities—a sanctity like to His, employing for that end all reasonable solicitude, removing far from everything that might displease his divine Lord, and thus becoming acceptable in His sight (1 Cor 7:34).

The saints were well persuaded that the sanctity of God could not require dispositions of any other nature in a soul whom He had united to Himself in a manner so particular, that it is no longer lawful for him to love his God in the common way, because he has renounced for His love what he might otherwise have lawfully loved, says Saint Augustine; that all his beauty should be interior, and that all the variety with which the prophet desires the soul should be adorned, is nothing else than the various number of virtues which should unite and accompany her withersoever she goes as her daughters and companions.[91]

Q. 4— If chastity is a virtue so extensive, and if it require such perfect purity; and as there is no sin that does not attack the purity of the soul, it seems reasonable to infer, that sin attacks the vow of chastity also, and consequently every sin is a violation of the religious engagement?

A.— It is true that every sin attacks this virtue, but it does not follow that every sin is a violation and destruction of the promises that were made at the time of profession. Though the law of chastity extends to every action of our lives and regulates all we do, as Saint Basil assures us, nevertheless, it contains only the protestation of a sincere will to acquire this perfect purity of soul. As long as this will is not revoked, the vow always subsists—though there may be some actions performed which are not conformable to it and which wound its integrity.

---

[91] S. Augustinus, *De Sancta Virginitate,* PL 40:427 / "If, therefore, ye despise marriages of sons of men, from which to beget sons of men, love ye with your whole heart Him, Who is fair of form above the sons of men; ye have leisure; your heart is free from marriage bonds. Gaze on the Beauty of your Lover: think of Him equal to the Father, made subject also to His Mother: ruling even in the heavens, and serving upon the earth: creating all things, created among all things. That very thing, which in Him the proud mock at, gaze on, how fair it is: with inward eyes gaze on the wounds of Him hanging, the scars of Him rising again, the blood of Him dying, the price of him that believes, the gain of Him that redeems. Consider of how great value these are, weigh them in the scales of Charity; and whatever of love ye had to expend upon your marriages, pay back to Him." Augustine. *St. Augustine: On the Holy Trinity, Doctrinal Treatises, Moral Treatises* (NPNF1/3:437).

But this vow may be criminally retracted in several ways: either by consenting to some impurity, whether the thing be executed or not; or by forming a will directly contrary to this engagement, for example, if a religious, hurried away by a licentious spirit, or wearied by the difficulties which the necessary vigilance in the pursuit of this perfection indispensably requires, should lay aside the resolution of laboring therein, or by any other spiritual sin; such as pride, hatred, envy or wrath. This vow may also may be retracted by inapplication—if by living in a slothful and negligent way, the monk takes no pains to advance in virtue, or to fulfill the duties of his state. For it is evident, that in all these cases he no longer tends to the state which he at first proposed to attain; that he has lost the will of doing it; that he fails in his promises to God, and that by such infidelity he violates the vow and protestation he had made to the Almighty.

But if he only falls into some light faults, though such faults are not conformable to that purity to which he ought to approach as near as possible, still it would not be just to say that by such faults he had violated his engagement, or that his sin was criminal prevarication, because his first will is still unretracted, and he perseveres in the desire of acquiring that purity which is contained in the essence of his vow.

I speak not of the chastity and the continency of the senses, because you are already sufficiently informed of the obligations they impose, and because there is no diversity of opinion on that subject. Only remember this, my brethren, that this virtue is the foundation of the building, which, if destroyed, the whole edifice must fall; and as it is insufficient for its own conservation if left alone, be always convinced that you carry a treasure in frail earthen vessels.

Avoid everything as destructive that might expose it to danger in the least degree; and consider every excess in a matter so very important as the greatest and most incurable of all evils; for though it is true that there is no fall from which the hand of God may not raise the soul; and that there is no disorder, however great, which the tears of true repentance may not heal while we are in this life, yet these cures are so very rare, that it may be said with truth that whoever has proved unfaithful in a state so holy shall not be able to find sufficient tears to bewail his misfortune, nor sufficient time to efface his sin.

Q. 5— All you have said concerning the virtue of chastity seems to be so worthy of the sanctity of God, that we cannot conceive how any person can entertain any contrary idea: but what should our sentiments be concerning religious poverty?

A.— The saints have considered poverty as the riches of monks. By it they are qualified to raise themselves above the things of the world—to consider them with an indifferent eye, and to contemn them. The being rich consists not in possessing much, but in desiring nothing. In effect, though a man were the master of many worlds, still his ambition would not be satisfied, for his desires would be as so many empty spaces, and he would be, of course, as yet in want (Ps 33:11).

On the contrary, they who renounce all things, like the Apostles, enjoy a real abundance (Ps 33:11), because they no longer desire anything, and they find in God, even in this life, a hundred times as much as they have forsaken for His love. They are so animated and filled with the hope of future things that they lose all esteem for, and even recollection of, everything created.[92] This disposition, my brethren, is so excellent that it can be the effect only of a perfect abnegation. He who desires to place himself in this happy state, must divest himself of all things. He must place himself the first in this number of things to be renounced. He must give no place to any created or transitory object in his heart, and finally, he must walk after Jesus Christ with such perfect disinterestedness that he may be able to say with the great martyr, Saint Ignatius— "Now I begin to be a disciple of Jesus Christ, since I desire nothing of those things which are in the world."[93]

What profit would a religious man derive from the renunciation of his goods and fortune, if, while he broke the chains of those affections by which he was bound to them, he suffered himself to be tied with other bonds? He should have no other motives in this renunciation but those of giving himself to God without division or reserve, and to serve Him in profound peace, and with an attention undisturbed by the anxiety and solicitude which always attend the administration and enjoyment of all earthly things.

Nevertheless, as it is a truth declared by the Son of God Himself, that where our treasure is, there our hearts are also. As the measure of our love for the things which we esteem becomes the link which binds us to them, it necessarily follows that he who reserves an affection for anything that is not God, or for whatever does not relate to Him, gives only a part of himself to God. Instead, then, of making His Sovereign Majesty completely master of all, he, on the contrary, contracts the dominion of His kingdom, which has no limits. Thus, by a kind of sacrilege, he resumes the dominion

---

[92] "Christian poverty is always rich, because what it has is more than what it has not. Nor does the poor man fear to labor in this world, to whom it is given to possess all things in the Lord of all things." *Pope St. Leo I. Leo the Great, Gregory the Great* (NPNF2 12:156).

[93] St. Ignatius of Antioch. *The Apostolic Fathers with Justin Martyr and Irenaeus* (ANF 1:76).

of that which he had previously offered to the Lord, and by immolating only an imperfect victim, draws down upon himself the divine wrath and indignation.

Now, how can a person of this character expect to find that peace and tranquility in solitude which he came to seek in it? For, besides the motives which demonstrate that this peace is a favor which our Lord reserves for those religious alone, whose only care is to study to know His will, and to fulfill it in all things, there is, moreover, a certain malignity inherent in the things of the world—chiefly when they are esteemed for themselves without any reference to God—which makes them incapable of satisfying those who possess them. They are desired with eagerness, they are sought for with ardor, they are enjoyed with anxiety. When men have them, they are tormented with the fear of losing them, and they never lose them but with sorrow and grief.

Thus the religious who gives himself to God with restriction and reserve may indeed be poor in the esteem of men, but he is not so according to the judgment of God. He neither enjoys the satisfactions of a worldly rich man, nor the consolations of the poor of Jesus Christ. He deprives himself of the false pleasures which are found in the possession of riches, and reserves for himself the real vexations which attend them. He is agitated by his passions in the cloister as much as if he were in the world. His heart is filled with envy, wrath, impatience, and sadness; and by a just judgment of God, that which he retained to himself for the comfort of life, becomes the instrument of his persecution and torment.

Be you, therefore, persuaded, my brethren, that a religious soul shall never find rest in his solitude, unless he gives himself up—without reserve—to Him from whom alone he ought to expect it; and unless he considers as so many dispositions of the Divine Providence all that he may have to suffer from privations, hunger, thirst, cold, from sickness, the government of his superiors, and from the various tempers of his brethren, his whole life will be nothing but a course of temptations, or rather a chain of falls and relapses. The enemy will inflict on him a thousand and a thousand mortal wounds by means of those things he had reserved. He may turn himself from one side to another to find some rest, but it will be to no purpose. He shall pass his days in bitterness, and finish a miserable life by a still more unhappy death.

It was this misfortune, my brethren, that the holy man Cassian deplored when he said that he had seen solitaries, who having generously forsaken great fortunes, after having stripped themselves of their goods, and given them to the poor for the love of Jesus Christ, fell into anger, and suffered

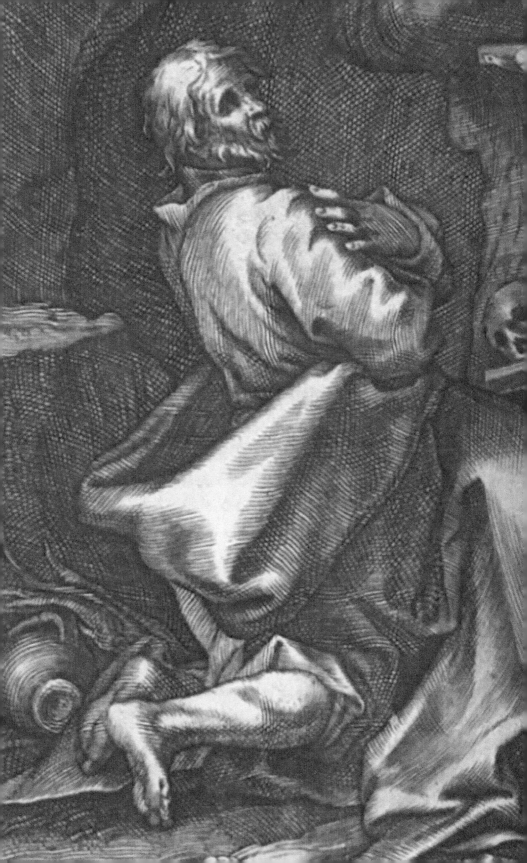

themselves to be carried away by passion for things of no account; and who, in this yielding to their former passions in matters of no value, made their first actions abortive, and destroyed their fruit, merit and recompense.[94]

Saint Syncletica was very far from confining religious poverty to a mere separation of worldly riches, since she required that a preparation should be previously made for that purpose by corporal austerities, such as fastings, sleeping on the bare ground, and many other penitential exercises, since she taught that voluntary poverty is something so great, that it belongs only to those who are already long accustomed to the practice of other virtues.[95]

Saint Basil, in answer to the question which had been proposed to him, namely, whether it is necessary to renounce all things before entering the service of God, could not explain himself more exactly on the subject than by saying:

> We believe that this command, addressed by our Lord to all those who desired to become His disciples, extends itself to many things from which it is necessary to separate ourselves. For first, we have renounced the devil and all carnal pleasures, having cast from us all such passions as conceal themselves, being of a shameful nature. In the next place, we have rejected all earthly kindred, all familiarity with the rest of men, as well as all customs which are contrary to the perfection of the Gospel, and to the affair of our salvation. Besides, that which is still more necessary, we renounce ourselves by divesting ourselves of the old man and of his works. In fine, we must renounce all affection to the things of this world, which are calculated to impede us in the acquisition of true piety. Hence perfect renunciation consists in disengaging oneself from all irregular passions—in having no attachment to life—in pronouncing on ourselves the sentence of our own death, and in placing no confidence in ourselves.
>
> This renunciation must begin by an entire separation from all exterior things; such as riches, vainglory, the usual mode of conversation adopted and practiced in our precedent life, and from all exterior and useless things, as we are taught by the example of the holy disciples of Jesus Christ; such as Saint James and Saint John, when they left their father Zebedee, and their fishing boat, which was the only property they had; Saint Matthew when he left the custom house to follow our Divine

---

[94] *Conferences* (NPNF1/11:297)

[95] Athanasius, *Vita S. Syncleticae*. PG 28:1485 / Pseudo-Athanasius, *The Life and Regimen of the Blessed and Holy Syncletica*, trans. Elizabeth Bryson Bongie (Eugene, Oregon: Wipf, 2005).

Savior . . . . . So true is it that when a man is inflamed with an ardent desire of following Jesus Christ, he can no longer find any pleasure in the affairs of this life, neither has the love of parents and relations power to make any impression, when this love is contrary to the love of God. For it is in such cases that this sentence of our Lord claims a full right: if anyone comes to me and hates not his father, mother, wife, children, brothers and sisters, yea, even his own life also, he cannot be my disciple . . .(Luke 14:26).

Hence, when we retain the possession of any temporal goods, or any of the corruptible affairs of this world, the spirit being as it were plunged in filth and ordure, becomes by an inevitable consequence incapable of divine contemplation so long as we remain in that miserable state, and thus its desires stand unmoved with regard to the eternal goods which are promised, and which we hope to obtain. For it is impossible to attain to the enjoyments of these heavenly possessions, if the soul be not elevated on the wings of fervent prayer to the region where they are reserved, and unless they are sought for with a fervor as may enable us to consider as matters of little or no importance the labors and sacrifices which we are obliged to undertake and to accomplish for the purpose of deserving to enjoy them.

So, as you may easily perceive, renunciation is nothing less than a bursting asunder the bonds by which we are confined to this transitory and mortal life; a deliverance from all commerce in human affairs, by which we become qualified and disposed to enter the ways of God. It forms an occasion the most interesting for obtaining the possession and enjoyment of which is more valuable than gold, and more excellent than the most valuable precious stones. In brief, to give you a short and comprehensive description of its worth in a few words, it is an admirable transport by which the heart of man is elevated to the sphere of heavenly conversation, and qualifies to say with the Apostle, Our conversation is in heaven (Phil 3:20).

The greatest of the advantages of this renunciation consists in placing us in the first degree of a perfect imitation of Jesus Christ, who being rich, became poor for love of us, a disposition so necessary that it becomes indispensable to all who desire to live in the full observance of the rules of perfection laid down in the Gospel. For without it, how is it possible to obtain either compunction of heart, humility of will, or means of overcoming anger, sadness, anxiety, and the other pernicious disorders of the soul, especially if we consider what opponents to this perfection are found in the goods and solicitudes of life, and in the violent propensities, as well as in the inveterate habits which bend us down to so many other things. [96]

Cassian treats the same matter in an extensive manner in his third conference, and proves from the authority of the holy scripture and tradition, that religious persons are obliged to labor with all their strength to attain the perfection of a threefold renunciation. The first is, according to him:

> To renounce the possession of all earthly goods and perishable riches; the second to renounce ourselves, our vices, ill habits, and all irregular affections both interiorly and exteriorly; and the third, to withdraw our hearts from all created things, and to fix them in a continual and undivided application to those which are invisible and eternal.
>
> Almighty God Himself teaches us this threefold renunciation by the command which He gave to Abraham (Gen 12:1), saying, go forth of thy county; that is, leave the goods of this world, and all the riches of this perishable life—leave thy relations; that is, forsake thy usual manner of life, and thy vicious inclinations, which adhering to us in our birth, and by the corruption of nature, are now become as it were a part of our existence—leave thy father's house; that is, efface the remembrance of the things of this world from thy mind, and turn away thy eyes from all visible and created objects. Hence, we ought to withdraw our eyes from the view of this earthly house, and raise them to the contemplation of the heavenly dwelling above, which is to be our eternal abode. This is, then, only accomplished, when, though living in the flesh, we by our actions evince that we are already become citizens of heaven; our conversation is in heaven (Phil 3:20).
>
> The accomplishment of the first of these renunciations, even with an humble and a lively faith, will produce but little advantage, unless we also attain the second with the same vigilance and fervor. Thus, the way being prepared to a full execution of the third, our souls are raised to a perfect disengagement, and all their thoughts and affections being placed on heavenly things, we depart from the ancient dwelling of our enemy, who became our father from the time we came into life, because we lived according to the maxims of the old man, and were children of wrath like the rest of men.
>
> We shall attain this third renunciation, when our souls being no longer

---

[96] *Saint Basil: Ascetical Works.* Vol. 9 (ed. R. J. Deferrari, trans. Sister M. Monica Wagner, C.S.C.; Washington D.C. : The Catholic University of America Press, 1962), 253-257.

weighed down by the contagion of this animal body, and their affections being purified from all earthly things, shall raise themselves to heaven on the wings of holy meditation, and shall be so absorbed in the contemplation of eternal truths, that they will no longer remember they are confined in the prison of the flesh: and when ravished in the contemplation of the divine perfections, they shall be so replenished with delights that they will no longer have eyes to see, nor ears to hear anything else, but being wholly wrapt in divine love, they shall be insensible to every other object.

Therefore, my brethren, if we desire to become perfect, we must, after having forsaken our parents and our country, after having renounced the riches and pleasures of this world, and even our own bodies, we must still disengage our hearts and our wills from all visible things, and never allow them to make one step towards the things we have forsaken. We must be careful not to imitate the Jews, whom Moses led out of Egypt. They forsook it in body, but soon returned back in affection. They renounced the true God, who, by so many prodigies, had delivered them from slavery, and adored the same idols of Egypt which they had before despised. They returned back to Egypt in heart and desire, says the Scripture: they spoke to Aaron, and said, make us gods to go before us (Exod 32:1).

Every religious, who, having renounced the world, return to their former desires and affections, are guilty of the same criminal request, at least by their thoughts and actions. Like them they say, alas! How happy we were in Egypt, and I am much afraid my children, lest there should be many amongst us at present who violate the law of God, like that ancient people in the time of Moses, and whose punishment was not less terrible than alarming in its application, for of six hundred thousand armed men who came out of Egypt, only two individuals entered in the land of promise (Num 14:30).[97]

Saint Benedict my brethren, gives us the same extensive idea of religious poverty, when he requires that his religious should have nothing in their possession or power, and they should give up everything without exception. He declares that their poverty ought to be so entire, that it should destroy in them every right and power of disposing of even their own bodies and wills. That is, that they can no longer do as they please, either in disposing of their interior or exterior actions, according to their own will and inclination, and that as to all such things as are of absolute necessity, whatever they may be, they are to address themselves to the superior, from whom they are to hope

---

[97] *Conferences* 1.3.6 (NPNF2/11:321).

to receive them, as the necessaries and conservation of life and existence are hoped for from the goodness of God.[98]

Saint John Climacus spoke on this subject in the same manner. He tells us:

> Voluntary poverty is a renunciation of all earthly cares; an exemption from all the anxiety of life; a way that leads to heaven with ease and facility, in which everything is cast off that might impede the advancement of the soul in the way of salvation; a deliverance from all grief and sadness. That the religious who is really poor is master of the whole world, for he commits all his cares to the providence of God, and all mankind becomes His servants; that he does not ask the necessaries of life of men, but receives, as coming from the hand of God, whatever he receives from the hands of creatures. He who is become voluntarily poor, enjoys tranquility of mind, which is to be obtained only by reducing the passions to a state of perfect subjection: that he considers those things he enjoys, with the same indifference as if they did not exist. That as soon as he retires from the world, he esteems all things as dung, and is affected when he feels the necessity of anything, because he believes he is not yet become entirely poor.[99]

From these sentiments of the saints you can only infer, my brethren, that religious poverty does not consist in a mere separation from exterior possessions, but that like chastity, it also separates the heart from everything visible and invisible that is not eternal; that it deprives us of everything, leaving us only God, and such things as may perhaps help us to attain the possession of His heavenly kingdom.

You will perhaps tell me, my brethren, that I am proposing to your consideration a state of perfection. I allow that such is indeed the case, but what should I propose to those who are called by God to be perfect, if not perfection itself? To whom should I present the state of sanctity but to saints, I would say, to monks, since Almighty God has raised them up and established them in His Church for no other purpose than that of becoming saints, of perpetuating in the mystical body of Christ the life of the apostles and of filling the place the martyrs formerly held therein. In a word, can anyone imagine, that those whose lives are nothing else than a literal imitation of Jesus Christ, are not obliged to live, not only according to His precepts, but also according to His instructions and counsels?

---

[98] *RB* 33.

[99] *Ladder*, 156.

Nevertheless, though this perfection be included in the vow of poverty, of which it is the essence, still it must be allowed that it has its beginning, its progress and its consummation. Every person who embraces the religious life is obliged to tend to this renunciation; but they are not obliged to have attained its perfection. They are indeed bound to endeavor to ascend to it by continual care and assiduity; but our Lord who requires all these who consecrate themselves to Him by the vow of poverty (from the observance of which He never discharges anyone), should thus be disposed, does not require that they should all possess it in the same perfection. He is satisfied with their will, when he beholds them sincere and effective, when they, on their part, neglect nothing, and when they make a faithful use of all the means and practices prescribed by the rules for acquiring it.

There are some to whom our Lord is become so habitually present, and whose disengagement is so perfect, that they have not the least thought of things created; others who are so faithful that they expel the thought of present things as soon as they perceive their minds attacked by them. Some are found with whom these thoughts remain somewhat longer; they even excite some desires; but they are so insignificant, and the impressions are so superficial, that they produce no consequence nor effect. Some others may be known, who, being weaker, are attacked by them with more violence and obstinacy, and who, during the combat and resistance receive some light wounds. In fine, these are the more imperfect who as yet remain attached to things of no consequence after having forsaken those of importance; but who endeavor by prayers and much weeping to obtain of God a deliverance entire and perfect, which they are persuaded is essentially necessary for them. Now we may say with truth, that these latter are indeed poor, that they have that.

But still, holding it as an incontestable truth, that a religious who does not join one or other of these different degrees of renunciation he may have made with respect to created things, is not really poor; that his poverty is not such as he should have promised to God at the time of his engagement; that he is poor only in his imagination, and in the opinion of such persons as know nothing of the perfection of his state. Hence, as he cannot say with those whose engagement and privations he is bound to imitate, "Behold we have left all things to follow thee" (Matt 19:27)—so he shall have no part in the reward which Jesus Christ promises them in these words: "Amen, I say to you, that you who have followed me, shall receive a hundred fold, and shall hereafter possess eternal life" (Matt 19:28). [100]

---

[100] Of religious poverty more in detail see vol. 2, chap. 21.

Q. 6.— Having now spoken of chastity and poverty, we request that you will instruct us concerning obedience.

A.—The greater part of men, my brethren, are neither more nor less exact in the opinion they form of obedience than they are in those which they conceive of religious poverty and chastity. They speak of it in a manner so opposite to that which the saints teach us concerning it that it seems as if they are zealous to make religious persons become the entire masters of their conduct as the holy fathers were of placing them in a state of dependence. The former, from mere human motive, endeavor to discover some specious reasons and expedients to discharge them from the necessity of obeying; but the latter—who consider nothing but the divine will—enforce the necessity of submission by the most holy and cogent arguments. The one regard obedience as an insupportable yoke; the others esteem it as a service full of benediction. The one imagines that a religious would enjoy more real felicity if his will had not so many contradictions to surmount; the others are persuaded that there can be no true happiness found in religion until self-will is entirely destroyed.

In fine, the saints being enlightened by the Holy Spirit, condemn every action of self-will in religious persons. They maintain that such as make profession in a state so holy are bound to live in subjection at all times, to be obedient in all things and in every circumstance of their lives, because they knew that there is nothing more essential to the monastic state than dependence, docility, and submission of the will.

But now there are persons found who are far from being saints, who being enlightened by the false light of human prudence, have discovered the means of fortifying self-love by enervating the virtue of obedience, and receiving this state so holy and excellent, they bring it down to a level with the common vulgar professions of life, and thus divest it of everything which might make it worthy of its primitive institution.

Without stopping to discuss the unfounded reasons of those who make it their principal study to throw a veil of obscurity over the most holy and most evident truths, it will be more profitable to you to hear the sentiments of the saints on this subject—provided that you hold as a fundamental maxim that it is necessary to reject as false coin everything which bears not the mark and character of the tradition of the holy fathers.

Saint Basil, after having delineated the portrait of a superior, says:

> As soon as you shall have found such a one, renounce your own will, and give yourself up to his conduct without reserve, that thus you may become like a pure vessel, and that you may partake in a profitable manner of the

goods which are distributed in such a state, and may employ them to your own advantage.[101]

Observe as a constant rule of conduct to do nothing without his advice. Everything you shall do independently of him is a sort of theft, and a sacrilege that leads to death, and can be of no advantage to you, whatever appearance of good you may imagine in it.[102]

True and perfect obedience demonstrates itself not only in abstaining from such things as are evil by the advice of a superior, but it moreover acquiesces to his orders in such as are good, so that it performs nothing independently of his commands. For although abstinence and every corporal mortification are useful, nevertheless, if a religious should undertake the practice of them influenced by nothing more than his own will and humor, and without consulting or submitting to the will of his superior, in such a case the evil he commits is much greater than the good he imagines he is performing, for he that resists power resists the ordinance of God (Rom 13:2).[103]

Saint Basil adds:

From the time a man is incorporated in a religious community, he should remember that though the orders which are given should seem to exceed his ability and strength, yet he is obliged to renounce his own judgment, and should on such occasions demonstrate his docility and obedience by submitting to the orders of his superior, and in using every effort to accomplish them, even to death, though, as I have just remarked, they should seem to be much above his strength and capacity.[104] He should remember that our Lord became obedient to death even the death of the Cross. To act in any other manner would be holding up to view, by the hands of his resistance, a frightful assemblage of vices which had before taken up their abode in his interior—such as a weak and imperfect faith, an uncertain hope, self-love, pride, and presumption. For no one ever

---

[101] St. Basil, *Ascetical,* 19.

[102] Basil, *Ascetical,* 20.

[103] Basil, *Ascetical,* 218.

[104] Editor's note: Today's Cistercians of the Strict Observance differ with St. Basil here, and for that matter with the entire monastic tradition as de Rancé has traced it. From the order's website, "Becoming a Trappist Monk or Nun": "'Blind obedience' is not much encouraged today. Abbots and Abbesses are held more accountable and expected to listen to and enter into meaningful conversation with their subjects." http://www.trappists.org/visitor-questions/how-have-contemplatives-changed-middle-ages. Accessed Aug. 31, 2018

comes to the point of resisting or disobeying his superiors unless he had
first conceived and nourished a contempt for him in his heart; and on the
contrary, a man who places all his confidence in the promises of God, who
patiently awaits their accomplishment with a firm hope, will always fly
with ardor to fulfill everything commanded, whatever difficulties he may
find in the execution, knowing, as the Apostle says, that the sufferings of
this life bear no proportion to the future glory that shall be revealed in us
(Rom 8:18).[105]

Therefore, every superior should be persuaded that if he does not direct his brethren according to the rules of truth, he will draw down on
himself a terrible and an inevitable chastisement from God, who requires
the most exact account of them for the loss of those who were committed to their care. Inferiors on their side must be so entirely subordinate
that they embrace without delay every order coming from their superiors,
however difficult it may be, being assured that our Lord prepares a glorious reward for them in His heavenly kingdom.

The same holy doctor teaches:

He who is commissioned to distribute the different works and manual
acceptations, should attentively consider the various capacities of the
individual, and regulate his orders according to their strength; but doing otherwise he should deserve to be reprehended for making unjust
arrangements, taking his own unmeasured reasons for law and justice.
"Thou framest labor in commandment" (Ps 94:20). But that he who receives the command should never contradict, death being the only limit
which true obedience knows.[106]

In another place the same saint requires:

He who embraces the monastic state, should be armed with a firm, constant, and unshaken mind and will, that his resolution should always remain unchanged, and even unmoved against all attacks of the enemy; that
his solidity and courage should be equal to that of martyrs; and that he
should persevere till death, whether there be question of keeping the com-

---

[105] S. Basil, *Ascetical*, 291.

[106] S. Basilius, *Brevius*, PG 31:1182c.

mandments of God, or of obeying the orders of his superiors, seeing that in such conduct alone the essence of his profession consists.[107]

He moreover teaches elsewhere:

A monk is not master of one single instant of his life; that as an instrument cannot give itself motion, but receives it from the artist's hands; and as a member loses it action when cut off from the body to which it ought to be inseparably united, so neither should the actions of a religious be at any time separated from the will of the superior from whom they ought to receive their first and last motion. If a religious finds that he cannot perform what is commanded by reason of physical or moral inability, let him declare it to his superior, and place the judgment of the whole affair in his hands; but as to himself, let him be always prepared to execute whatever his superior shall decide, being mindful of the words of scripture: "You have not as yet resisted unto blood" (Heb 12:4). [108]

Cassian tells us that the rule of obedience which the monks of his time observed was so extensive that they were not allowed to do the least thing, nor to supply the most trivial wants, without having obtained the permission of doing so from their superior, that they executed all his orders without discussion and with as much promptitude as if they had received them from God Himself, and that they received the orders which were given them, even in things impossible, with so much piety and devotion that they employed all their force and abilities in endeavoring to execute them. So great was their veneration for him from whom the commands proceeded, that it did not allow them to examine whether they were or were not impossible.[109]
Saint Jerome says:

A religious ought to be subject in all things. His will should not exist for itself. He can neither will nor refuse to will, but according as he receives orders from his superior; he should find no difficulty nor repugnance in

---

[107] S. Basilius, *Constitutiones,* PG 31:1387a..

[108] S. Basilius, *Constitutiones,* PG 31:1418.

[109] "And so [the juniors] are quick to fulfill without any discussion all those things that are ordered by him, as if they were commanded by God from heaven; so that sometimes, when impossibilities are commanded them, they undertake them with such faith and devotion as to strive with all their powers and without the slightest hesitation to fulfill them and carry them out; and out of reverence for their senior they do not even consider whether a command is an impossibility." *Institutes* (NPNF2/11:221).

anything that might be commanded him, though the orders might be quite contrary to his inclinations. He who is truly obedient, and who has once divested himself of his own will, for the love of Jesus Christ, knows no longer what it is to say this is difficult, that is unjust. He continually remembers, that from the moment he came into religion, he has placed his will in the hands of Jesus Christ, and that he renounced all right to will, or not to will, for the remainder of his life; and that consequently he possesses nothing at present, but the necessity of obeying our Lord in the persons of those who hold his place. For he knows that when he obeys his superiors, it is Jesus Christ Himself who is the object of his submission.[110]

He concludes by these words: "Therefore there is no monastery, there are no monks, when the inferiors refuse to obey their superiors, as they are by their profession obliged to do."

Saint Fulgentius used to say, "They are truly monks, who, having renounced their own will, are in a perfect indifference, and determined to do nothing of themselves, but to observe exactly in all things the will and advice of their superiors."[111]

Saint Gregory teaches us:

True obedience neither examines the intentions nor the commands of superiors, because he who has committed the care and direction of his conduct and life to the wisdom of another, finds matter of joy in one thing only, which is, to fulfill what is commanded him. He who has learned to obey perfectly does not judge his superiors, for he knows one good thing only, which is to accomplish the sole will of his superior.[112]

Saint John Climacus says:

Obedience is an immunity or emancipation from all fear of death, a perfect abnegation of ourselves, a simple motion by which we act without discernment. It is a voluntary death, a life exempt from every species of curiosity; for obedience lays self-will in the tomb and calls humility into existence. He who is truly obedient forms no contradiction, nor considers things whether they are good or evil, no more than if he no longer existed,

---

[110] S. Jerome, *Regula Monachorum*, PL 30:400 (1846).

[111] *S. Fulgentii Episcopi Ruspensis Vita*, PL 65:143 (1849).

[112] S. Gregorius Magnus, *In Librum Primum Regum*, PL 79:131 (1849) / Gregory the Great, Commentary on the First Book of Kings, Book II, Chapt. 4.

unless the things commanded were so evidently contrary to the law of God that there could no longer be any doubt. He who has had the happiness of dying this happy death will have nothing to fear when he is called before the tribunal of Christ to give an account of his actions. In brief, obedience is a virtue, by which through a plenitude of discernment, we renounce all other discernment.[113]

Saint Benedict enjoins in his own rule:

Superiors are to be obeyed with the same exactitude as if their commands were those of God Himself; the religious are to follow their advice in all things. They must obey with simplicity, sincerity and affection, and this obedience must be entire and universal. [114]Thereby they may imitate our Divine Redeemer, who became obedient even to death; when there is question of obeying, everything, however painful and humiliating it may be, is to be endured with patience and tranquility. In a word, he requires that, Our obedience should have no other bounds than those which an evident and demonstrated opposition to the law of God might prescribe; and that even impossible things are to be undertaken with love and confidence, when they are commanded.[115]

Saint Bernard teaches:

Perfect obedience knows no law or limits, save the law of God; it is not confined within the strict bounds of perfection; it soars high on the wings of a full and entire will in the vast space of divine charity; and being animated with a free unrestrained disposition, it embraces with vigor and joy everything commanded. The obedience which is divested of these qualities is an imperfect, slothful, and servile obedience. [116]

He says:

The rule of Saint Benedict enjoins religious to submit themselves without reserve to their superiors; and that this virtue will not allow them to restrain its action to a literal observance of the promises they made at the

---

[113] *Scala*, PG 88:679 (1864) / Ladder, 68.3.

[114] *RB* 7:34.

[115] *RB* 68.

[116] *De Praecepto*, PL 182:868a (1854). / *Treatises I*, 114.

time of their profession; but that the rule requires they should extend their obedience beyond their vows, and that they should obey in all things, even in those which are impossible. He says, True obedience examines not the command, but that it is sufficient to know that it is commanded.

The saint could not declare his thoughts on the exactitude of obedience better than by saying:

> If the superior commands me to be silent, and I speak a word without reflection, I acknowledge that I have committed a fault, but this fault is only venial; but if I should infringe the law of silence through contempt, and with deliberate knowledge, such disobedience would be a criminal prevarication; it would be a mortal offence, and if I should persevere in it without repentance until death, it would be the cause of my eternal damnation.[117]

Hence when Saint Bernard says that a religious is not to be forced—that a superior cannot oblige him who is engaged in a life so holy to do anything more than what he promised at the time of his profession, his design is only to restrain the power of those who govern, and to deter them from abusing the authority with which they are invested, from conducting their brethren according to the false rules of their own fancies, from indiscreetly requiring extraordinary things, and from annulling the holy observance which they had found divinely established under the pretext of a greater perfection— the holy doctor not alluding to any particular action, but to a change of state in general.

For though a superior cannot compel his religious to descend to an observance inferior to that which they have professed, on the contrary, the religious in such a case are not obliged to obey him. Nevertheless, he may on certain occasions when his intentions are founded on pure and holy motives, command them to do something less perfect, and it must not be doubted but that in such cases, they are obliged to obey him. In like manner, the superior can order some things to be done which are of greater perfection than that which the state requires; and, when he does, the inferiors are equally bound to obey.

Saint Thomas says that the most essential virtue,[118] and that which constitutes the essence of the monastic state in the most particular manner,

---

[117] *De Praecepto*, PL 182: 878b (1854). / *Treatises I*, 128.

[118] Aquinas, "Eighth Article: Whether the Vow of Obedience is the Chief of the Three Religious Vows?" STh., II-II q.186 a.8.

is obedience; that when the superior's will is known in any way whatever, it becomes a tacit precept and command; and that perfect obedience requires that a religious must obey in everything that is not contrary to the law of God, or forbidden by his rules.[119]

From all these different testimonies and instructions, you may clearly perceive, my brethren, that though the saints seem to extend the limits in a different way, some more and others less, though some allow no other bounds than a criminal opposition of the command to the divine law, and others contract its duties within a more gentle sphere, yet they all agree in asserting that when a religious is truly obedient he no longer possesses his own will; that the will of his superior is to him a rule by which he regulates his whole conduct, together with the actions and circumstances of his life; that he then receives with an entire submission everything commanded within the bounds of his profession, which tend to his perfection, and are according to the spirit of his rule, though they may seem impossible, unless they are evidently contrary to the will and law of God.

Hence every one who aspires to perfection in religion, must endeavor to acquire this perfect obedience, which knows no limits but those above stated; and unless they were so disposed, whatever idea they may form of their virtue, their obedience will be no other than that which Saint Bernard terms base and servile, [120]and which is consequently unworthy to be found in the character of those whom God calls to the practice of everything that is most holy and sublime in religion. Hence again, they must accept with a lively faith, without reflecting on what they can or cannot do, everything enjoined by their superior as coming from God Himself, considering that he holds the place of our great master, and speaks to them in His name, and is the living interpreter of the divine law in their regard.

As to such persons who pretend that there is nothing comprised in the practice of obedience but such things as are absolutely essential to the state; that those which are of less importance may be omitted without scruple or sin; that with regard to the orders of superiors there is no sin, but when they enforce their commands with the adjunct in virtue of holy obedience, or when their orders are opposed by a positive resistance; that it is allowed to examine the motives and intentions of things commanded; that to maintain a remote dependence on superiors is sufficient for the preservation of the virtue of obedience, that it suffices to require their permission in the more

---

[119] "Peracta obedientia est, ut simpliciter in omnibus obediat quae non sunt contra regulam, aut contra Deum".–*Questiones Quodlibetales,* Quest. 8. Art. 1.

[120] *De praecepto,* PL 182:868a (1854). / *Treatises I,* 114.

considerable circumstances and occasions, and that every other subjection is quite useless, such maxims are so contrary to reason and to the piety of the cloister, as well as to the doctrine and maxims of the saints; and to maintain them would not be less extravagant than rash and scandalous.

We cannot, my brethren, sufficiently deplore the unhappiness of our times, and our own wretchedness, seeing that this virtue which in the primitive ages sanctified the deserts, converted the most frightful solitudes into so many paradises, and elevated the religious of those happy times to an equality with angels, is so entirely banished from religious houses that it is only with difficulty that we can find a few vestiges of it in the best and most regular communities. Obedience is practiced with such reserve, and so distant from what the saints inculcated by the term obedience, that it seems as if those who perform something of it did it merely to save the name from complete oblivion; or perhaps, that our Lord preserves it for our confusion, and in order that our infidelity might constantly appear before our eyes or perhaps that the view of it might produce in us a true repentance and a salutary fear, and that thus we might deplore in a profitable manner the misfortune of having forsaken the paths in which our fathers walked before us, and of thus being deprived of a means, in itself so powerful and effectual, in which the essence, the repose, the glory of our state consists more particularly than in any other.

I say the essence, because by the virtue of obedience alone when perfect, a religious is formed to and really confirmed in his state. By it he consecrates and immolates himself to God. By it he gives the blow by which he expires in the arms of that blessed death, which makes him live to God at the same moment in which he ceases to live to the world (Gal 2:20). I say the glory, because a monk has no longer any other glory than that of Jesus Christ; and as there is nothing by which he can honor that Divine Savior more, or by which he can better contribute to the exaltation of His holy name than by obedience, so there is nothing which can more redound to His own particular glory. In effect, though he were to sacrifice a thousand hecatombs, he would offer much less to God, and render Him a much less agreeable homage, than by immolating his own will by the vow and practice of obedience. [121] For, as Saint Gregory explains it, in that exterior sacrifice he would only offer up strange flesh; whereas in the other oblation, he immolates his own person, he himself becomes both host and victim. [122]

---

[121] "Obedience is better than sacrifice." 1 Kings 15:22.

[122] "For obedience is justly preferred to victims, because by victims the flesh of an-

Moreover the life of an obedient man is a chain of victories.[123] In effect, the virtues have, in particular, a vice and an opposite defect, which they attack: thus, poverty opposes avarice; meekness anger; chastity impurity; fervor sloth; but obedience triumphs over all vices at once, and by destroying self-will, which is their principle and support, he puts the whole army to flight. Thus it is a well founded truth, that the religious man who has taken upon him the yoke of perfect obedience, has gained as many battles, defeated as many enemies, and won as many crowns, as he had different vices and passions against which he had declared war at the moment in which he took up the successful arms of obedience.

Behold here the precise reason why we find this heavenly tranquility, this sacred repose in the silence of the cloister, for as all the passions are there either brought into subjection or completely destroyed by the power of obedience, as this virtue eradicates them and dries up their sources, so there can be no longer anything found in such an abode that may foment agitation or excite confusion. Peace is there profoundly established, and Jesus Christ (who is the king of peace, and who is delighted to dwell in every place where it is found–Isa 9:6) erects His throne in it; He there reigns without opposition, conserving good order, and maintaining everything in an invariable concord. His place is in peace (Ps 75:3).

From the hands of obedience alone the monastic state receives those favors. From it, and from it only proceed these precious advantages which never fail to enrich this happy state while that essential virtue is preserved in health and vigor, such as it formerly was, when it flourished amongst the ancient monks.

However, as it contains so many benedictions, and as it is at once the essence, the repose, and the glory of this holy state, so is it equally true that the malice of the devil is principally irritated against it. Nor does he cease to attack it with the greatest obstinacy and violence. He has inspired inferiors with the love of independence, and instilled into the minds of superiors an aversion to that submission which is so necessary, and by which the functions and marks of obedience are demonstrated. The former are no longer docile, and the latter are without solicitude; thus they have mutually conspired by opposite means, but equally contrary to the designs of God, to destroy this principal virtue. They have enervated its strength, they have changed its substance, and quite annihilated it. And every species of monastic sanctity

---

other, but by obedience our own will, is offered up." Saint Gregory the Great, *Morals on the Book of Job*. Vol. 3.(Oxford: Parker; 1850), 681.

[123] "An obedient man shall speak of victory." Prov 21:28.

which cannot subsist when separated from this virtue is enveloped in its ruins.

Behold, my brethren, the cause of all our evils: but still it would be to no purpose to know it, nor even to deplore it, if we did not labor to repair it. Therefore, let us beseech our Lord by continual prayers and sighs to revive the spirit of His saints and of His faithful servants in His church; to create in the pastors the bowels of paternal tenderness; to reanimate their charity and vigilance with such fervor, that forsaking every other occupation, they may solely apply themselves to the direction of those whom Divine Providence has committed to their care. And as to our part, my brethren, that He may enable us to enter into this perfect renunciation and abnegation of ourselves; to replenish us with that confidence, with that simplicity and cordial docility, without which obedience is nothing but a constrained submission, a political dependence, an exterior deference that contains nothing supernatural, and is consequently no virtue, but a mere human production.

It seems to me, my brethren, unnecessary to say any more on this subject, and that I have sufficiently answered the question you have proposed; nor can I doubt that you now evidently see, that, as all the greatness, splendor, and advantage of the monastic profession are contained in chastity, poverty and obedience, but more particularly when these three virtues are considered in all the perfection which the saints discovered in them, so nothing can be more unreasonable nor more unworthy this holy angelic state, than to attempt to persuade one's self or others, that it suffices to consider these three virtues in a common imperfect way, and to observe no other exactitude in practicing them, but that which results from such a mode of acceptance, and that thus we may attain to sanctity and perfection. For though it be true, as I have said above, that these three virtues are the foundation and basis of this state, yet, they not only are incapable, when alone, of adorning it with its essential holiness, but they are even sometimes thus found amongst persons whose irregularities and excesses render them abortive and unprofitable.

For, might it not happen, or rather does it not frequently happen, that a monk is chaste, that he possesses nothing in this world, that he obeys his superior in everything, observing all the exterior conditions we have noticed above; and yet, notwithstanding all these apparent virtues, he is full of pride, anger, envy, ambition, a slave of intemperance, of murmuring or of sadness; inclined to, and frequently falling into, the sins of rash judgment, and unfavorable suspicions of his brethren; the victim of sloth, of negligence, of vain thoughts, unmortified, haughty, impenitent, and untrue. In a word, it is possible that such a religious might be a slave to all the passions of the mind, to every vice and irregularity, and that his soul, though quite deformed,

might conceal from the eyes of the world all its filth and abominations under the appearance of a sanctity of which he no longer possesses the least essential. Could there be anything more unjust than to imagine, that such a man (who, to speak correctly, is nothing better than a professed hypocrite, and a deceiver cloaked with specious appearances), because he is chaste, poor and obedient, in the manner above described, that he is on that account adorned with all the qualities essential to his state; that is to say, that he is a true monk according to the judgment of God, in the same manner as he may be in the opinion of men, who judge only according to his habit?

We read in the monastic rule of which Saint Jerome is thought to be the author:

> The renunciation of riches, which may be acquired and lost in a moment, is not sufficient for him who is called to the practice of perfect and con-summate virtue; for many pagans, though corrupt and vicious, have done the same; but a disciple of Jesus Christ should do something more than the heathen philosophers, who like vile slaves had nothing in view but the approbation of men and worldly applause. It is not sufficient for you to forsake exterior goods—you must also follow Jesus Christ; He requires a living victim, adorned with every qualification that may render it agree-able to Him. In a word, He seeks not your treasures, but yourself.[124]

The holy scripture teaches us the same truth, when it tells us, as we have already remarked, that the chastity of the foolish virgins was of no advantage to them (Matt 25:1-13); that the poverty of him who has distributed all his goods to the poor, will be unprofitable to him without charity (1 Cor 13:3), and the other virtues which are its inseparable attendants; nor can our obedience be acceptable, as the same sacred oracles inform us, unless it be like that of our divine model, expressed in the words: "I came down from heaven not to do my own will, but the will of Him that sent me" (John 6:38). "He humbled Himself, becoming obedient to death, even the death of the cross "(Phil 2:8). Which words demonstrate an obedience marked with the characters which the saints inculcate as necessarily requisite for its perfection, and without which it would not deserve even the name.

You may learn from this, my brethren, that the blindness of some monks is very great, and that there are few among them sufficiently instructed concerning the sanctity and excellence of their state. In effect, these truths are so weakened by the customs which the corruption of the times has introduced into the most holy states, that they are no longer recognizable.

---

[124] Epistola LXVI, *Ad Pammachium*, PL 22:644 (1845).

Each individual has closed his eyes and no longer considers his principal duties. They regulate their conduct according to the practices they find established; every one thinks he is secure when he lives as others live; and thus they find an imaginary assurance in doing what others do, as if the greatness of the number were a sufficient warrant for security, and as if iniquity were justified as soon as it became public.

6

THE PRINCIPAL MEANS BY WHICH RELIGIOUS PERSONS MAY ATTAIN TO THE PERFECTION OF THEIR STATE

God, whose wisdom and mercy are infinite, and who, in forming the different states of life to which He calls His elect, has also provided everything necessary for their sanctification, and prepared the means by which they may fulfill the duties of their profession. There is no state, except such as are unlawful, to which He has not annexed proper means, and particular graces by which their end may be attained. For God does not tempt men, nor does He lay snares before them; He does not command impossible things, so that their duties never exceed their strength. Hence, as the religious state becomes a command for those whom He is pleased to call to it, so does He always prepare for them in their rules and exercises every necessary assistance, and the most effectual means to sanctify them in their journey to the term to which He calls them. Now, though it is certain that each religious order in the Church has means of sanctifying its members peculiar to itself, yet those common to all may be safely reduced to the following heads, namely—

1. The love of God, or divine charity.
2. Entire confidence in the superior.
3. Charity and vigilance on the part of superiors.
4. Fraternal charity, or mutual love of the members for one another.
5. Fervent assiduous prayer.
6. The love and constant practice of humiliations.
7. Frequent meditation on death.
8. Habitual attention to the presence of God, remembering His judgments.
9. The spirit of holy compunction.
10. Exact solitude and retirement.

11. Profound silence.

12. Corporal austerities and mortification of the senses.

13. Manual labor.

14. Night watching.

15. Evangelical poverty.

16. Patience in sickness and corporal infirmities. These, my brethren, are the most certain and the most effectual means to obtain the perfection of the monastic state, and you may be firmly convinced that a faithful and practical attention to all these articles will succeed in raising the members of the cloister to the sanctity and perfection to which they are called. By them they will ascend to the summit of the patriarch's mystical ladder; by them they will run a good race, fight manfully for the palm, vanquish their enemies, and deserve to receive from the hands of the just judge the crown which, according to the apostle, He has promised to all who shall persevere in the combat, keep the faith, and steadily finish the work which He had commissioned them to perform.

But if in the great multitude of persons consecrated to God we can discover only few whose conduct is in harmony with the sublime dignity of their state; if we behold the greater part of religious houses languishing in such lamentable debility, abandoned to the spirit of licentiousness, and indulging in a mode of conduct so directly opposite to that first adopted by the holy founders of the religious state, you may without difficulty be convinced that this never too much to be deplored disorder proceeds from our infidelities alone.

Yes, this is the empoisoned source of all our evils: we have forsaken the ancient practices;[125] we have strayed from the paths which our fathers sanctified; indifferent to their zeal and labors as well as to their holy example, we have lopped off from our rules everything that stood in opposition to our irregular desires, and we have finally dismissed truth, so that we may live generally according to the maxims of our degrading sensuality. The yoke of Christ, though in itself so amiable, and the necessary duties which it enjoins, have appeared divested of all beauty and deformed with the features of a disgusting and insupportable aspect. We have at length exemplified that which the prophet expressed in these words: "You have cast off my yoke, you have broken the bonds by which you were bound to my service, and you have insolently declared, I will no longer serve" (Jer 2:20).

Thus, having pulled down and destroyed the rampart which the hand of the Lord had raised for our defense, we are become a prey to our enemies.

---

[125] St. Ephrem, Serm. Ascet. de Vita Monachorum.

It would not be just that He protect those who have withdrawn themselves from His orders and appointments, and who make a public profession of breaking His law, since He has promised such a favor to those only who observe it

Hence, it should be no longer objected that this perfection is not possible at the present day; that such a state is vainly proposed, since no one is now qualified to attain its completion; that God forms no more saints, as if His power or goodness were now impeded by limits which they never knew before; as if men had acquired an invincible obduracy and the church had lost her accustomed fertility. For the Lord teaches us by the mouth of His prophet, that His arm is not shortened, and that His mercy is always the same (Isa 59:1). But we have first closed our hearts, our contempt of His holy law and our iniquities alone have suspended and impeded the current of His graces (Isa 59:2). And we may say in the same sense as the prophet: "O that thou hadst hearkened to my commandments: thy peace had been as a river, and thy justice as the waves of the sea" (Isa 48:18).

When we shall be more pious and exact in the observance of our rules, when we shall obey the commands of the Lord more respectfully, when we shall be more attentive to please Him than to satisfy our passions, and when we shall prefer this happy subjection to the false liberty which flatters and deceives us, then we shall perceive that Divine Providence will defend us as it did our fathers in former times. He will pour out upon us the plenitude of His graces as He did in those ages with abundant effusions and communications; we shall then attain the perfection of our fathers, we shall enjoy that profound peace which is the reward of those who do His holy will with invariable constancy, fidelity, and exactitude.

Fields become sterile by continual production, but the Church is a field whose fecundity never ceases. Its fertility is inexhaustible; Jesus Christ is the source and principal of it. It is still watered daily with His blood, and doubt not but it is capable even in our age to produce men as famous for sanctity as were the ancient Pacomiuses, Anthonies, Hilarions, and Macariuses.

As to those who are insensible to this essential duty, and who, instead of aspiring to perfection, content themselves with an effeminate and relaxed mode of conduct, bewail their misfortune, my brethren, but do not condemn them. Lament their error, as if the evil had attacked your own souls. And let this be a maxim, which you shall always hold as general and constant, that the life of a religious who is indifferent to advancing in perfection, and who neglects to observe his rules which are the means to arrive at that end, that such a life opposes and even resists the will of God. It strays from the way appointed by Him, out of which salvation is not to be obtained. Still, never apply this maxim to any particular person unless you are compelled to it by some indispensable necessity. It is not sufficient to be certain unless we are obliged to by necessity.

Here then you see, my brethren, that all those different practices of virtue, of which I have just spoken, are as it were so many steps by which a solitary may ascend to this perfection that appears so far elevated above us; and that the whole face of the monastic state has been deformed, only because its members had forsaken these holy observances so much venerated by our holy fathers. Hence, I think it necessary to speak of each of them in detail in order that we may be more solidly instructed in our duty. Let us therefore begin by treating of the love of God and consider how far this duty obliges religious persons.

7 | ON THE LOVE OF GOD—CONTENTS

7

ON THE LOVE OF GOD

QUESTION 1 —*Tell us what is the principle and source of the first of these duties, which is that of loving God ?*

ANSWER..—As there are none of the divine commands more indispensable than that of loving God, for it holds the first and principal rank, so no precept can be found the obligation of which can be more clear and evident. It seems that none can mistake it but those who are so blind and miserable that they will not know it. It seems, I say, that only such as these can ever be ignorant of this amiable and interesting duty; and I may safely affirm that the heavens, and everything enclosed within the circle of the universe, continually announce the divine glory and magnificence (Ps 18:1), and inculcate the duty by which we are bound to adore Him. For, can it be possible that men acknowledge Him to be the author of all these astonishing productions; that all these wonders proceed from His power and goodness; that they have borrowed from that infinite source of all riches whatever beauty and splendor they possess: can this be admitted, I repeat, and at the same time doubt for a moment, whether we are obliged or not to love God?

We may say of the love of God what we say of the adoration due to Him, if indeed it be certain that love and adoration are two distinct actions. His Supreme Majesty is the object of our adoration, and His infinite goodness is the motive of the love that we owe Him. As the precept of adoring God is only the confirmation of the essential duty that every rational creature contracts at the instant it is formed by His hands, so the commandment which obliges us to love God is nothing more than an act which corroborates the immutable law under which we come into existence, so that if the Lord had never uttered these words,

"Thou shalt love the Lord thy God" (Deut 6:5), we should not be less obliged to love Him.

But without dwelling on these general considerations, enter into yourselves, and you shall find this truth in the sentiments of your hearts much easier than you could by any human reasoning. Moses told the people of God, whose obduracy he well knew, to address themselves to their ancestors.[126] But as for me, I will send you no farther than yourselves. Interrogate your own consciences, consider with a holy attention everything that our God has done for us, as well in the order of grace as in that of nature. Reflect that He shields you under the wings of His divine protection against an infinite number of invisible enemies; that He preserves you from a thousand accidents which threaten you; that He pardons you all your sins, heals all your infirmities (Ps 102:3), delivers your soul from death, satiates your desires with good things, and fills you with the effects of His paternal tenderness; that He revives your youth like that of the eagle, stands up in your defense against those who would injure you; and, in a word, that He places no bounds to His mercies, but heaps them on you without measure.

Consider all this, and a great many other particular motives which everyone who thinks seriously will not fail to discover, and then you will find your whole interior set in motion. You will then know no other duty, no other precept, but that of love; all your joy and happiness will consist in pouring out your hearts in His divine presence. You will neither have sufficient time, nor sufficient means, to testify your gratitude; and you will exclaim with the prophet in continual transports: "Bless the Lord, 0 my soul, and all that is within thee, glorify His holy name; bless the Lord, my soul, and never forget His benefits " (Ps 102:1).

Now, although it is true that this law is immortal, and that we bear it deeply engraven in our hearts; though it be a duty as essentially necessary to every rational creature to love God, as to adore Him; nevertheless the Almighty formed it into a precept which He was pleased to corroborate with several important circumstances, so that it might make an impression on the heart of man sufficiently profound to withstand the influence of human corruption, and to stem its consequences.

Nor was He content merely to enforce the necessity and obligation of this command; He was pleased to point out its extent also. He did not confine Himself to tell us simply, "Thou shalt love the Lord thy God" (Deut 6:5); but in order to teach us that our love should have neither limits, measure or

---

[126] "Ask thy father and he will declare to thee: thy elders and they will tell thee." Deut 32:7.

reserve, He adds the following words, "with your whole heart, with all your soul, with all your mind, in fine, with all your strength" (Deut. 6:4,5,6).

These words which are so essentially connected with this precept, the most important of all precepts, the most necessary as well as the most holy, are found in a great many parts of the Old and New Testament.

Moses, whom Almighty God was pleased to make the first instrument to promulgate this law of love to men, took particular care to inculcate and enforce its observance. He tells the people in the sixth chapter of Deuteronomy—"Thou shalt love the Lord thy God with all thy heart, with all thy soul, and with all thy strength" (Deut. 6:5):

> The commandment that I give you this day thou shalt lay up in thy heart; thou shalt teach it to thy children; thou shalt meditate on it continually in thy house, on thy journey, when thou art lying down, and at thy rising up (Deut 6:6, 7).

The holy legislator continues in the 10th chapter:

> "And now Israel, what does the Lord thy God require of thee, but that thou fear the Lord thy God, and walk in His ways, and love Him, and serve the Lord thy God with all thy heart and with all thy soul" (Deut 10:12).

In the 11th chapter—

> "If then thou obeyest my commandment which I command thee this day, that thou love the Lord thy God, and serve Him with all thy heart and with all thy soul"(Deut 11:13).

In the 13th chapter—

> "Thou shalt not hear the words of that prophet or dreamer, for the Lord thy God tryeth thee, that it may appear whether thou love Him with all thy heart, and with all thy soul" (Deut 13:3).

And in the 30th chapter—

> "If thou hear the voice of the Lord thy God, and keep His precepts and ceremonies, which are written in this law, and return to the Lord thy God with all thy heart and all thy soul . . . " (Deut 30:10).

We find this precept confirmed in the book of Joshua:

"Observe attentively," says he, "and in work fulfill the commandment and the law which Moses the servant of the Lord commanded you, that you love the Lord your God, and walk in all His ways, and keep all His commandments, and cleave to Him, and serve Him with all your heart and with all your soul" (Josh 22:5).

And a little before his death, he recommended the same thing to the people: "This only take care of with all diligence, that you love the Lord your God" (Josh 23:11).

The Royal Prophet inculcates nothing more forcibly than to love, serve, and seek the Lord with our whole hearts. His sentiments, his expressions, his inflamed words denote the ardor of his love. He ceases not to praise and confess the name of the Lord with all his powers and faculties: here he is inebriated with the abundance of His graces; there he considers Him as his father, and expresses the tenderness of a child to Him; now he sighs for the possession of his God, as the tired hart pants after the fountains of refreshing waters; and again his soul pours itself out like water in the divine presence, and quite dissolves like wax by the ardor of the fire with which he is consumed. He tells us in the 118th psalm, that those are happy who, being without spot or stain, walk in the law of God, study His precepts, and seek Him with their whole hearts (Ps. 118:1). He declares in many places, that those who love God enjoy abundance of everything good, and rejoice in the charms of a profound peace.

"Fear the Lord with all thy soul," says the wise man, "and love Him who made thee with all the powers of thy soul" (Ecclesiastic. 7:31-33). Again in the 13th chapter, "Love God all your life, and call upon Him for your salvation" (Ecclesiastic. 13:18). And in the 30th chapter, "Have mercy on thy soul, studying to please God, gather your heart together with all its virtue" (Ecclesiastic. 30:24).

The prophet Isaias requires that the conversion of a sinner should be as complete and entire as his former licentiousness was unbounded; that is to say, that as sinners separated themselves from God with all the force of their irregular desires, they should return to Him with all the extent of their love.[127]

Almighty God promises, by the mouth of the prophet Jeremiah, to hear the prayers of His people, on condition they return to Him with their whole

---

[127] Isa 31:6: "Return as you had deeply revolted, O children of Israel."

hearts, and that they shall find Him when they shall seek Him sincerely (Jer 29:12,13).

This obligation, which is so clearly expressed in the Old Testament, appears vested with so much strength in the New, that Saint Augustine does not hesitate to affirm that the new law commands only one thing, which is to love. It is certain that there is nothing more remarkable in the doctrine of our Divine Redeemer, Jesus Christ, in all the circumstances of His life and death, and in the instructions transmitted to us by His apostles; in every part this important declaration pronounced by the sacred mouth of our divine Savior for the consolation of men, appears with dignity. By it He affirms that He came to cast fire on earth, the fire of divine charity; and that His greatest desire is that it should inflame every heart (Luke 12:49).

The Pharisees having asked which was the greatest commandment of the law, He answered that it was to love the Lord our God with all our heart, with all our soul, and with all our mind (Matt 22:37) and in Saint Mark He adds, with all our strength (Mark 12:30). He confirms the same precept in Saint Luke, where, speaking to all men in general He says, "If any man desires to come after me and hates not his father and mother, his wife and children, yea even his own life, he cannot be my disciple, and whoever does not take up his cross and follow me, cannot be my disciple" (Luke 14:27). It is impossible to require a more extensive or a more ardent love.

This interesting truth which Almighty God announced by His sacred oracles has been again taught by His beloved son during His mission here on earth, and from hence we may infer that since He has loved us even to the sending us this divine pledge of His love, that "whosoever believes in Him may not perish, but may have eternal life" (John 3:16). From hence, I say, we may infer that our love for Him should be without bounds or limits, since we know that an infinite favor requires an infinite gratitude. Gratitude is a composition formed both of charity and justice; it is a sensation of the heart which is regulated and treasured by grace, by the quality of the motive, and of the person who confers it; and as the donor is every way infinite, the gift being nothing less than Jesus Christ (Isa. 9:6) as we receive Him by the charity of the Father (Eph 2:4, 5). Consequently our gratitude to be proportionate should be also infinite. However, since that is not possible, because man being limited in his nature is so also in his sentiments and dispositions, it must be at least allowed that he is bound to offer to his benefactor and his God the tribute of that acknowledgment of which he is capable, and that he should, of course, love Him with his whole heart, with all his powers, and with all his strength.

The same thing is quite remarkable in every circumstance that accompanied the birth of our blessed Lord. Nor is it less striking in the incidents attendant on his mortal life, especially in every stage of His dolorous passion, since it was no less a martyrdom of love, than a martyrdom of blood, and moreover, since charity alone was the cause of His sufferings (John 13:1). Thus the Church, desiring to excite the love and piety of her children, not finding anything more tender nor better adapted to the purpose, after recalling to our memory the great favors we have received from the mercy of God, she concludes by this, which is the plenitude and perfection of all the rest, and in the impulse of her tenderness cries out to the Lord in the Easter Vigil, "Thou, O Lord! hast delivered up thy only son to death to redeem thy slave."[128]

Saint John the disciple of love, in his first epistle, speaks of nothing but of charity and love. "Let us," says he, "not love merely in words and with the tongue, but in truth and in deed" (1 John 3:18), "He that loves not, knows not God, for God is charity "(1 John 4:8).

Saint Paul in his first epistle to Timothy says, that charity is the end of the precept; that is to say, that a Christian is made only to love (1 Tim 1:5).

After all this I think it is evident that it is unnecessary to ask in what manner we ought to love God, since all these considerations, like so many tongues, speak clearly of themselves, and if they are not sufficiently understood, it is because they are the language of the heart—we must possess them if we desire to understand them, and the misfortune is that the greater part of men know nothing of them. But as to the saints, who received of God that new heart and new spirit which He promises to give us by His prophet (Ezek. 36:26), they were penetrated with these truths, and we find by the instructions they have left us, as by so many impulses of the greatness of their love, that they made the deepest impressions on their souls.

Saint Basil teaches us, that the charity we ought to have for God is not a thing that can be taught; for, says that great doctor:

> We want no instruction to be informed that we ought to rejoice at possessing the light; nor do we want to be taught to love life, to cherish those by whom we have received existence or education: with much more reason should we be convinced that no human instruction is sufficient to teach us the love of God, but that in the moment in which that rational animal called man was found, a reasonable soul was then given him, by which we

---

[128] From the *Exsultet*.

find within us this innate propensity to love God. But it must be remembered that although this commandment is simple, yet in power it embraces every other, and its accomplishment is the perfection of all the rest. For he who loves me, says our Lord Jesus Christ, keeps my commandments (John 14:23).

"We have no need of instruction," continues Saint Basil:

To teach us to love that to which we are affected by domestic consideration, by natural engagements, and we feel inclined as of ourselves to do good to those to whom we are indebted. What is there more admirable than the infinite beauty of God? Can we form a more agreeable idea in our minds than that of His magnificence? Can anything be conceived more impetuous, or of greater violence, than the fervent desires which the Spirit produces in a soul purified from all malice, and who may with truth repeat with the spouse in the canticles, I am wounded with divine love.

He moreover says:

The love of God is a debt which we are obliged to liquidate in His favor; and that the being deprived of that virtue is the greatest evil that can possibly happen to a soul. . . .That if all animals naturally love those which gave them birth, as it appears in beasts, and in children towards their mothers, let us not suffer ourselves to become more unreasonable than children, or more savage than beasts, by remaining without any sentiment of love for Him, who by His power called us out of nothing and gave us the noble being which we enjoy out of the treasures of His infinite goodness. For, though we should allow our minds to be enveloped in a total forgetfulness of the other effects of His goodness, this only consideration, that He is the author of our existence; that we have our being and all we have, not only by Him, but of Him, as our first principle; this I say, should make us love Him with all possible affection above all things created, possible or imaginable, and attach us to Him continually, as little children are about their mother's neck. [129]

In brief, the saint having elaborated with much detail on the benefit of creation, and on our duty to God in consequence—which becomes yet more forcible by the redemption He has given us through the blood of His

---

[129] Basil, *Ascetical,* 233.

only son—he concludes, "With justice therefore does this God of goodness and love expect as an acknowledgment for so many benefits, that we should give Him at least all our love."

Saint Macarius, after having spoken of the attachment with which worldly people remain steadfast in their fidelity to those who do them any kindness, as well as to transitory greatness, says:

> If those who are guided by the sentiments of the flesh are animated to desire and to seek those things which belong to the flesh with so much ardor, it ought not to be considered astonishing, if those souls who are enlightened with the spiritual and enlivening ray of the Holy Spirit are inflamed, and burn in that sacred fire which our Lord came to cast on earth, that they are, as it were, enchained by the celestial beauty, by the ineffable glory, by the incorruptible magnificence, and by the incomprehensible riches of their true and eternal king, and in fine, they are so set on fire with the desire of enjoying Him, that all earthly affections being consumed in the flame, they have no love but for Him, they wholly belong to Him.[130]

Saint Augustine says that God is the source of our beatitude, the end of all our desires. He tells us:

> It is He alone whom we ought to choose, or rather to retake, since we lost Him in neglecting to love Him. That we must go to Him by the way of love, to the end that when we arrive, we may find our rest and happiness in Him, for they who attain this end want nothing more—hear His own words.[131] We are commanded to love this sovereign good with all our heart, with all our soul, and with all our strength, and we should suffer ourselves to be conducted to it by those who love us, as we should also lead those whom we love to the same happy term. Thus we shall accomplish the twofold precept on which the whole law and the prophets depend (Matt 22:37). . . Therefore, that man might learn to love himself in a proper manner, this noble end has been assigned him to which he ought to refer all his actions. The love of God is an act of rectitude, which fixes its eye on God without intermission; it is the bond of souls, the society of the faithful.[132]

The commandment that is given you is short; love, and then you may

---

[130] St. Macarius, *Fifty Spiritual Homilies of St. Macarius the Egyptian*, A. J. Mason, trans.(London: Macmillan, 1921), 72.

[131] *de Civitate Dei*, PL 41:280-281 (1845).

[132] In epist. Joan. c. 7.

do whatever you will; if you keep silence, let it be for love; if you speak, let it be for love; if you reprimand, let it be for love; if you forgive, let it be for love. Let divine charity be planted deep in your heart, nothing but good can spring from that root.[133]

This holy doctor was so convinced that the love of God should influence all the actions and every part of a Christian's life, that he teaches us that in order to live well there is nothing to be done but to love God with our whole hearts, with all our soul, and with all our strength. He reduces all the virtues to charity alone. He says that charity assumes different names according to its different motions, its applications and exercises. Sometimes it is called temperance, when it defends our souls from being corrupted with any impure love. It is called fortitude, when it so strengthens us that no adversity can separate us from the love of God. It is called justice when it allows no division in our services, and prudence when it is attentive to distinguish the nature of things, lest we should be deceived by artifice and dissimulation.[134]

Saint Fulgentius says, that our thoughts are where our treasure is, according to this sentence of truth itself (Matt 6:21). If we desire, therefore, to possess a treasure in heaven, let us love heavenly things. Do you desire to know where your treasure is? Examine your thoughts. By this means you will find your treasure by your love, and you will discover the nature of your love by the qualities of your thoughts.[135]

Saint Paulinus says:

The goodness of God is such that He is pleased to forgive our past iniquities, on condition that we serve Him for our own profit, as we formerly served the devil for our own disadvantage, according to the words of the apostle (Rom 6:19). That is to say, that we take as much satisfaction in the Lord as we have found pleasure in sin; that we seek the kingdom of God with as much ardor as we formerly sought worldly dignities; in brief, that we have as much affection and solicitude for the things of heaven as we had for those of earth.[136]

What shall we return to the Lord for all the evils He has endured for the love of us? What thanks shall we give Him for His incarnation, for the

---

[133] *In Epistolam Joannis ad Parthos,* PL 35:2033 (1845).

[134] S. Augustinus, *De Moribus Ecclesiae.* PL 32:1326.

[135] S. Fulgentius, "De Dispensatoribus Domini," In *Sermones Genuini* PL 65:724.

[136] S. Paulinus Nolanus, *Epistola XXXVIII,* PL 61:363 (1847).

outrages and ill-treatment He endured in His scourging and other stages
of His bitter passion, for His death and burial? Let us therefore pay this
great debt by love; let us give Him our charity as a gift, our acknowledgment for His wages, but woe to us if we do not love.[137]

Saint Bernard, speaking of the love of God says, "Do you desire to
know why and in what manner we ought to love God? I answer, that the
cause why we should love Him is no other than Himself, and as to the
measure of loving, it is to love Him without measure."[138]

Saint John Climacus says:

The love of God never fails, it never stops in its course; the soul being once
pierced with its arrows knows no repose but in its effulgence, the soul is
transported with a holy intemperance. A mother, says the same saint, does
not take more pleasure to hold in her arms the child whom she feeds with
her milk, than the soul whom we may properly name the child of divine
love takes in being united to God, and to live as it were in the embraces
of this father of love. He who truly loves, represents to his mind without
ceasing the image of his beloved, and considers it with such joy in his
thoughts, that he cannot forget it even when asleep, his affection being
such that he beholds his beloved even in his dreams. Thus it happens in
spiritual things; this gave birth to that expression which I admire of the
spouse in the canticles: I sleep by a natural necessity, but my heart watch-
eth by the greatness of my love. [139]

*Q. 2.—Tell us precisely in what manner we ought to understand
this precept of loving God; and what we are bound to do in order
to accomplish it?*
A.—The solution of your question, my brethren, is so easy, that it is not
necessary to adduce the testimony of the Holy Scripture, nor the sentiments
of the holy fathers, because it is natural to infer, that when Almighty God
announced this commandment: "Thou shalt love the Lord thy God "(Deut
6:5), He desired to instruct and inform us concerning this great duty of
love, and to point out to us the extent of this beautiful law; He desired to
show us that by it we are bound to love Him with all the affections of our

---

[137] S. Paulinus, *Epistola XXIII*, PL 61:285 (1847).

[138] *Tract. de diligendo Deo*, PL 182:974a (1854).

[139] *Scala*, PG 88:1155 (1864) / *Ladder*, 244.3; 245.12;13.

hearts, and with all the extent of our powers and faculties; that is, as much as we possibly can according to our capacities.

But, that I may yet make it more clear, permit me to add, that we love God with all our heart, when we advance towards Him and unite ourselves to Him by the motions of our will, and when we concentrate all our affections in Him. We love Him with all our mind, when our mind is employed in those things which exclusively belong to His service, or rather, when He alone is the principal object of our thoughts, and when we make the contemplation of His infinite perfections and His eternal truths the principal object of our reflections. We love Him with all our soul, when He alone is the end to which we direct all the acts of our memory, understanding and will, and when we employ the entire man interiorly and exteriorly in the accomplishment of His holy will. We love Him with all our strength, when we obey exactly everything He has commanded us by His holy law, and when keeping ourselves in His holy presence, observing exactly the most minute precept He is pleased to enjoin, we direct our intention to Him alone, and make Him the ultimate end of all we do, according to these words of the apostle: "Whatever you do, do it in the name of our Lord Jesus Christ" (Col 3:17).

Do not imagine, my brethren, that you can accomplish the end of this commandment by an obedience which is merely exterior, or by an observance of the law, by exercises of piety, or by a literal discharge of the duties enjoined by the precepts. For however exactly they may be performed, if they do not spring from a supernatural source, if God is not their principal, and if they are not animated with His love, and tend to Him as to their ultimate end, they are abortive, and nothing at all to the purpose.

Again, do not persuade yourselves, that however full and entire your observance of your rules may be, however exact your fidelity may be in your watching, fasting, manual labors, silence, mortifications, and in your other austerities, that there is nothing more required to fulfill this obligation. The love of God is a disposition inseparably belonging to the interior, and though it manifests itself by works, and demonstrates its existence by sensible action, or the operation of the senses, nevertheless its principal residence is in the heart. It is the heart which really loves. Love is an affection. When the heart is not moved toward the object one pretends to love in action, there is not, there cannot be any true love.

In effect, what would you think of a courtier, who having received a thousand demonstrations of his prince's kindness, would tell him, "My greatest pleasure shall be to obey your majesty in all things, my chief happiness shall consist in accomplishing your orders with the greatest exactitude; but my heart is frozen in your regard. I find no sentiments of affection in it for your person." Would you not say that he would be the be the most unjust, and the most ungrateful of men, and that he would deserve to lose for ever the favor and kindness of his sovereign?

Can you then judge more favorably of a Christian, who being indebted to Jesus Christ, the King of Kings, for his being, for his life, for his salvation, and for every other good, and who in return contents himself with a mere legal submission, who obeys the commandments only exteriorly, and who in reality keeps them literally, but who has neither sentiment, affection, nor tenderness for their author, and who persuades himself, moreover, that he is not obliged to have such dispositions? Would not such a character deserve that his Divine Master should ask him in the words of the Scripture, how he dared to appear in his presence without being clothed with the nuptial garment, that He the King should drive him from His presence with ignominy, and that He should inexorably reject both his person and services?

You know, my brethren, that our divine Lord has told us that since the establishment of the new covenant His Father must be adored in spirit and in truth (John 4:23). By this, the new law becomes more excellent than the old; and Saint Augustine teaches us that piety is the true worship that we owe to God, and that we adore Him only in loving Him.[140] We must therefore love Him in spirit and in truth, if we desire to offer Him a true and spiritual adoration.

We shall love God in spirit when we shall love Him with the tenderness and affection of our hearts, when our souls are borne towards Him, their sovereign Good, on the wings of holy thoughts and the affections of peace and divine charity. We shall love Him in truth when our love shall be effective, conformable to His divine will in all things, and according to all its rules, by which He has declared that He requires that we should love Him. These rules, says Saint Augustine, are the words, "Thou shalt love," etc. (Deut 6:4-6).

Hence that our love may be true and effective, and that we may love God in that truth He requires, we must love Him according to the sense of these words, "with thy whole heart." That is to say, we must love Him with all our powers, with all our efforts, at all times, in all places, and in every circumstance of our lives. We must, as the same holy doctor explains it, direct all our thoughts, all the actions of our minds, and the whole tenor of

---

[140] "Pietas est cultus Dei, nec colitur ille nisi amando." - St. Aug. Epistola 140 caput 18, ad Honorat, PL 33:558A (1902).

our lives to Him, as to their ultimate end. These terms, says he, with all thy heart, show clearly that all belong to Him. They leave no void, nor do they allow any strange affection the least entrance to occupy the smallest place in our hearts. On the contrary, if anything else should present itself to our mind, and solicit a place in our hearts, they ought to turn immediately to the point whither the impetuosity of our love should carry them. [141]

Nothing can be more pressing and positive than what Saint Francis of Sales teaches in his treatise on the love of God, where he says:

It was by a very particular effect of Divine Providence, that the Council of Trent expressed the heavenly commandment of loving by the word charity, rather than by that of love; for although charity is love, yet it is more than simple love; it is a love accompanied with choice and election, as the word itself signifies, according to the remark of Saint Thomas. For this commandment enjoins a love chosen among thousands, as the well beloved Sunamite takes notice in the Canticles. It is a love that should prevail over every other love, and should command all our passions.

And this is what God requires of us, that His love should be the most cordial among all our loves, and that it should reign over the vast empire of our heart; the most affectionate, occupying all our soul; the most general, employing all our powers; the most elevated, filling all our mind, and the most firm, exercising all our strength and vigor. . . .He continues, saying, The love of God is a love without equal, because the goodness of God is a goodness without comparison. Give ear, O Israel! thy God is alone the Lord, therefore thou shalt love Him with all thy heart, with all thy soul, with all thy mind, and with all thy strength, and because the Lord alone is God, and His goodness is high above all goodness; therefore He must be loved with a love, high, excellent, and powerful above every other love.

And he concludes:

Now do you not see, Theotime, that whoever loves God in this manner, has dedicated all his strength and his whole soul to God, since he is so disposed that at all times, and in every circumstance, he prefers the love and favor of God to all things; and is always disposed to forsake the whole world, if the charity he owes to that Sovereign Goodness required the sacrifice; in sum, it is a love of excellence, or the excellence of love, that be-

---

[141] Si quid aliud diligendum venit in animum; illuc rapitur quo totus dilectionis impetus recurrit.—St. Aug, lib,. I. de Doct. Christ, c. 22., PL 34:27 (1845).

comes a duty to every rational creature in particular, and to all in general as soon as they possess the full use of reason. A love sufficient to each individual in particular, and necessary to all in general, who desire to attain to the possession of eternal life.[142]

Thus, my brethren, did that great disciple of love enlarge on this delightful subject, and hence, we ought again infer that if we desire to accomplish this precept of loving God, we must love God as children love their father, unite ourselves to Him by the fervor and desires of our hearts, and allow nothing to enter these seats of divine love that is unconnected with the glory of His holy name. Endeavor, as much as the weakness and inconstancy of human nature will permit, to make this amiable Lord the sole object of all your thoughts, the end of all your words and actions. Neglect nothing that He has commanded either in His Gospel, or in your rules; be careful that in being solicitous to fulfill His adorable will in all things, the desire of pleasing Him alone may be your first and last intention. Let the interior eye of your mind be ever turned to Him in things even the most natural and indispensable, as the great apostle commands, saying: "Whether you eat or drink, or whatever else you do, do all for the glory of God" (1 Cor 10:31). Let your interior and exterior be mutually united in your actions; join the spirit to the letter in your obedience.

By this means you will walk in the paths of security, by it you will avoid the opposite extreme into which they fall who think it sufficient to multiply a great number of actions, who are punctual in fulfilling all the duties of a piety that is nothing more than an external appearance, and who make the love of God consist in a mere legal justice without admitting the necessity of loving Him from an impulse of the heart. The illusion of the former is condemned by these words of the Holy Spirit: "He who says he knows God, and keeps not His commandments is a liar, and the truth is not in him" (1 John 2:4). And the error of the latter is no less reproved by those words of our Lord: "This people honor me with their lips, but their heart is far from me" (Matt 15:8).

Moses told the people of God that they could not cover their infidelity in the observance of this precept by any reasonable excuse, because it was neither above them nor far from them, and that they could not say, "Who can ascend up to heaven to bring it down to us? . . . Which of us can cross the sea and bring it unto us?" since they had it before their eyes, and in

---

[142] Lib. 10. c. 6.

their hearts, and consequently, that there was nothing more required to fulfill it but the will and resolution (Deut 30:11). But you, my brethren, will be still more inexcusable than the Jews, if you should fail to observe it; nor will it suffice to observe it in a common way, for in consequence of the special graces, means, and advantages, which you have received from the divine goodness, He expects that you accomplish it with all possible sanctity and perfection.

The reason why the love of God is so rarely found amongst men is that their hearts are either divided or entirely enslaved by other loves; the almost infinite number of sensible objects that surround them form continual snares, which enervate, or completely destroy their fidelity to God. Everything that strikes their senses imprints its image with the same facility on their minds, and from thence generally finds its way to their hearts. Besides, their propensity to the love of creatures is so great and so continual, that they allow themselves to be vanquished on the first attack, as if they had neither strength nor means to defend themselves. If sometimes they escape the attacks of ambition, they are overcome by those of avarice; if they despise pleasures, the desire of glory and human applause are sure to become conquerors in their turn, and it frequently happens that those who have surmounted the most violent and most lively passions are in the end vanquished by that of sloth.

As to you, my brethren, Almighty God by calling you into solitude has removed all those obstacles, and preserved you from those temptations. The world is to you as if it no longer existed. It is effaced from your memory, as you are from its thoughts. You know nothing of what passes in it. Its most important events and revolutions never pass the barrier that separates you from it and you only think of it to sigh over its miseries before the Lord. Even the names of those who govern it would be unknown to you, if the prayers which you pour out before the throne of mercy did not point them out.

In fine, in forsaking the world you have renounced its pleasures, its affairs, its fortunes and its vanities, thus by one act you have trodden under your feet those things which they, who love and serve it, have laid up in the midst of their hearts. Hence, my dear brethren, let nothing prevent you giving your hearts to Jesus Christ without reserve, and in a manner worthy the obligation you have contracted with Him. Let your grateful love answer the excess of His goodness. Let your souls ever live in Him, let them advance to Him by continual efforts. Let them, if possible, experience in themselves that happy fainting of which the prophet speaks when he says, "My soul longeth and fainteth for the courts of the Lord" (Ps 83:3).

In a word, let your actions be done with purity and sanctity. Make such use of your poverty, of your solitude, of your silence, of your austerities, and of so many other gifts which you have received from the goodness of your heavenly Master, that they may appear in His presence like so many sacrifices of immortal praise, which you immolate to His greater glory and honor, as thanksgivings for all the graces and favors He has mercifully communicated to you.

Q. 3. *What judgment can be formed of a Religious who neglects to observe certain things prescribed by his rule, pretending that they are of little importance, and who makes no scruple to commit faults which seem to him to be light?*

A. It may be affirmed with every reason that a religious who lives in that manner does not truly love God, that he has forsaken the way of salvation, and that he walks in a path that leads to death. For first, Almighty God pronounces a malediction on him, who serves him with negligence (Jer 48:10).

Secondly, we learn by the word of God, that whoever neglects small faults, will by the same most assuredly fall into greater (Ecclesiastic. 19:1).

Thirdly, such a religious lives in a fixed and determined rebellion against the will of God. Almighty God in calling him to a life of purity, sanctity, and perfection, requires that he should constantly advance towards that end, but he, unhappily forgetful of his high destination, has formed to himself an opposite will. Content in his miseries and imperfections, he not only will not become perfect, but even cherishes his evil dispositions, and loves his sin. Woe to those miserable religious, says Saint Bernard, who are contented with their imperfections and defects, or to speak more properly, with their poverty and indigence, for who can be found among such persons that aspires to the perfection we behold recommended to us in the holy Scripture.[143]

In fine, what is the reason why this religious does not commit great sins, and yet makes no difficulty about committing small ones? The meaning of his conduct is no other than this: he knows very well that the former are punished with the greatest severity; but as to the latter, he persuades himself that either they will be taken no notice of, or upon the whole that some inconsiderable chastisement will be abundantly sufficient to efface them. Thus, he fears the punishment but hates justice, and hence, were there no pains to be feared, he would not hesitate to commit the crimes he seems to avoid. Thus this man called by God, and obliged by the duties

---

[143] Sermo XXVII, PL 183:614b (1854). / *Monastic Sermons*, 153.

of his state to ascend to the perfection of the Apostles, unfortunately languishes in a state inexcusable to a common Christian, considering as a thing of no consequence the injuries he offers to the majesty of God, provided that he can flatter himself that the Lord will not vindicate His offended honor, and that His judgments will not overwhelm him.

But senseless as he is, he deceives himself, for, although his sins are but venial in themselves, yet the desire of committing them, and this voluntary hopeless depravity is, in itself, a state of mortal guilt. It is a sin against the Holy Spirit and the broad road to final impenitence, which, as you know, if continued, will lead to an eternal irremissibility. "Let no one say to himself, " cries out Saint Bernard, "these are but small faults, I am not much concerned about them, nor will I take any care to amend my conduct; surely it is a thing of no great consequence to remain in those faults which are only small and venial. Even such a mode of expression," continues the holy Doctor, "is an impenitence, it is a blasphemy against the Holy Spirit—it is an unpardonable blasphemy. Saint Paul, indeed, was guilty of blasphemy, but it was not against the Holy Spirit. Because he was not enlightened with the gift of faith, he sinned by ignorance, and hence he obtained forgiveness".[144]

Be therefore convinced, my brethren, that to speak correctly there is nothing small when it offends God, and that to oppose and combat His holy will is by no means to be considered as an insignificant action or disposition. Every sin is a disobedience to the divine law, and those which seem light when viewed comparatively with more enormous evils become considerable when they are examined in their relation to God, or when regarded in their consequences and effects.

Saint Gregory of Nazianzen, after his return from the solitude of Pontus, was so grieved for having hurt his eye in turning an ozier branch to amuse himself, that he would not celebrate the holy mysteries until he had expiated his faults by prayers and tears.[145]

We read that the holy abbot Moses, for having disputed with vivacity against Saint Macarius, which is a thing almost inevitable when contrary opinions are maintained, was immediately punished by God, who permitted the devil to take possession of him; the possession was violent, and he was delivered only by the prayers of Saint Macarius.[146]

---

[144] S. Bernardus, "De conversio Sancti Pauli," PL 183:363a (1854)

[145] Greg. Nazian. Carmine 1 in vita sua.

[146] Cassianus, *Collationes,* PL 49:706 (1846) / Cassian, Conferences 1.7. 27 (NPNF2/ 11:372).

Saint John Chrysostom teaches that we should strenuously endeavor to root out these small faults. And that instead of attending to their apparent insignificance, we should consider them as the sources of great evils. He says that it is astonishing how we can be more careful to avoid great sins than little ones; for the former naturally inspire horror, whereas the latter plunge us into a state of sloth and tepidity; we despise them but never forsake them nor take the necessary paints to eradicate them: hence they become great by our negligence.

No person suddenly perpetrates great crimes, because a natural shame prevents the immediate transition from virtue to vice. But the journey is performed insensibly. One laughs at an improper time, another undertakes just as improperly to reprehend him for it. He immediately replies, what harm is it to laugh? and what evil consequence can proceed from it? Nevertheless, they soon pass from thence to injurious words, from thence to indecent expressions, and at length to actions no less scandalous.[147]

Saint Augustine speaking on this subject, compares small faults to rain water, which though falling only in drops, still fails not to fill and to swell into rivers, the inundations of which bear away trees and their roots, spreading desolation over fields and whole countries. What matter, says the same saint, whether the ship perishes by the shock of a violent wave, or by the water entering little by little through a chink, which, by the negligence of those who should attend to it, insensibly increases, at last plunges it into the deep, and thus completes the shipwreck.[148]

And in another place, he says, you have thrown off the load of great sins, take care that you be not overcharged with a multitude of small ones[149].

The sentiments of Saint Gregory on this matter are well known. He says that the loss of all virtue usually begins by the smallest faults; and that sinners passing on to greater soon arrive at the most enormous crimes, and that the soul having been cast down from its throne of justice, rolls from sin to sin, from one abyss to another, by the weight of iniquity with which it is impelled, until at length it concludes its criminal fall by being plunged into the profound receptacle of unlimited crimes.

He says in another place, that when souls neglect to correct small failings, they sink into a languishing state of base and worldly actions; that they then commit many sins imperceptibly, that they consider many sins of which

---

[147] *Saint Chrysostom: Homilies on the Gospel of Saint Matthew.* 1888. (NPNF1/10:513-514).

[148] In Ps 129; PL37

[149] Enarratio in Psalmum CXXIX, PL 37:1699 (1845).

they are guilty as things of no consequence, and esteem vain discourse and useless thoughts as mere trifling faults. But when they are once inflamed with the fire of true compunction, they then consider as grievous mortal offenses those actions which they formerly imagined to be nothing more than little failings.[150]

Again, these faults not only seem important when viewed collectively, or in their consequences, but they are so even when they are examined separately and in particular. If a man had done an action that deserved to be punished by death, would it not be ridiculous to say he had committed only a small fault? Could such an excess seem to be an insignificant affair to any man of sense? Surely not: nevertheless, those who make no account of such sins as they please to call light, and who commit them without any remorse, are much more unreasonable and unjust, since it may be affirmed with all truth that every one of such offenses deserves a chastisement much more grievous than death, for such as are not washed away with the tears of repentance shall be punished by avenging flames. For, as Saint Augustine says: [151]

> The sins of the elect which shall not have been effaced by penance during their lives, shall be chastised after their death by the same pains by which the crimes of the reprobates are punished; but with this difference, that they shall terminate for the former, and be eternal for the latter.[152]

Therefore let men say what they please in order to conceal from their view a truth that appears to them so disagreeable and insupportable. All they can say cannot obstruct the rays of faith, by which we learn that everything that is not effaced by penance shall pass through fire (1 Cor 3:15).

If we may judge and decide on the enormity of the least sin by the severity with which we know that the justice of God punishes it in the other life, it is no less possible to form the same judgment and decision by the rigor with which he has frequently chastised it in this. Who could imagine that the Bethsamites, who were guilty of nothing more than looking at the ark of the covenant as it passed by, which seemed to be only a holy curiosity and an act of piety, could have been so severely punished as to lose, in consequence thereof, the number of fifty thousand men; and that Oza's fault could be

---

[150] PL 75:896 (1849); Saint Gregory the Great. *Morals on the Book of Job.* Vol. 1. (Oxford; Parker,1844), 544.

[151] *Enarratio in Psalmum LVIII.* PL 36:701 (1845).

[152] *Obitu Domni Humberti, Monachi Clarae-vallensis Sermo.* PL183:518C (1845)

considered so great, that he should deserve to be immediately struck dead on the spot, for only putting his hand to support the same ark when it seemed to be in danger of falling (2 Kgs. 6:6, 7). Yet, that boldness which might be thought to be an effect of his piety, was considered and punished by God as a criminal rashness.

Moses, the well-beloved friend of God, was deprived of the consolation of entering into the promised land on account of one word that he spoke without much reflection at the waters of contradiction; and the angel of the Lord at another time was on the point of putting him to death, because he had not immediately circumcised his son (Exod. 4:24).

Almighty God was so displeased at the order given by David for numerating his people, that He punished it by the death of seventy thousand persons (2 Sam 24:15).

But our Lord Jesus Christ could not more clearly demonstrate how earnestly He expects we should obey the least of His commandments, than by those astonishing words which he spoke to Saint Peter: " If I wash not your feet, you shall have no part with me "(John 13:8).

"I will not contend at present," says Saint Basil,

> That the cause of this terrible menace which Saint Peter heard from the sacred lips of Jesus Christ, was any negligence or contempt of his divine master; no—but the reason of it was the resistance he made, though it proceeded from his profound respect for our Lord, was nevertheless an opposition to the divine will, and was therefore so much reprehended by our Lord. [153]

In fine, the supreme majesty of God, that infinite excellence requires of men such profound acknowledgment, so extensive and continual respect, that the least offence they commit against Him contracts an incomprehensible deformity. If our faith were more lively, and our charity more ardent, we would be more terrified of committing one only sin, than of suffering ten thousand deaths. Be not astonished, therefore, my brethren, if Saint John Climacus made his cave to resound with his sobs and cries;[154] if Saint Catherine of Siena was so terrified at the view of these faults—which some will take no notice of—that she was willing to cast herself alive into

---

[153] S. Basilius, *Fusius*, PG 31:894.

[154] Daniele, monachus de Rhaitheno, *De vita S. Climacus*, PG 88:602 (1864) / *Ladder*, 35.

flames. Be not amazed that there are Christians to be found, who, knowing that Jesus Christ will judge even justice (Ps. 74:3), have neither fear nor apprehension in committing sin.

The great Saint Theonas used to say that the reason why we fall into this error is that we are not sufficiently informed of the extent of the obligation which bind us to live in sanctity and justice; and that being as it were bewildered in a maze of darkness and obscurity, we cannot perceive the almost infinite number of stains and filthy spots which defile our souls.[155] Stupefied, for example, by an evil sadness, we are unable to feel the stings of a salutary compunction; we are in no manner afflicted, when we are attacked by a subtle temptation of vainglory; we do not lament that we have been too negligent, too remiss, or too slothful in prayer; we do not imagine that we have committed any sin, when we are willfully distracted in the time of prayer, or of the divine office, or when we think of everything else but of the psalms or prayers with which we seem to be occupied. In a word, we do not believe that we have lost anything when we forsake the remembrance of God, and employ our thoughts on created things; so that these words of Solomon may be justly applied to us —"They have beaten me, but I have not suffered; they have mocked at me, but I have not perceived it" (Prov 23:35).

True solitaries, says the same saint, find all their joy, all their pleasure, and all their happiness in the contemplation of divine and spiritual things. When they are withdrawn for a moment from this sweet occupation against their will, by the rapidity of their thoughts, they punish that distraction as a kind of sacrilege; and finding no means to console themselves for having preferred a creature before their creator, to whom they turn their mournful eyes, they consider themselves as nearly guilty of impiety. As they feel an extreme joy in always contemplating the glory and majesty of their God; so they cannot endure those earthly thoughts, though they should continue only a moment; and they abhor everything that might withdraw them ever so little from contemplating the splendor of their heavenly King.[156]

---

[155] Cassianus, *Collationes,* PL 49:1253 (1846) / Cassian, *Conferences,* 3.23.6 (NPNF2/11:523).

[156] Cap 2.

8 | OF LOVING THE SUPERIORS AND HAVING CONFIDENCE IN THEM

Question 1.—*Is it necessary to have an entire confidence in our superiors?*   109

Q. 2.—*What qualities are necessary in a superior that the religious may have an entire confidence in him?*   113

Q. 3.—*Would it not suffice that a religious confide in and manifest themselves to some other member of the community besides the superior?*   113

Q. 4.—*Are we therefore to conclude that those who direct in communities are not doing the will of God?*   116

Q. 5.—*Is there not reason to fear that such an entire dependence on the superior's will should weaken the exact observance of the rules, and produce many relaxations?*   118

Q. 6.—*Does it not appear in many places of Saint Bernard's works that he taught maxims entirely opposite to this truth?*   121

Q. 7.— *Explain to us what are those charitable reasons and real necessities which are according to the rule.*   125

Q. 8.—*What did saint Bernard mean when he said that a superior might grant dispensations for some time, in some places, to some persons, and for some particular reasons?*

Q. 9.—What should a religious do who being desirous to lead a life more exact and perfect, but who is prevented from doing so by his superior?   126

8

OF LOVING THE SUPERIORS AND HAVING CONFIDENCE IN THEM

QUESTION 1 —*Is it necessary to have an entire confidence in our superiors ?*

ANSWER.—The superior is the prince and chief of the community. He is the head of a body of which all his brethren are the members and parts; and as the proper function of the head in the human body is to govern and direct, to form all the motions and actions, and everything that relates to it, all things must proceed from it as from a source and principle. In like manner, everything should be performed in a religious community according to the orders, and in the spirit of an entire submission to the will of the superior. Let him regulate all things for the public good, and for the benefit of each individual; let him place his brethren and furnish them with employment and exercise; let him direct their consciences, regulate their piety, and let there be nothing to which his vigilant direction does not extend. This is his duty; Saint Benedict inculcates it, when he says that the superior holds the place of Jesus Christ in the monastery, that all things are subject to him, and that there is nothing exempt from his jurisdiction in the house he governs.[157]

This sovereign and absolute government requires that the superior should perfectly know the persons who are under his charge, without which the authority he has received for no other purpose than to preserve good order would produce nothing but trouble and confusion. Without the aforesaid knowledge, he would act without light. He would, consequently, act without prudence; he would be directed by nothing but humor and

---

[157] "Christi enim vices agere in monasterio creditur." / "He is regarded as the Vicere-gent of Christ in the Monastery." RB 2.2.

fancy; his conduct would be like to that of a blind man who does everything by conjecture, or like that of a physician who undertakes to cure the sick, of whose maladies and constitution he remains entirely uninformed.

It is therefore evident that the superior, in order to be properly qualified to direct his brethren, should have a perfect knowledge of them. This being admitted, it naturally follows that they ought to have an entire confidence in their superior, for without such a disposition on their part, it is impossible he should know them; since it is equally certain, that unless he acquires this knowledge, either by some extraordinary means, or by revelation, he can form only some uncertain notions of them founded on mere conjectures. Hence the brethren must certainly give him a full description of the state of their interior, manifest the motions of their hearts, and unfold clearly its most latent recesses, which can never be the case, unless they have an entire confidence in him.

It is thus a perfect unity is formed, in which all the beauty and solidity of a monastic society consists. And as this union is not only its chief ornament, but also its principal conservation, there is nothing so strenuously recommended to us by the Holy Fathers. The ancient superiors taught it to their disciples with particular solicitude, and their true disciples practiced it with all possible fidelity and exactitude.

Saint Basil says,

A prudent superior knows how to discern with exactitude the manners, interior passions, and motions of those who are under his charge, and to employ in their favor whatever he esteems best calculated to promote their real advantage. . . . As men conceal in themselves a fund of self-love, and a propensity to follow their own unenlightened judgment which prevents them from discerning the solid principles of truth, so nothing can better obviate all difficulties, and facilitate the access of divine light, than to manifest themselves, and to follow their lawful guides. For self-love does not obscure the light of truth, nor disturb the judgment of those who are invested with the authority of directing the souls who are committed to their care. And as long as this union of mind and heart shall subsist in a religious community, between the superior and inferiors, so long shall peace be conserved therein, and each individual will apply himself to the great affair of his salvation, with constant tranquility and love.[158]

The same saint having proposed this question to himself, namely,

---

[158] *Constitutione Monasticae*, Caput XXII, de Obedientia Uberius, PG 31:1410 (1857).

"Whether the prioress ought to be present when one of her sisters accuses herself at the tribunal of penance," answers no; but that it would be more decent and more sure, if the prioress would declare the fault of that sister to the superior, who by her spiritual knowledge might prescribe the proportionate satisfaction for the past, and effectual remedies for the penitent's future conduct.

Cassian informs us that the Holy Fathers in the eastern monasteries, in order to raise the solitaries to the perfection of true humility, taught them to be careful never to conceal any evil thoughts that came into their minds through a pernicious shame, but to disclose them without delay to their superiors. And that they should consider everything as good or evil, according to the decision of their spiritual guides, without attending in any manner to the decisions of their own judgment. He moreover says that the devil with all his artifices can never succeed in deceiving a religious, though young and inexperienced, until he prevails on him to conceal his thoughts by an impulse of pride; and that the holy monks considered it as an evident demonstration that a thought came from the devil when a person feels a repugnance to declare it to his superior.[159]

He adds in the thirty-seventh chapter of the same book, that a solitary in order that he may persevere in the service of Jesus Christ, must take hold of the head of each temptation, that is, the beginning, and show them to his superior, who is his guide. You are, my brethren, undoubtedly acquainted with the history of the abbot Serapion, who was delivered in a manner no less visible than miraculous, from the devil of gluttony, by whom he was possessed, at the very moment in which he acknowledged his sin to his superior; and in what manner that holy abbot requires that we should walk in the steps of the ancient fathers, and declare the secrets of our hearts to our superiors.[160]

Saint John Climacus requires before all things that a religious should acknowledge his faults to his superior, and to him alone; and that he should be ready to declare it publicly, if his superior should command it.[161]

He says that a religious ought to be able to represent in spirit, and with sincerity to Almighty God, his confidence and love which he cultivates in his soul for his spiritual father. He adds that he who manifests all his temptations, and places all these serpents naked before his superior, evinces to the enemy the strength of his confidence; and that he who keeps

---

[159] *Institutiones,* PL 49:161 (1846) / *Institutes,* 4.9 (NPNF2/11:221).

[160] *Collationes,* PL 49:538 (1846) / *Conferences* 1.2.11 (NPNF2/11:313).

[161] *Scala,* PG 88:682 (1864) / *Ladder,* 70.10.

them concealed in his heart remains in error, and walks in the ways of perdition.

Saint Benedict enjoins in his rule that his religious must be careful to declare humbly all their faults and evil thoughts to their superior; he requires that they destroy the evil imaginations they perceive within them by confidence in our Lord, and that they discover them to their superior, whom he calls their spiritual father.[162]

Saint Bernard taught the same doctrine. He declares that a religious ought to have a sincere confidence in his superior, and to offer him the tribute of a cordial submission and respect; and that an exterior literal obedience is insufficient.[163] That great saint taught nothing more repeatedly; he demonstrated it by the whole tenor of his conduct. He principally enlarges on the subject in one of his sermons, where speaking on these words of the Canticle of Canticles, thy teeth as the flocks of sheep (Cant 4:2), he compares religious persons to teeth. Among many proportions and affinities of which he takes notice in his comparison, he says that good religious, like teeth, can suffer nothing to remain concealed within them, that they cannot allow their conscience, or that of their brethren, to remain charged with the smallest fault. This is the cause, says he, from which that opportune importunity proceeds, which is indeed useful to you, but at the same time no less troublesome to us; this it is, that leads you so often to us, and that, even without any necessity you frequently employ the whole day in the discussion.[164]

If you consult the rule of Saint Fructuosus, you will there learn that the brethren are obliged to declare with tears, compunction of heart, and humility, all their thoughts, negligences, and everything else they may have committed, to the abbot, or to the superior who governs the monastery.

While this spirit reigned in religious communities, Almighty God poured down His blessings on them in abundance. The simplicity and submission of the members of those holy solitudes became the guardians and preservers of their innocence; and I may add, that they were perfect men, as long as they remained faithful to the practice of this holy puerility.

---

[162] "The fifth grade of humility is for a monk to manifest to his abbot, by humble confession, his evil thoughts and the sins he has committed in secret . . . ." *RB* 7.44

[163] S. Bernardus, *De adventu Domini*. PL 183:45c (1854). / "It is not enough to show ourselves externally obedient to those in authority, unless we also entertain feelings of respect and veneration for them in the interior of our souls." St. Bernard, *St. Bernard's Sermons for the Seasons and Principal Festivals of the Year*, (Vol. I., trans. a priest of Mount Melleray; Westminster, MD:: Carroll, 1950), 26.

[164] Sermo XCIII, De dentium proprietatibus. PL 183:716C

Q. 2.—What qualities are necessary in a superior, that the religious may have an entire confidence in him?

A.—If a superior knows the sanctity of his state perfectly well, if he possesses its true maxims, if he observes his rule with exactitude, if he loves his brethren and demonstrates his charity by laboring with assiduous care to assist them in the great work of their eternal salvation, in fine, if his conduct in the monastery is so edifying that these words of Saint Benedict may be justly applied to him—The superior is to be considered in the monastery as the vicegerent of Christ[165]— then the religious should attend to his doctrine in all things; place themselves in his hands, and give themselves up to his direction without reserve.

But if, on the contrary, his incapacity, his negligence, his indifference for his state, and the impropriety of his conduct are such as to produce sufficient motives to distrust his direction, it is then necessary to walk more cautiously, and to consider the superior's manner of life with much exactitude. Saint Bernard teaches us that in such a case we ought to possess prudence and liberty; prudence in order to discern whether there is anything in his orders contrary to the law of God; and liberty so that we may be able to resist the order, if any such opposition should be evidently found in it.[166]

You must take notice that when he speaks in the name of Jesus Christ, that is, when he proposes nothing but truth and the will of God, that then he must be obeyed as Jesus Christ Himself. Moreover, you should evince by all your words and actions that you respect his person and character though at the same time you find it necessary to adopt different sentiments from those he inculcates.

Q. 3.—Would it not suffice that the religious should have confidence in, and practice that manifestation of conscience to some other member of the community besides the superior?

A.—My brethren, to superiors alone the care of souls has been committed, they are invested with the entire government of the house. Hence it is necessary that they should have an entire knowledge of their brethren, without which, as I have said before, it would be impossible for them to succeed in their ministry. The brethren should, of course,

---

[165] RB 2.2

[166] Epistola VII, ad Adam, PL 182:100c (1854). / "Prudence also is necessary to notice if anything does so contradict, and freedom firmly to pronounce against these." Saint Bernard of Clairvaux. *Life and Works of Saint Bernard.* John Mabillon, ed., Samuel J. Eales, trans. Second Edition. (Vol. 1. London; Burns, 1889), 151.

address all their wants to the superior and place all their confidence in him. The consequence is just, nor can it admit any modification— much less alteration—without becoming at the same time the parent of much inconvenience and disagreement.

It is certain that as there is a particular benediction annexed to a faithful stability in the order established by God, to remain in the state in which He has placed us, and conserve the things He has been pleased to give us in the same appropriation as they came out of His hands. Consequently, it is certain that when we forsake the plan laid down by the wisdom of Providence, and transpose the order He has established, we deprive ourselves of much good, and of a great number of heavenly favors.

Now as He has appointed that the members of a religious community should be directed by their own superiors, under whose inspection they continually live, and as these members are consequently obliged to repose an entire confidence in their superiors, it follows that if this direction and confidence are transmitted to other persons, a derangement must take place, which will infallibly enervate the strength of the community, and set the whole body in a state of suffering. Besides, such a mode of conduct, not being that which the hand of God has pointed out, will neither be so enlightened, nor so useful, nor so charitable; for the brethren cannot find in an extraordinary ministry the same consolation as they might have found in their true pastors.

Moreover, a community is a body that cannot subsist unless the members and parts are properly connected with one another, and the whole are in perfect union with the head. It is almost impossible to preserve this concord and union, if the brethren forsake their superior's direction, and follow that of another. Also, it will be very difficult to find a means to prevent the diversity of direction from producing a division of hearts.

In the first place, there is scarcely any man who has not his own particular opinion, his own spirit and way of directing; this spirit and mode of conduct is always communicated, and becomes partial to those with whom we maintain habits of strict communication.

Secondly, there is nothing more usual than to link one's self in strict friendship with those persons whose advices we adopt in practice, and in whom we place all our confidence. Hence, disunion becomes inevitable in a community, when the difference of direction gives birth to the occasions, which seldom fail to be— by reason of the attachment which the brethren naturally feel for the sentiments or interests of those who are their guides— so, that if the directors have any difference or misunderstanding with the superior, the brethren will certainly range themselves with the former, become partakers in their resentment and displeasure, and thus form a party in the monastery. Thus it will become a house divided against itself, and consequently be exposed to complete ruin.

As to the superior, as virtue is necessary to lead to a just submission, and as authority has something in it that makes it repugnant to the views of corrupt nature, inferiors are generally much pleased when they discover a means to conceal themselves both from the knowledge and direction of their superiors. Hence it is that they are happy when they can disclose their anxiety, and confide themselves to persons who are in some degree no more than their equal, thus using such communications as flatter their inclinations. Those conversations they might have had with their superior become of course insupportable to them; they avoid him, their hearts are entirely closed to him. Thus all commerce being interrupted they irrecoverably lose the respect they owe him, like those rivulets which flowing into the apertures they meet in their course, leave their ordinary channel, to which they never return.

There is another difficulty in this matter which is no less common, nor of less fearful consequence. It frequently happens that religious persons forsake their superior's direction, not for the purpose of adopting that of another person, but in order that they may become undisturbed masters of their own conduct, either because they make little account of their superiors, or because the repugnance they have for all manner of subjection makes them skeptical of their advice. Whatever may be the real cause, such persons as these place themselves in the hands of their own counsel, and follow no other rule than their own irregular passions and desires.

Hence you see, my brethren, how important it is that religious communities should be governed by their own superiors; that nothing should be concealed from them; that everything should move according to their direction, and in a real dependence on them. Here you may discover the reason why parties are formed in the cloister, from which arise murmurings and intrigues. This is why divisions become manifest with so much scandal, why piety, union and peace, simplicity and the other religious virtues become so attenuated in it.

It is because the flock is no longer with the pastor. They no longer listen to his voice. The brethren have withdrawn themselves from the authority of their superior. They have despised his character instead of loving him as their father and fearing him as their master—according to the words of Saint Macarius—and in fine, instead of considering Jesus Christ in His person, and placing an entire confidence in Him as holding the place of our great master on earth.

Q. 4.—Are we therefore to conclude, that those who direct in religious communities in the place of the superior are not doing the will of God ?

A.—A state may be according to God in two ways; either by being such as He has instituted by the inspiration of His Holy Spirit, or when it derives its origin from the divine permission by a sort of toleration. The superior of a monastery is in the first rank; he holds the place of Jesus Christ Himself. His state derives its origin from the divine will and institution. But as to those who direct and exercise the functions of the ministry in the tribunal of penance; there are some who are thus deputed only by reason of the indocility of the brethren, who not having the esteem and confidence they should have for their superior, are unwilling to be directed by him. These directors are to be placed in the second rank, because they are nominated only in condescension for the weak and imperfect, and merely allowed on account of their hardness of heart. It was thus that the government of Judges among the Jews was according to the appointment of God and His own institution, but the institution of Kings was only a concession, by which the divine will was pleased to acquiesce to that of men.

It is evident, that though the first king was chosen by the Lord, and though he received the royal unction from the hands of the Prophet Samuel, yet it was a thing so far from being pleasing to the divine Majesty that He complained of their inconstancy and ingratitude, showing thereby that such a form of government was not agreeable to Him.

Hence we may infer, that those religious, who by their indocility, anxiety, contempt, or unfounded diffidence, forsake their lawful superiors, and oblige them to appoint confessors and directors according to their fancy, we may, I say, conclude that they have reason to apprehend hearing the same reproach from Almighty God, as He formerly made to His people by His Prophet, saying, "It is not thee they have forsaken but me, they have rejected my government, not thine" (1 Kings 8:7).

There are others who have the care of souls in monasteries which are governed by abbots, who are entitled priors, deans, ancients, or presidents, as we find in the ancient monastic rules. But it is to be noticed that it was neither the indocility of the brethren, nor any other illegal cause that gave birth to such an arrangement. The superior established them so that dividing his pastoral charge with them, they might assist him in his functions, when on certain occasions he found it impossible, by reason of the many indispensable impediments which occur, to attend to the wants of his brethren.

The person thus chosen is always a man of much piety, who not only acts by virtue of the commission he has received from his abbot, but is influenced in his ministry by the same motives, who is always careful to give the abbot an exact account of the brethren's dispositions, even to their least thoughts. Thus confidence is not injured, but remains entire, unity is preserved. This subordination does not enervate in any manner the first and principal authority; and the superior being informed of everything, is by that means personally enabled to prescribe proper remedies for every disorder, to calm every anxiety, to dissipate every dangerous thought, which might disturb the brethren. In a word, he rules all, and the whole community regularly moves under his direction. But here you easily remark, my brethren, that I speak not of sacramental confession, the secret of which is inviolable, as you all well know.

The same thing is spoken of in the rule called the Rule of the Master, in which it is exactly commanded that if any dangerous thought arises in the mind of any of the brethren by which his soul is troubled, he is to inform the president immediately; and the president on his part, after having prayed for him, is to give account thereof to the abbot, so that if the temptation should prove obstinate, the abbot may do that which he may judge best calculated to destroy it, either by the application of the Holy Scriptures, or by calling in to his assistance the charitable penance of the whole community.[167]

Whether we consider this mode of government as it relates to the superior, or to the brethren, we must allow that it is most innocent and pure. It is according to God, conformable to His designs, and entirely different from that which makes the brethren forsake the authority of their superior, and which derives its existence only from the disorder of their minds, the impropriety of their conduct, and from the unfounded aversion they entertain for his person and mode of conduct.

There may be found other directors in monasteries, who have been commissioned to supply the inability of the principal superior, which inability proceeds either from non-residence (Such as was that of our holy father, Saint Bernard, who, when the affairs of the church required it, was frequently obliged, against his inclination, to wrest himself from the embraces of his brethren) or whether it proceeds from the superior's incapacity, infirmities, or disorderly life. Such a mode of direction is just,

---

[167] Ex Regula Magistri (cap.XV). In *Concordia Regularum*. In *Sancti Benedicti Ananiensis Opera Omnia*, PL 103:850 / Luke Eberle, O.S.B., trans. *The Rule of the Master* (Kalamazoo: Cistercian, 1977),

it is founded on lawful principles, and there is no danger in believing that the inferiors shall derive from it every necessary assistance and comfort.

My intention, in all I have said, is not to enervate the ecclesiastical power, to which all spiritual direction naturally belongs, and which is so usefully maintained in many religious congregations. Much less do I mean to alienate anything from that which the wisdom of the church has established, by which she regulated that extraordinary confessors should be empowered from time to time for the greater ease and security of the consciences of religious persons. She prescribed that confessors should be authorized and properly commissioned in every monastic community by the superiors, to whom a free access should be allowed, and that such as desired to be guided by their ministry might have such liberty as they pleased in that respect. And that the superior should admit such as addressed themselves to him for the sacrament of penance, but that he should not force anyone.[168]

By these regulations, the church sought to prepare a remedy for the weakness of the brethren, and to provide a means of supplying the inapplication, or ill conduct of improper pastors. But that ought in no wise prevent us from wishing that both the one and the other might adopt the ancient practices, and the primitive simplicity, without which it is almost impossible that the union which should bind the members of the cloister should be as close and as constant as it ought to be.

Q. 5.—Is there not reason to fear that such an entire dependence on the superior's will, should weaken the exact observance of the rules, and produce many relaxations?

A.—There is nothing to be apprehended of that nature, my brethren, if you conduct yourselves according to sound principles. The superiors hold the place of Jesus Christ in our regard; they are His ministers and vicegerents. They have been commissioned by Him; they govern us in His name; and they are invested with authority, and by virtue of the same they are obliged to make those committed to their care respect that of God, accomplish His commandments, fulfill their duties, and advance continually in the way of salvation. Hence the accomplishments of the precepts and of the law of God, as well as our sanctification, is the end of monastic authority—it has been instituted for no other.

Almighty God has placed men over us to no other purpose than that we might find in their care and vigilance all the assistance and means necessary for our sanctification, that thus we might obey his orders and

---

[168] Concil. Trid. Sess 21. ch 10. Clem VIII.

render ourselves agreeable to him. So superiors, when their commands are according to the divine law, enjoined for your perfection, formed by the spirit of the rules, and within the sphere of your profession, should find in you a submission without bounds. So, in like manner, when they require anything contrary to the law of God, when they withdraw you from the ways of perfection instead of assisting you to advance, and when they aim at the enervation and destruction of the rules, for the preservation of which they have received their authority, in all these cases, I say, you are not bound to obey them. You should remember that He who said: "He that hears you hears me, he who despises you, despises me" (Luke 10:16), declares in another place that it is better to obey God than man (Acts 5:29); and that when the blind leads the blind, both fall into the pit (Matt 15:14). Saint Basil says, that as God, who is the father of all men, and who is pleased to be called such, requires of all those who serve Him a most perfect obedience, so also, he who fills the place of the spiritual father among men, when he directs his orders and commands according to the rules of the divine law, obliges those who depend on him to an entire and indisputable obedience.[169]

The same saint tells us that if the orders of the superior are in harmony with the law of God, we are bound to obey him, even at the expense of our lives. But if there be anything contrary to the divine precepts, or which cannot be executed without violating the law, though it were commanded by an apostle, or even an angel from heaven, though he might threaten us with death, or promise us eternal life; we ought not to do it for the fear of the one, or the hope of the other. [170]The great apostle having already declared, that if even an angel from heaven announces to you another gospel, let him be accursed (Gal 1:8).

He tells us, in another place, that superiors are appointed to teach truth and justice, and that the inferiors must obey them, when their commands are lawful.[171]

You admit, my brethren, without doubt, that your rule is the law of God in your regard, and that it contains His holy will. The saint, by whose ministry you have received it, proposes it as His orders and commandments. Give ear to his own words, "Hear, my son, the precepts of thy master." [172]And Saint Bernard tells you, that this rule, which, before your profession, was proposed to you as a matter of choice, which you were free to embrace or

---

[169] S. Basilius. *Constitutiones Monasticae*. PG 31:1387 (1857).

[170] *Brevius*, PG 31:1159.

[171] S. Basilius, *Constitutiones* c. 21, 22.; PG 31:1402, 1403.

[172] *RB*. Prol. 1.

reject, is now become an object of your duty; and that you are bound to fulfill everything it prescribes, with exactitude and fidelity;[173] and in the same chapter, he says, the rule obliges those who profess it, and to them transgression against it is criminal.

Hence, though the superiors can give you a dispensation as to some points of your rule, when real necessity, or some important consideration requires it. Nevertheless, if they should propose to enervate or destroy it, you ought not to be influenced by their counsels, nor obey their command, because, in such a case, you could not conform to their will without acting in opposition to the holy will of God.

The same Saint Bernard confirms this doctrine, when he says:

> We consecrate ourselves to God in the presence of our abbot, but not to do everything he might judge proper, whether good or bad; he is our superior, to assist us in fulfilling our duties, but not to impede us in the execution; to punish our transgressions, but not to authorize them. If I place what my mouth has promised, [says the saint, speaking of the form of profession, in the hands of my abbot], and what my hand has signed before God and the holy angels, I must observe it exactly, knowing that my rule declares that if I should fail to do so, the Lord, whom I deride, will not fail to condemn me. So, that if my abbot, or even an angel from heaven should command me to do something contrary to it, I would consider myself obliged to refuse him an obedience which, I could not execute, without transgressing the vows I made to the Lord, and becoming a prevaricator. The scriptures inform me that I shall either be justified or condemned by my mouth, and that a lying tongue kills the soul. . . . In fine, my abbot should reflect in what manner he ought to answer, when he shall be examined concerning these words: that he should maintain the exact observance of this rule. And likewise if this general command addressed to every one, who had made profession to observe the same rule, without any exception of persons—that every one in all things should observe the rule from which no person shall deviate in anything. My resolution, therefore is, to follow him (the abbot) in all things, and in every place, with this only proviso, that I am never commanded to do anything whatsoever contrary to the rule which I have promised and sworn to observe in his presence. [174]

Saint Bernard in every part of his writing establishes the same

---

[173] *De praecepto*, PL 182:862b (1854). / *Treatises I*, 105.

[174] Epistola VII, ad Adam, PL 182:103a (1854).

principle, he declares that the superior must be obeyed, but without doing any injury to the vows we have made to the Lord; he should keep within just bounds; he should be careful to be neither above nor below the rule; he ought not to impede his brethren in the fulfilling what they have promised to God; he should not require anything beyond what they have promised; he should add nothing without the will and consent of his inferiors; and in fine, he should diminish nothing without a true and lawful necessity.[175]

Q. 6.—Does it not appear in many places of Saint Bernard's works, that he taught maxims entirely opposite to this truth ?

A.—I allow, my brethren, that such an idea is but too common in the cloister, and that perhaps nothing is more frequently heard from the mouths of relaxed monks. They endeavor to conceal the irregularity of their lives under the authority of so great a saint; and that which he spoke with so much light and truth, serves only to plunge them into darkness and error. The passage that seems to speak most for them is taken from his forty-first sermon,[176] where Saint Bernard says that there are goods and evils that are such naturally, and that there are others which hold a medium, and are sometimes good and sometimes bad, according to their peculiar circumstances; such as walking, sitting, speaking, being silent, eating, fasting, sleeping, watching and other things of the same nature, which, being done with permission of the superior deserve a great reward. . . . That, in cases of such a nature the religious should obey their superior, without asking the reason why they act in this or that manner (1 Cor 10:25); because God has not decided anything positively concerning such matters, but left them to be regulated by the authority of superiors, and that we should not be anxious whether they are men of capacity, whether learned or ignorant, but simply attend to the orders they give.

Behold the reason of those who conclude, from the words above cited, that superiors can dispense in the observance of rules with impunity, and that their inferiors are obliged to obey them in all such cases without reply. But their opinion is entirely different from that of Saint Bernard.

That great saint seeing that there might be superiors so rigorously religious, so exact and scrupulous, that they would adhere to a literal observance of their holy rule, at all times, and in every point, without any consideration; or reflecting that it is not only lawful sometimes to dispense in their observance, but that there is an obligation to do so on many occasions;

---

[175] *De praecepto*, PL 182:867b (1854). / *Treatises I*, 113.

[176] *De praecepto*, PL 182:867b (1854). / *Treatises I*, 113.

the saint, I say, endeavored to clear up all doubts, remove the difficulties, and to communicate to both the one and the other such information as might serve to guide them with security in these cases.

This was the reason why he distinguishes three different sorts of precepts. [177] Some he calls immutable, because they are founded on eternal truths, these are always the same and never change, others are invariable, and can neither be changed nor modified, but by a particular command of God; there are others which he calls fixed precepts, that is, such as are to be religiously and exactly observed, from which, nevertheless, the superior may dispense. He places in the first rank everything contained in the holy scriptures, or in particular rules which relate to meekness, charity, humility, and the other virtues, the duties of which are all interior and spiritual, and which are to be observed at all times and by all persons. He places among the second, murders, thefts, and other such like actions, which, though prohibited by the law, were sometimes permitted by God, as we read in the sacred history.

Others are exercises, practices and observances of mortification and penance, which are prescribed by the rules of some particular saints, as fasting, watching, manual labor, hard beds, abstinence from flesh; over these latter the superior has authority, and may grant dispensations. But he declares at the same time, that superiors have the power to dispense only, but not to destroy; that they are the subjects of the rule and not the masters, and that if they are to be obeyed when they dispense for just motives, they are not to be attended to, if they do so without lawful and just reasons.[178]

He declares that all those points of which we have just spoken depend not on the superior's will, that the power of dispensing has been given to his charity, his piety, his faith and prudence, but not to his fancies and his inclinations; that the abbot is subject to the rule, to which he is obliged by his profession; that he has been invested with power to prevent his brethren from transgressing it, and not for destroying what has been established by the institution of the holy fathers.[179] Moreover, he declares that it is said for him as well as for others: let all follow the rules as their guide, and let no one rashly deviate from it, but if none can deviate without rashness, then the abbot himself cannot lawfully transgress it; [180]that the obedience which the religious promise him is not general, but limited, and precisely

---

[177] *De praecepto*, PL 182:863 (1854). / *Treatises I*, 107.

[178] *De praecepto*, PL 182:863-64 (1854). / *Treatises I*, 107.

[179] *De praecepto*, PL 182:866a (1854) / *Treatises I*, 111.

[180] *De praecepto*, PL 182:866b (1854) / *Treatises I*, 112.

according to the rule;[181] that he ought not to consult his own inclinations in the things he commands, but that which is appointed by the rule; that a good intention is not sufficient, for the good he proposes must be chosen according to the rule, and to what Saint Benedict instituted; and that if he leave these conditions and goes beyond the limits prescribed by these constitutions, those who are under his charge are not obliged to follow him.[182]

In brief, Saint Bernard teaches that the superior can grant dispensations only when real necessity requires it, and then they must be according to the rule, for some particular time, place or person; and that every dispensation that bears not these marks, and is not granted in these circumstances, is to be considered not as a dispensation, but as a prevarication.[183]

Hence you may perceive, my brethren, that Saint Bernard has said nothing contrary to the principles I have laid down above. I have shown you clearly that he teaches that we are not obliged to obey superiors when they propose either the enervating, or the destruction of the rules; but we should also remark that he speaks of those evil superiors whose aim is a total abolition of the rules, and of the cases which are so evident that there can be no doubt. For in all other circumstances when they dispense in the observance of rules for just reasons, through motives proceeding from charity and true necessity, we are bound to obey them, though these motives and reasons may be concealed from us. This is exactly Saint Bernard's decision and sentiments on the subject.

All that Saint Bernard wrote on this matter ought to be understood in this sense, and those who understand him in any other manner presume on themselves, and attribute to the saint, without any foundation, maxims which he never taught.

Q. 7.—*Explain to us what are those charitable reasons and real necessities, which are according to the rule.*

A.—Saint Benedict, my brethren, has left us a rule not less conspicuous for discretion than for sanctity. He would have it to be austere; but he would, at the same time, form it within the bounds of a just moderation, and he squared it so exactly that excepting the extraordinary things practiced by the first solitaries in the desert, there has been no rule in the Church more penitent and exact

---

[181] *De praecepto*, PL 182:866c (1854) / *Treatises I*, 112.

[182] *De praecepto*, PL 182:866d (1854) / *Treatises I*, 112.

[183] *De praecepto*, PL182:867c (1854) / *Treatises I*, 113.

than his; and yet he, like a tender father, did not forget to provide for the necessities, inabilities, and infirmities of his children.

In the third chapter he orders that those who have professed his rule shall observe it exactly in all its points. He exempts no person, he binds the superior more strictly than any other, and nevertheless, in the thirty-sixth chapter, he recommends the care of the sick above all other things; he enjoins that the severity of the rule be relaxed in their favor. In the thirty-seventh chapter he declares that his intention is to have the same consideration for children and aged persons as for the sick. When the heat of the season is excessive, he exempts the religious from the regular fasts. In fine, his will is that everyone should be treated according to his needs, and that each individual be allowed more or less in proportion to his infirmities and particular necessities.

It is in these cases, in these necessities, and in all such like circumstances, that the superiors have power to grant dispensations in the observance of the rule, and to mitigate its austerity. Those are the well founded reasons which point out the time and moments in which charity should be preferred to the letter of the law. [184]Then it is that a superior may, without fear of offending, dispense in fasting, manual labor, watching, hard beds, abstinence from flesh, and other painful and laborious regularities, and that he ought, like a true pastor, regulate and dispose all things for the consolation and sanctification of the souls which our Lord has committed to his care.

Every person will agree that unless these modifications are carefully observed when necessity requires it, monastic observances, which ought to be the most powerful means and sure havens of salvation, would become places of disorder and confusion; that there would be more danger than advantage in religious houses, and more spiritual infirmity than remedy and succor. Some carried away with the force of indiscreet zeal would undertake excessive practices against the holy will of God; others, of whom the number would be incomparably greater, not being able to walk in an uniform manner amidst the vicissitudes and inequalities of sickness and health, and feeling themselves overpowered with the weight of austerities which surpass their strength, would fall into dejection, murmuring and repining.

Q. 8.—What did Saint Bernard mean when he said, that superiors might grant dispensations for some time, some places, some persons, and for some particular reasons ?

---

[184] *De praecepto*, PL 182:866a (1854). / *Treatises I*, 111.

A.—There is this difference, my brethren, between the abrogation of a law, and a dispensation of the same law, that the abrogation is for all times, for all places, and for all persons; whereas, a dispensation is limited to some specific time, persons, and places, and also to the alleviation of some particular necessities, so that when this latter is just, it does no injury to the rule, and continues no longer than the cause for which it has been given.

This evidently proves that the dispensations which some monastic superiors claim to be authorized to grant to entire orders are abusive, because they are general. According to Saint Bernard, they ought to be considered as so many prevarications and destructions, as well as those which are granted to particular communities and individuals when they are not founded on just reasons, and delivered with the circumstances of limited time and real exigency. Such superiors as these cover their conduct under the veil of charity; but, in reality, it possesses nothing of that virtue, for charity cannot be in contradiction with truth. Charity is ever subject to the will of God; it respects His orders and never militates against the integrity or sanctity of His holy law.

Nevertheless, there are many persons to be found who either do not sufficiently reflect, or have not sufficient light to discern, that though our Lord Jesus Christ teaches us that we must lose our lives to save them, that is, forsake our lives in order to save our souls, yet, they make no difficulty to sacrifice the souls of their brethren to the pleasure and satisfaction of the senses, to deprive them of the assistance and of the fruit of penance, and by a deceitful compassion, and an effeminately cruel condescension, engage them in a way leading to inevitable perdition.

Q. 9.—What should a religious do, who being desirous to lead a life more exact and perfect, is prevented from doing so by his superiors?

A.—Saint Bernard says[185] that if the religious of whom you speak is in a community where piety, temperance, and justice are observed, and where the rule is exactly followed, he ought or may yield to his superior's opinion, content himself with the common life of the community, and endeavor by his interior piety, as well as by the secret dispositions of his heart, to repair whatever he may find wanting in his exterior conversatio, lest by forsaking his house he might disturb the repose of his brethren, or expose himself to temptations of vanity by living in a manner different to them, which

---

[185] *De praecepto*, PL 182:885 (1854). / *Treatises I*, 139.

is a thing almost inevitable when an individual pretends to a particular exactitude in a well regulated community.

Nevertheless, if his desire increase, if his will become more strong after many long and solid proofs, he ought to follow the holy impressions which influence him; and without being intimidated by the opposition of his superior, retire to another community, in which he may lawfully attend to the perfection he aims at. He ought to remember that the spirit of Jesus Christ is free, that He breathes where He pleases, that He endures neither violence, nor constraint; that nobody has any authority to oppose Him.

Moreover, he should remember that the Church[186] has given her children a perfect liberty in this matter; and that, if she have given any privilege to some orders, by virtue of which they prohibit such translations, it was only for the purpose of stemming inconstancy, so frequently the disposition of persons who live retired in the cloister, but not to impede their advancement in piety, oppose any obstruction to the motions of grace, or deter them from ascending the summit of a more perfect life.

If the monastery is in disorder, if instead of living according to the true spirit of the institute and maintaining an exact discipline, relaxations have been introduced, or if those unhappy mitigations, which the church never authorized, are adopted and preferred, and which, though they present nothing to the public view that might inspire horror, are nevertheless, almost as completely opposite to the sanctity of the rules and to the salvation of souls as the more scandalous excesses, there is no time to deliberate, the religious must attend to the voice that calls him, and believe that the prophet addresses the following words to him : "Fly from the midst of Babylon, and let every man save his own soul" (Jer 51:6). He must fly from his monastery as from a Babylon; and literally accomplish the advice addressed to a man of the world by Saint Bernard in these words: "Go from them, lest otherwise you should be obliged to live singularly amongst them, or perish by following their example."[187] Let him forsake his brethren and seek refuge in a well regulated community, lest he should expose his salvation by leading a life different from theirs, or by following their bad example be in danger of perishing with them. If circumstances should make this impossible, if such a transition was absolutely impracticable, he should remember that it is better to live in singularity than in relaxation.

If it should be objected that in thus separating himself, he scandalizes his brethren, that he wounds charity, he may answer with Saint Bernard,

---

[186] Innocent III in decret.

[187] Bern. Epist. 2.; PL 182:0086D (1854).

that we should not be concerned about scandalizing those whom we cannot heal without making ourselves sick.[188] Let him remember that the Apostle commands us to separate ourselves from every one who lives in disorder and confusion (2 Thess 3:6); and let him boldly declare that the charity which unites us to the society of the wicked, and which prevents us from breaking, I do not say communion, but commerce, with those who have separated themselves from Jesus Christ, and who are no longer in the way He has appointed, such a charity he should maintain is false and pernicious. He should affirm that the greatest proof of a true and sincere charity is that which he intends to give them. For by forsaking their society he endeavors sincerely to make them enter into their interior, so that seeing themselves in a condition disapproved by those who desire to serve God in good earnest may fill them with a salutary shame, open their eyes, affect their hearts, and produce in them sentiments more proportionate to the sanctity of their state.

Saint Basil gives us the same advice. He says that when a religious is determined to forsake his brethren, because he finds their mode of life pernicious, he should previously declare his intention to them, so that if they hear him and amend their ill conduct, he has gained his brethren, and then he has no necessity to dishonor the community by a retreat. However, if they continue in their evil state, he ought to consult some persons capable of deciding the affair, and if they agree in favor of a change of place, he should then withdraw without fear, for he forsakes not brethren, but strangers—our Lord Himself having declared that whoever perseveres in his sins, ought to be considered as a heathen and publican.[189]

If some persons are not sufficiently bold to attack and condemn the transition from a disorderly observance, with the superior's permission, to one more holy and exact, the most general opinions unite in opposing those who desire to pass from a regular observance to one more pure, more austere, and more perfect. Here again the Saint's authority is alleged, who in his book of the precept and dispensation, says, that he would not advise a religious of a well regulated observance to leave it without the consent of his superior, more especially if the members thereof live in piety, temperance, and justice, nor to seek another of greater perfection and austerity. [190]

To this we may reply, my brethren, that Saint Bernard only meant to lay down some general rules, as I have said above, so that thereby he might

---

[188] Bern. Epist. 2. / PL 182:0086D (1854).

[189] S. Basilius, Fusius, PG 31:1007 (1857).

[190] De praecepto, PL 182:885d (1854). / Treatises I, 139.

curb the anxiety, inconstancy, and wanderings of the minds of religious persons, as well as the too great facility of superiors, who otherwise might be induced to receive indifferently all those who should present themselves for admission into their communities. But these rules have some exceptions, and Saint Bernard evinced this every time he found an occasion, and judged it reasonable to do so, as may be easily seen by consulting many of his letters.

He had received several regular canons of the order of Saint Augustine without any permission of their superiors. He told them by letter that they ought not to be anxious concerning their brethren's salvation, that they had embraced the order of Citeaux by the advice and counsel of judicious persons, that they were admitted only after reiterated petitions, and that their intention in thus changing their former state was to lead a more strict and austere life than that which is observed in the order of Saint Augustine.

He also wrote that they ought not to take it ill if his order admitted and detained them, provided, that if their minds should change during the year of their noviceship, and that they desire to return to their former observance, they may be allowed to do it without any impediment; and that they, the superiors, would err, if by inconsiderate excommunications, they should oppose the liberty of the spirit by which they were inspired.[191]

He writes to Drogon, religious of the abbey of Saint Nicaise of Rheims who retired to the abbey of Pontigny; he approves his conduct, he confirms him in his designs, he praises him for having lived with such piety and virtue in his former monastery that he acquired the reputation of a man consummate in sanctity, and yet animated with zeal for greater perfection, he embraced a life more holy and eminent. He tells him that he is imperfect who does not endeavor to become still more perfect and that if others are scandalized at his departure, he ought not to make himself anxious at their unreasonable conduct, according to those words of our Lord: "Let them alone, they are blind guides of the blind" (Matt 15:14). He adds, that if they threaten him with anathema and malediction, the patriarch Isaac will answer for him, in the words he spoke to his son: "Let him who curses thee be himself cursed" (Gen. 27:29). He writes also that he ought to depend on the purity of his conscience as on an impregnable fortress and say with the royal Prophet: "If whole armies should stand against me my heart shall not fear"(Ps. 26:3). And in fine, if he resist the first efforts of

---

[191] Epistola III, Ad Canonicos Regulares De Aildicurte, PL 182:89a (1854) / Bernard, Works, 131–133.

those who attack him, he shall tread the old serpent under his feet (Rom 16:20)

In a letter which the holy abbot wrote to Aluise, abbot of Auchin, he excuses himself for the fact of having received one of his religious by only telling him that he did not allure him, nor invite him, and that he did no more than consent to the repeated entreaties of the brother in question.[192] It is to be remarked that the above monastery was just then reformed and established in exact discipline, and, of course, wanted good subjects to maintain good order, which seemed sufficient to deter Saint Bernard from admitting him into his community, and yet he did it, being persuaded it was an action that was lawful and good in every circumstance.

I might adduce a great number of similar facts, but those I have cited are sufficient to demonstrate that Saint Bernard did not observe a strict uniformity in this matter, and that he neither admitted nor refused all those who presented themselves to be united to his community; and though prudence and discretion were the usual rules he observed in this affair, as well as in every other, yet it is certain that he never refused admittance to any person who came to him bearing sufficient evidence that they were guided in their undertaking by the spirit of Jesus Christ, who is the author of our true liberty.

Again, if this sentiment which is attributed to Saint Bernard was so general as some pretend, it could be said with truth that it was never adopted in practice; nevertheless, we find that the Carthusians, even at the time when both these orders were in their vigor, came over to the Cistercians; while the Cistercians also imitated them by embracing the order the others had forsaken; and that at length, it was found necessary to form a mutual agreement, not to receive any person coming from either side, without the consent of their superiors; no other means being thought sufficient to obstruct the progressive abuses of the above liberty.[193]

We read moreover, that Stephen, abbot of St Genevieve, and afterward bishop of Tournay, wrote to Robert, abbot of Pontigny, on the subject of some members of the order of Grandmont, who, after they had retired to his monastery, were much afflicted with scruples concerning what they had done; but, instead of acquiescing to their doubts, he encourages them; he assures them that their translation is lawful; and that, having changed

---

[192] Epistola LXV ad Alvisum Abbatem Aquiscincti, PL 182:170 / Bernard, Life, 1:247.

[193] Distinctio XI. De personis in Ordine recipiendis. Caput Primum. De Novitiis de Calatrava, de Cartusiensibus, et aliis recipiendis. In Nomasticon Cisterciense seu antiquiores Ordinis Cisterciensis constitutiones. (Paris: Alliot, 1664) 555.

their state for their spiritual advancement only, and for the purpose of advancing in perfection, their enterprise advanced them much in the way of life; that the canons of the Church allow virgins to change their first institute for one more austere, and that, according to Gratian, religious men must be understood to enjoy the same privilege.[194]

He cites a canon of the council of Autun, and a constitution of Urban the Eleventh, which forbids regular canons to leave their state, or to embrace the monastic; but he adds that this prohibition has been moderated by Pope Alexander, and he doubts whether some regular canons who had embraced the order of Citeaux, could be recalled by the force of the above constitutions; that as to his own particular conduct, if any of those who are under his authority should desire to embrace it, he would endeavor to dissuade them from the undertaking, but that, if they were already retired, he would not advise or force them to leave it, lest, by so doing, he might resist the Holy Spirit, interrupt His operations, and impede that holy liberty, which he communicates to the souls whom He inspires.

But that which we read in a decretal of Innocent III evidently shows what the practice of the Church has been concerning the present subject. In it he declares that though the see apostolic may have granted privileges to some religious persons, regular canons, hospitaliers, and templars, by which those who are engaged in their congregations are forbidden to forsake them, for the purpose of embracing other religious orders against the will of their superiors, in order that, as the apostle admonishes, each person may remain in his vocation; nevertheless, that the Church did not intend to resist the Holy Spirit by such an ordinance, nor to do violence to those whom He is pleased to inspire; that there is no constraint where the spirit of God resides, and that those whom He actuates and inspires, are not subject to the law (2 Cor 3:17); that these privileges were granted in order to prevent those inconsiderate transitions, so common amongst religious persons, under the pretext of embracing a more perfect state; so that, this great pope adds, he who desires to embrace a more perfect state is at liberty to accomplish his design, by a particular law, by which he is discharged from the obligation of the general law, and hence he may freely pass from a less perfect to a more perfect life without being intimidated by the indiscreet opposition of his superior.[195]

Hence, my brethren, as no person can better understand the sentiments of the Church than he who is her visible head, so she never

---

[194] Stephen of Tornai, Epistola 1; PL 211:309 (1855).

[195] Innoc. III, decret. I. 3. de Regul. et transl. tit. 31. c. licet.

prohibited, nor does she prohibit a religious at this time, to leave his first state to embrace a more perfect life, when he is influenced by a pure and sincere intention of consecrating himself to a life more holy and excellent.

9 | OF THE CHARITY AND DUTY OF SUPERIORS—CONTENTS:

attribute to himself any exemption or dispensation from the regular common exercises, by which he might be distinguished from his brethren?   145

Q. 8.—What excuse can be adduced, therefore, in favor of those superiors who maintained revenues, coaches and equipages?   146

Q. 9.—Tell us precisely to what the duty of watching over those who are committed to their care obliges superiors.   149

Q. 10.—Do you then require that the care of a superior should be continual?   150

Q. 11.—Do you require that the superiors should not have any care of temporal things?   152

Q. 12.—How shall superiors be able to assist their brethren in all these ways if the brethren on their part are unwilling to seek even their advice, and if, as is usually the case, they have no confidence in, or respect for them?   157

Q. 13.—We desire to be informed concerning the obligation by which a superior is bound to pray for those who are under his care: in what does it consist?   158

9

OF THE CHARITY AND DUTY OF SUPERIORS

QUESTION 1.—*Tell us precisely how a superior should conduct himself, in order that in his actions he may accomplish the sense of these words—Christi vices agere: the representative of Christ in the monastery, and in what manner they are to be understood?*

ANSWER.—That a superior may accomplish the duties which these words enjoin, it is not sufficient, my brethren, that he hold the place of Jesus Christ, that he govern in His name, nor that he be invested with His power and authority for that purpose. It is, moreover, necessary that he do everything in the monastery as our Lord would do, if He were there in person; that he should exert himself for the salvation of his brethren, as Jesus Christ did for the sanctification of His disciples; that he ought to evince the purity of his faith and charity in all his works; and that he should, if I may be allowed the expression, so fulfill the duties of his ministry with such piety and exactitude that the invisible pastor may in him become visible.

Jesus Christ, so that He should omit nothing that might render His disciples more pleasing to His heavenly father and worthy of the distinction and choice He had made of them, was pleased to form them not only by His word, but also by His example. As He watched over their conduct with unwearied application, and never ceased to sustain their weakness by the strength of His prayers, so should a true superior labor, without intermission, to form his brethren. So should he instruct them in their duties, both by word and work. Thus he should apply himself to regulate the order and state of their lives, with constant vigilance, and also should he, above all, join fervent prayer to his labor and solicitude.

Be convinced, my brethren, that the words of a superior are usually unfruitful unless they receive strength and vigor from his example; that example, alone, is dry, languishing and dead, unless it be enlivened by words, from which it may derive that power it cannot possess of itself; and that both word and example will be equally abortive, unless the superior unites his vigilance to them, and consecrates himself without reserve to the care of the souls which Divine Providence has committed to his charge.

Moreover, having faithfully performed all his duties, he must acknowledge his incapacity, being equally convinced and penetrated with this great truth, which the apostle inculcates when he tells us—"It is not he that planteth, or he that watereth, that is anything, but God who gives the increase" (1 Cor 3:7). Hence, addressing his fervent prayers to the Lord, accompanied with sighs and tears, he must beseech His Divine Majesty to look down with pity on the flock of which He was pleased to make him the pastor, that His gracious bounty may bless his solicitude and communicate to his labors that holy fruitfulness which can be the effect only of heavenly grace and the operation of the Holy Spirit.

Behold, my brethren, the duty of a superior, who desires to be worthy of his ministry, and to fulfill the import of these words, "Christi vices agere." [196]To this, St, Benedict declares, he is bound by the station he fills in the community, when he tells him, that he ought to instruct his brethren, both by word and example; that they should find as much edification in his example as in his discourses; and that he shall be absolved at the tribunal of Christ only when it shall appear that he has communicated to his brethren every assistance that was possible to him.

Finally, our holy legislator requires of superiors so much care, application, assiduity and diligence, that there is no possibility to doubt but he requires that they should be disengaged from every employment, occupation and affair, that might impede them from a continual vigilance over the souls placed under their direction, and which have been redeemed by the precious blood of the Son of God.

Q. 2.—*Is it necessary that a superior should be very learned, in order to be sufficiently qualified to instruct his brethren with advantage?*

A.—Science should be regulated and measured, according to the state and condition of the persons who are to be instructed. Therefore it can be asserted without danger of erring that a man who knows everything

---

[196] RB 2:2

relating to his profession, who understands its principles, its nature and its rules, that such a man, I say, possesses all the knowledge proper for him, and that God requires in him. Consequently, he is sufficiently qualified to fulfill the duties and obligations which his state imposes on him.

There is a great difference, my brethren, between a superior of religious persons, and a doctor, or an ecclesiastical pastor. The latter is a lamp set up to enlighten the world. He is a man appointed by God to instruct the people and direct their consciences. He is a debtor to all those who apply to him for light and instruction, and he cannot refuse to answer every doubt, and clear up every difficulty, from whatsoever point they come. His knowledge, of course, cannot be too great, nor his capacity too far extended. He ought to know, perfectly well, all the dogmas and mysteries of faith, the holy scriptures, tradition, ecclesiastical history, the decisions and rules of the Church, a profound knowledge of the writings of the holy fathers, and be so qualified, that these words of Ecclesiasticus may be, with propriety, applied to him—"He will keep the sayings of wise men, and will enter withal into the subtleties of parables " (Ecclesiastic. 39: 2, 3).

But as to the former, my brethren, he is, to speak correctly, nothing more than a light concealed under the bushel, a man destined to direct only a few persons, whose life ought to be spent in retreat, in silence, in the mortification of the senses, and who, having his mission only for the purpose of teaching piety, and not for expounding doctrine, has no want for such profound learning, nor of that science which can only be acquired by assiduous reading and study. And we must agree that he possesses that measure of science sufficient to qualify him for his ministry, if he can say with the apostle, "I judge myself not to know anything among you but Jesus Christ, and Him crucified" (1 Cor 2:2).

In Him, my brethren, in the great book of Christ crucified, the superior may easily learn in what a true and unbounded obedience consists, as well as the insatiable desire of contempt and humiliation; an invincible patience in suffering; an entire resignation to the will of God; poverty without reserve; charity amidst injustice; an invariable attachment to things eternal, and a perfect renunciation of all perishable goods. In brief, in that source he may find every other virtue which forms the essence, the truth, and perfection of his state, and which have been so divinely exemplified by our Lord, in the different positions in which that Divine Redeemer was pleased to appear in order to satisfy His own infinite love, and to purchase eternal life for man. In this, the knowledge of a man who is the guide of monks should consist. This is, indeed, the science with which he may sanctify his flock. And if you inquire in what manner he may still attain to a greater knowledge of Jesus crucified, I answer, that it is by a constant study of holy scripture, for which reason the holy fathers recommend it to every one of his character, in very express terms.[197]

Q. 3.—Do you then allow superiors no other studies but that of the Holy Scripture?

A.—Superiors being established only for the purpose of guiding those whom our Lord had committed to their direction in the practice of everything most elevated, pure and holy in religion, it cannot be doubted but that they are obliged to have a perfect knowledge of it; and as the whole system of religion consists in the truths of faith, and in the holy maxims laid down and delivered to us by Jesus Christ for the direction of our lives; it is equally certain, that the duty of a superior is to read, to hear, and to meditate on the sacred writings, since they are the sources from whence these maxims and divine truths flow.

To this sacred occupation he must join the study of the works of the holy fathers, which treat of the conduct and rule by which we should square all the actions of life. Moreover, since he ought to understand his state in a perfect manner, and in its fullest extent, he must read with care and attention whatever the saints have written concerning his obligations, and the history delivered down to us by ecclesiastical writers of the lives, actions, rules, and doctrine of the ancient holy monks. Behold, my brethren, the precise circle of the sciences necessary for a superior.

Should it happen that he possesses a greater store of learning, he is to reduce it all to the accomplishment of his duties. He should not extend it beyond the limits of his profession, and he should be careful not to attend to desires, which are but too common to persons of learning, or to such as are qualified to make a progress in it, which is to apply himself to the study of things that are foreign to his state and so, unfortunately, lose the love and even the remembrance of those matters which are of obligation, and of which he is persuaded he must one day give an account to God.

It is certain that superiors may be guilty of great abuse in matters of learning; and that if their occupations were regulated by necessity and duty, a great many of the hours which they employ in the study of unprofitable things would be spent in the meditation of the holy law of God. Then they would not deserve to be so justly reproached in these words, spoken by our Lord to Martha, "Thou art troubled about many things, but there is only one thing necessary" (Luke 10:42).

Q. 4.—May it not be objected, that if a superior should confine

---

[197] S. Basil, in asset, c. 3. 1 tract.

himself to such a narrow sphere, and of course, having less knowledge, that he would be less qualified to assist his brethren in their spiritual advancement?

A.—Such an objection would be ill-founded. Is there anything more unreasonable than to say that a man is not qualified to teach others his art and trade, because he has no knowledge of the arts and trades of other men? No one ever heard it said that this lawyer, though so completely skilled in his business, yet is unqualified to teach it to others, because he is not an astronomer or a divine. Indeed, nothing would be more insupportable than to imagine that a religious, shut up in his cloister, and a stranger to everything except those which belong to his state, having Jesus Christ crucified constantly before his eyes, meditating on His truths day and night, having no other occupation or affair but that of watching over those whom the Lord has placed under him—it would be, I repeat, foolish to conclude that such a man were disqualified to discharge the duties of his state, or to guide his brethren with less success, because he is not fully acquainted with the traditions of the Church, nor accurately skilled in its history, nor well versed in all the writings of the holy fathers.

Is it not a fact that the Anthonies, the Pacomiuses and the Hilarions, who laid the foundation of the monastic state, and who filled all the East with innumerable solitaries, extracted their learning from no other source but from that of truth itself by their profound meditations on the sacred writings? The same thing may be said of Saint Benedict, who has been the father and founder of all the western monks, for he confines all the learning of a superior to the knowledge of the holy scriptures. We learn from Cassian that all the learning of those men who were then so eminent for their sanctity, and who made the desert flourish in perfection, was no other but the sacred books. Saint Basil requires no other in a superior—and it is certain, that no one better understood what qualities were necessary for such a man than that holy doctor.

Saint John Climacus, who ought to be considered as a master by every monk, was of the same opinion, for he tells us that a true director seeks his instruction and knowledge of divine truths in the book written in his heart by the finger of God, and in the heavenly inspirations communicated to him by the goodness of our Lord; and, that he has no necessity of seeking wisdom in natural and sensible books, since he is taught by so great a master.

If anyone should maintain that ecclesiastical learning is necessary, and might very much assist a superior in the acquisition of that knowledge we require in him, we can reply that such a proposition would prove on the one side a great error in the mode of reasoning on the subject, and on the other, that we might complain with sufficient motives of the conduct of Divine Providence, who, in such a supposition, would have refused an essential quality to the Anthonies, Hilarions, Palemons, Saints Sabas, Auxentius and to a great number of others, no less famous for their wisdom and abilities in the care of souls. Let us rather say that God by His mercy preserved them from that which might have been capable of enervating that amiable simplicity, and profound humility, which became their great glory.

Q. 5.—*Do you therefore believe that a superior ought not to apply himself either to the study, or to the acquisition, of such things as are not of his profession?*

A.—No, he ought not, unless he is determined to do so by a particular order and disposition of Divine Providence. I will here add some other reasons to those I have already adduced on this subject. First, religious are penitents, who advance towards the possession and enjoyment of God by simplicity, by silence, and by the continual practice of everything calculated to humble them. Their superior is obliged to walk at their head continually, he is bound to practice first himself what he teaches them.

Now, as there is nothing so well adapted to acquire the praise and esteem of the world as study and learning, so, there is nothing more adverse to the profession of a solitary life. Nothing allures those who are engaged in it more speedily from the essence of their state, nor dissipates their minds and sentiments with more success. Consequently, as he who governs them is at the same time their model, nothing should be more prohibited to him, because he ought to instruct them more by his example than by his words. His actions should be such that the brethren might read in them, as in a living book, the whole system of rules by which their lives are to be directed.

Secondly, if the superior feels the weight of his charge, if he knows the extent of his duties, if he be persuaded, as certainly he cannot doubt, that he belongs no more to himself, but that his time, his person and his life belong to his brethren—in a word, if he love them as he ought, and as much as he is obliged—his days will appear too short to fulfill the whole extent of his duties, and to satisfy the efforts of his love. Hence, so far from engaging himself in any affairs that have no connection with his state, he will not, without scruple, deprive his brethren of one single moment of his time, since he will be persuaded that they should be all employed in their service.

Thirdly, I say, that the study even of holy things has its dangers as well as its advantages. Such persons as are called by God to it never fail to find much advantage and utility in the application, but as for those who engage therein without any other vocation save what they receive from their own imagination, they derive from such labors nothing but loss and disadvantage. All the passions of the mind are thereby nourished and strengthened. Pride, vainglory, presumption, anxiety, envy, contempt of others, and curiosity are almost inevitable excesses to such persons as these.

And if the superior, who thus exposes himself beyond the bounds of his profession should by chance escape these disorders, there are others from which he shall not be able to defend himself. His heart will become dry, his mind dissipated, his imagination filled with a thousand illusions. He will lose all love for his state. The duty of watching over his brethren will seem to him an insupportable burden. He will regret the few moments he will have given them by constraint; they will become a load to him. In fine, that mutual communication that should exist between them being interrupted, his ministry will be useless to them. He will be then in the community confined to himself, instead of being all to all; and he will, of course, do everything else but what he is obliged to do.

Perhaps you will oppose the example of Saint Bernard to what I have said, and corroborate your argument by adducing the example of some monks of the order of Saint Benedict, who applied themselves at former periods to the public ministry of announcing the word of God. But I answer, that as to that holy doctor, it is well known that he was an apostolic man, who had received infused knowledge, and whom God elevated above the sphere of his profession for the edification and support of the universal Church.

As to the others, they yielded to the pressing necessities of the people, that there were not, at that time, any public colleges, nor persons sufficiently qualified to instruct. They were forced by charity and necessity to engage in an occupation that did not agree with their state. And, may I not add, that if we are to guide ourselves by example, it would be much more to the purpose to imitate an infinity of religious men who served God in solitude, in simplicity, in abjection and in forgetfulness of creatures, than a small number of persons whom it pleased God to lead by extraordinary ways.

In a word, my brethren, if a superior regulate his life as he ought; if he give to every exercise the portion of time it requires; if he be careful to instruct his brethren by his exhortations, and to edify them by his strict observance of the common regular practices; if he watch over them like a charitable pastor; if he give them the time necessary to comfort and strengthen them in their different wants and necessities, so far from having

time to employ in the acquisition of learning, he will scarcely find a few moments to sigh before the Lord over the faults he shall have committed in his functions, to recommend the salvation of his brethren to the divine protection, to implore wisdom and strength for himself that he may be able to fulfill the duties of his state, which are so much above his weakness, and which even angels could not consider, though vested with so much light and sanctity, without fear and dread.

Q. 6.—*What is a superior obliged to do, and how far should his exactitude extend, in order to fulfill the duty of instructing by his example?*

A.—His life, my brethren, must be so exact, he must observe his rule with so much fidelity, and be so punctual in performing everything it prescribes, that his brethren in beholding his conduct, may learn therein all their duties. For this purpose it is necessary that they should find in his actions everything they are bound to practice, and nothing of that, which they ought not to do. Give ear to Saint Benedict,[198] " Let the abbot by his actions, much more than by his words, inculcate everything good and holy, and moreover, whatever he censures by his words, let him not recommend by his actions." That is, that except in those actions which are peculiar to himself, as superior, he ought to appear in all the regular exercises of his state and observe his rule in all its points, in order to form his brethren's exactitude by his own, their piety by his piety. This not only because the best means he can make use of to make them respect their rules is to show them that he respects them himself. But also because without that demonstration, every other would become abortive and of no utility.

In effect, my brethren, of what advantage would the care of a superior be, if he does not observe his rule himself ? Can he recommend exactitude if he himself be not exact? How can he teach any truth that condemns his own conduct, or forbid what he does himself? Can he reasonably excite others to penance and austerity, while he lives in softness and good cheer? or exhort to regularity in the exercises, while he discovers a thousand reasons to exempt himself from them? or inculcate the necessity of religious poverty, while he is followed by an entourage, like the great ones of the world? In a word, to what purpose would he labor to prove the necessity of a disengagement from the world and its maxims, and to explain what Saint Benedict signifies by these words: " I have become a stranger to the

---

[198] RB 2.

maxims and ways of the world, "[199] while on his own part he studies all the maxims of the world, follows its vanities, does everything in his power to appear like it, and shows forth by his profane exterior that the spirit of religion is almost extinct in him, and that he no longer possesses its principles.

If he sometimes speaks to his brethren on the observance of a rule he so much neglects in his conduct, can it be thought that he will do it with that vigor and zeal without which no one can ever persuade? Though he should speak of the difference of the good and bad servant, expatiate on the recompense laid up for the one, and the punishment reserved for the other, what more would he do than pronounce his own condemnation, and give our Lord full reason to say to him: " Out of thine own mouth I will judge thee, thou wicked servant " (Luke 19:22).

Let us moreover suppose that a superior, such as we are discussing, applies himself with all his strength to the duty of instructing his brethren, what effect can his futile instructions produce, since they are destitute of good works, which are their chief support ? What impression can that man make on others, who by his actions condemns all he says, and who, while he points out the right way to those whom he directs, walks in a contrary one himself? It is certain that he asperses himself with confusion in proportion as he proves the truths which he inculcates; and the contempt he purchases for himself, by living in opposition to his own lights, and betraying the sentiments of his own heart, makes him unworthy of any attention.

Hence, it is impossible that he should communicate a persuasive love of good to those souls, when he has no vestige of it himself; and on the other side, he will almost inevitably destroy it in those who possess it, since we know there is no incentive more powerful to bad actions than wicked example, more especially, when it is exhibited by persons of rank and authority. Inferiors, as Saint Gregory says, are more inclined to imitate the evil they observe in their superiors, than to practice what they hear recommended only by words. [200]

This was the inconsistency that Saint Benedict had before his eyes, and to which he desired to apply a remedy, when he commanded him

---

[199] RB 4:20

[200] "Subjecti non sectantur verba quae audiunt, sed sola quae conspciunt exempla pravitati"- S. Greg. past. p.1. c.2. / Liber Regulae Pastoralis, PL 77:15 (1849); "They do not attend to the words they hear but imitate only the depraved examples that they observe." St. Gregory the Great, The Book of Pastoral Rule, trans. George Demacopoulos (Crestwood, NY: St. Vladimir's Seminary Press, 2007), 31.

who is chosen to be the guide of the monastery to show his superiority by his actions as well as by his rank,[201] when he tells him, that he ought to instruct his brethren, and lead them on, in the way of holiness, more by his actions than by his words;[202] that he should corroborate his words by his example; that he ought to point out to his brethren, by his conduct, how they are to abstain from every appearance of evil.[203] In brief, the holy legislator teaches him that he ought to be as much above his brethren by his exactitude in the observance of his rule, as he is by his dignity and authority.[204]

Saint Basil was undoubtedly of this opinion.[205] When informing us what a superior ought to be, he requires in him a perfection so consummate that nothing can more effectually terrify those who have the care of souls, nor more forcibly deter such as are free of such an office from seeking to be engaged in it. He requires that he should be so strong in virtue as not to err himself, nor to be the cause of others going astray; that he should know how to conduct those to God, who seek Him; that he must be adorned with every virtue; that he ought to prove his love for God by his actions; that he ought to understand the sense of the holy scriptures; that he should never allow himself to be carried away by distractions.

Saint Jerome says that the conduct of a superior should be so well regulated, that his smallest actions and most common motions ought to be impressed with it; that all his deportment ought to evince the truths he has laid up in his heart; and that his entire life ought to be a continual instruction to the souls has under his care.[206]

Saint Gregory declares that he who is appointed to govern others should be elevated in holiness of life, so that his direction may be useful to those whom he commands. [207] He says, in another place, that he who by his good life is not qualified to direct, ought not accept the government of souls, lest he should become guilty of the same faults for the correction

---

[201] "Majoris nomen factis implere." RB 2:1.

[202] "Omnia bona et sancta factis ampliusquam verbis ostendere." RB 2:12.

[203] "Omnis vero quae discipulis docuerit esse contraria in suis factis indicet non agenda.." RB 2:13.

[204] "Quanto praelatus est ceteris, tanto cum oportet sollicitius observare praecepta regulae." RB 65:17.

[205] S. Basilius, Renunciatione, PG 31:631, 634; Basil, Ascetical, 19, 20.

[206] S. Hieronymus, Epistolae XLIV, Ad Fabiolam, Pl 22:622 (1845).

[207] Homiliarum in Ezechielem Prophetam, PL 76:907 (1849)

of which he has received his authority.[208] He says that a superior ought to excel in his actions in order that by his life he may point out to his brethren the way of peace; and that the flock, who ought to follow the voice and steps of their pastor, may advance more by his example than by his words.[209]

Saint Bernard says that the superior must add the voice of example to his words; that is to say, that his actions must agree with his words, or rather his words with his actions; and that he should be careful to do, before he begins to teach. It is a beautiful and salutary measure, says he, to carry the load first yourself, before you lay it on others. The example that is given by actions is a living and effectual instruction; and it is easy to persuade when that which is taught is shown to be possible by the teacher's actions.[210]

Saint John Climacus could not better point out what a superior ought to be, than by telling us that he ought to be divested of every passion; and that it is a shame for him to ask those graces of God for others which he has not as yet obtained for himself.[211]

This opinion will not appear too severe, if we consider a little what the holy apostle says when he speaks of the qualities and dispositions which ought to meet in the person of a bishop; for he requires that he should be holy, irreprehensible, and that in all things he ought to be the example of those whom he governs (Titus 2:7).

Notwithstanding the variety of his employments, the extent of his solicitude, and that dissipation which is almost inevitable in the multiplicity of his affairs, what dispositions ought we not desire in a superior of religious persons, whose functions and duties are all enclosed within the bounds of his cloister; and who being of the same state and condition as those who are under his charge, should consequently be in all his actions, and in every circumstance, their rule, their model, and their example.

Q. 7.—*Do you then believe that a superior ought not to attribute to himself any exemption or dispensation from the regular common exercises, by which he might be distinguished from his brethren?*

A.—From the moment a superior receives his authority he should apply these words of the Holy Spirit to himself: "If they have made thee a ruler

---

[208] Sanctus Gregorius, Librorum Moralium, PL 76:318 (1849).

[209] S. Gregorius, Regulae Pastoralis Liber, PL 77:28 (1845).

[210] Epistola CCI, Ad Balduin. PL 182:370a (1854).

[211] Liber ad Pastorem, PG 88:1171 (1864) / To the Shepherd, in Ladder, 251.

be not lifted up, but be amongst them as one of themselves " (Ecclesiastic. 32:1). He ought to be with his brethren in all the common exercises, in labor, in watching, in fasting. Moreover, he ought not to think it improper to embrace the meanest occupations. He must observe the same austerity in his food, and the same simplicity in his clothing. Let him be distinguished only by his virtues, or by such actions as are annexed to his ministry. He ought to remember, on all occasions, that in imitation of Jesus Christ he is appointed to serve his brethren, and not to receive services of them (Matt 20:28). Nor is it permitted him to affect any human differences, or to seek any other preeminence, but such as are established by the rules, and confirmed by the example of the saints.

Q. 8.—*What excuse can be adduced, therefore, in favor of those superiors, who maintain retinues, coaches and equipages?*

A.—Such a mode of living is so entirely opposite to all monastic piety, to the maxims and examples of the saints, that it can be considered only as the consequence of extreme disorder. In effect, what connection is there between such conduct, and that which should naturally result from the idea of men, who, by the appointment and order of God, ought to be clothed in sackcloth and ashes? Who are obliged by their state to spend their lives in tears and mourning; Who make public profession of poverty and abjection? And yet these are the men who walk in the ways of the world, and imitate, without scruple, its pomp and vanity; and what reason can they find to excuse such scandalous and palpable excesses?

The principal and chief superiors will, undoubtedly, allege the necessity of performing their regular visits, but is it not well known that such visits were made before any such equipages appeared in the world? That many generals of religious orders, even at the present time, acquit themselves of the same duty, and go from one nation to another, and from kingdom to kingdom, using such means only as contain nothing contrary to the simplicity of their state, nor derogatory to the edification they owe to the Church?

Some will adduce their infirmities as sufficient reasons for their conduct, and will pretend that not being able to perform the duties of their charge by any other means, it is lawful for them to make use of this. But they deceive themselves, and they ought to know that the good to which we cannot attain by proper ways is not of the number of those which God requires of us. After all, there is nothing to prevent anyone from using carriages, or other simple vehicles, by which they may enjoy the same accommodation as they could in coaches, without having the same ostentation and pomp. If those who make to themselves imaginary necessities reflect that eighty years ago there was only one coach in the capital of the kingdom; that fifty years back, nobly born persons travelled on horseback only, and nevertheless, superiors at that time made their visits as well as they do now, they will find that our opinions are founded on solid reason and justice, and that they are duped by custom, fashion, or too great a fondness for their own ease, or by the spirit of the world.

Others will say that their motives are founded on decency, and on the necessity of supporting their dignity. But what sort of decency must that be in which there is neither relation, proportion, nor analogy between the persons and their state? Or rather, can there be a deformity more scandalous than to see men, who, according to their state and condition, are obliged to hold up to others the example of humility, mortification and self-renunciation, appear in public surrounded with the superfluities, luxury and pomp of worldlings ? If it be alleged as a pretext that there are some countries in which that simplicity would injure the superior's authority, would it not be more proper, in such a case, to disabuse the world of such an error, and to begin immediately, than to make to one's self a perpetual necessity of yielding to it?

And ought we not to hope that religious persons, who are children and disciples of the saints, would follow the example of their fathers and masters without much difficulty? Saint Bernard considers it as a monstrous thing when a man, in an elevated dignity, nourishes base sentiments in his mind. [212]But what would he not say if he saw the vanity of the world revive in a person who is no longer of the world, who forsook it for the love of Jesus Christ, for the purpose of imitating his humility, his confusions and contempts? What would not that holy saint exclaim at seeing such things, he who feared no exaggeration, when he declared that to conceal a secular heart and mind under a religious habit is real apostasy.[213]

It is well known with what force he condemned the ostentation of Suger, Abbot of Saint Denis, who walked with a train and equipage, which was not proper for a man of his condition, and that the saint declared his conduct to be the greatest scandal of his time, though the abbot was prime minister of state, and was invested with a distinguished authority and rank in the kingdom.[214]

This was so much the sentiment of his whole order, that we read in a

---

[212] De consideratione, PL 182:750c (1854) / Saint Bernard of Clairvaux and George Lewis, Saint Bernard on Consideration. (Oxford: Clarendon Press, 1908), 52.

[213] Sermo III, in Psalmum XC, Qui Habitat, PL 183:193b (1854).

[214] Epistola LXXVIII, Ad Sugerium, PL 182:191a (1854).

statute of a general chapter held in the second century after its foundation, which declares that the excellency of the religious state is so great, that what might be innocently used by other Christians is prohibited to monks. And the general chapter being informed that some abbots were become so sensual and effeminate that they made themselves be drawn in carriages and litters, the chapter condemned such conduct, and forbade any abbot or religious of the order, from thenceforth, to be guilty of such an excess. In case any should be so presumptuous as to do the like, that he should fast on bread and water during the same length of time as he shall have remained in the fault: I will here copy the part of the statute, word by word.[215]

As to what concerns the supporting their dignity, they must be strangely blind who imagine that they can support the dignity of a state, which as we have said many times, is nothing but abjection, poverty and penance, by human magnificence and splendor. The holy monks, our fathers and predecessors, attracted the esteem and veneration of men by the sanctity of their lives, though they desired nothing less. And it is a fact that the monastic state was never so much considered and venerated by the world as during the time that it conserved its primitive simplicity and virtue. All its beauty ever flows from its interior piety. [216]

But now when its chiefs and members have no longer either its virtue or merit, they are ashamed to belong to a state which has nothing but what is vile and contemptible. This they endeavor to cover by having recourse to the assistance of a strange apparatus, and by a deplorable illusion, they seek to content themselves with a false and apparent glory, because they cannot procure that which is true and solid.

It will be alleged as a third reason that the times are changed, that things are not to be taken according to the letter of their primitive institution, and that they are not now as formerly. It is true that the times are corrupted, but it is no less true that the sanctity of the cloister ought not to cede to the cupidity of men; that the salt of the earth ought not to partake of the corruption of the earth, and that the darkness of the world should not obscure those who are set up to be its lights, What fellowship hath light with darkness (2 Cor 6:14) ?

Hence you see, my brethren, that this custom is founded on no solid reason; it sprang from the corruption of the heart; cupidity is its true parent, and it is nothing better than the real production of the spirit of

---

[215] He does so, but it is a long passage in Latin, omitted here.

[216] "Omnis gloria filiae regis ab intus."– Ps 44.

the world. This ought not to astonish you, for when religious persons lose the desire of pleasing God alone, they are hurried on by their thoughts to the study of pleasing themselves and to that of pleasing men. They have no well-regulated conduct nor fixed dispositions, contrary to the precept of the apostle who forbids us to conform ourselves to the world (Rom 12: 2). They follow all its maxims, its customs and ways; they extract from it whatever is pleasing to them; they learn its manners; they imitate its mien, its looks, its conversation, at table, in their dress and equipages; and it may be said that they have retained no marks of their profession, but those which the fear of public infamy prevented them from abdicating.

Q. 9.—*Tell us precisely to what the duty of watching over those who are committed to their care obliges superiors.*

A.—A superior ought to be persuaded that among all his duties that of watching over his brethren is the most peculiarly essential; that vigilance is the first and most important quality of a pastor; and that the fruit of all the labors he endures for the preservation and increase of his flock depends on the care he takes to have an exact knowledge of its necessities, that thereby he may be enabled to procure for his sheep everything useful and profitable, and avert from them all that might injure or destroy them.

The farmer who having cultivated and sowed his fields but who neglects to watch over it, takes no care to prevent the birds from destroying the seed he had sowed, or suffers it to be choked with the weeds which are usually most abundant in the best land, would certainly be much disappointed if he expected to gather an abundant harvest. Similarly, when a superior contents himself with merely instructing his brethren, though he should even confirm his words by his example, he still fails in his duty unless he takes care that the divine seed is not destroyed by the winds of temptations, or by the malignant impressions of the devil from which the most holy souls are not exempt.

Therefore the superior must watch over his brethren without ceasing, imitating thereby the example of the Lord, who according to the prophet never slumbers nor sleeps, but keeps His eyes continually open on His elect (Ps 120:4). He must support them by his pastoral vigilance, be present in all their wants, and assist them in the different states and conditions in which they may be. He must strengthen the weak, enlighten the blind, raise up those who are fallen, comfort the afflicted, excite the indifferent, encourage the pusillanimous, correct the negligent, moderate those who advance too rapidly. He must lead those into the right way who stray from it, rectify the impudent zeal of some, correct the faults of others, and keep all in a just balance. He must transform himself into a thousand shapes, so that he may render his ministry as profitable as the brethren have a right to expect it should be, so that he himself may say with the apostle: I became all to all in order so that I might preserve for my Lord and master Christ, the souls whom He was pleased to commit to my care (1 Cor 9:22).

Q. 10.—*Do you then require that the care of a superior should be continual?*

A.—No person considers it strange that a magistrate should consume all his life and employ all his time in the duties of his charge; that a divine should pass whole days and nights in the study of ecclesiastical learning; nor that the minister of a prince should apply himself, without reserve, to the interest and government of the state. A superior ought, in like manner, apply himself with unwearied zeal to the discharge of his duties which are much more important, since, as the saints tell us, the care and direction of one soul is of much greater consequence than the government of the whole world. Hence, he ought to consider his charge as the only object of his solicitude; and, by continual vigilance, prepare himself to give a strict account to the Lord who will one day demand of him the sacred treasure of which He had made him the depository.

Saint Benedict requires that the superior should continually reflect on the great account he is to give to Jesus Christ of the souls committed to his care; that this consideration should influence all the tenor of his conduct, and regulate every action of his life. To this thought he calls his attention on every occasion, in order that his duty may be so present to his mind that nothing may be able to avert it from his thoughts. [217] He declares that if the father of the family does not find all the profit in his flock that he expects, he will impute the loss to the negligence of the pastor.[218] And that he shall not be discharged from the great tribunal, unless he can prove that he neglected nothing, but applied every possible remedy to heal their disorders, so that he may be qualified to say with the prophet, "I have not concealed thy justice in my heart, I have announced thy holy will to them; but they have despised my words."[219]

Saint Basil says, that he who loves God gives himself without reserve to the instruction of such as are under his care; that he employs every means to become useful to them, and that he ought to persevere in this application, both in public and in private, as long as he lives.[220]

---

[217] RB. 2:37.

[218] RB. 2.7.

[219] RB. 2.8; Ps 39:10

[220] *Moralia*, Regula LXX, Caput XVIII, PG 31:831; Basil, Ascetical, 174.

Saint Chrysostom teaches that a pastor should possess much prudence and wisdom; and that he cannot have too great attention, nor too much light, in order to dispel the shades of obscurity from the souls whom he directs

Pope John III to show what the vigilance of a superior ought to be, relates what Jacob said to his father-in-law:

> I have served you twenty years, during which time your flocks have not been sterile; I have not fed myself with the flesh of your sheep; I have never shown you the marks of any ravages committed by wild beasts; you have suffered no loss; and I repaired whatever might have been stolen. I have been burned with scorching heat, and pierced with excessive cold; I have passed entire nights without sleep.

If Laban's shepherd endured so much fatigue and pain for the temporal good of his master, what vigilance and labor should not the pastor of the sheep of the Lord endure, says this holy pontiff, since the effect is to be eternal.[221]

Saint John Climacus, in his letter to the pastor, requires so much vigilance, and such an invariable exactitude in a superior, that it is evident he means to inculate the duty of a constant attachment to the direction of the community of which he is the head and guide.[222]

In effect, if the superior does not make it his only affair, how can it be possible for him to accomplish what this great saint requires of him? How can he enter into a detail of everything that regards his brethren, know their characters, their dispositions, their good or bad qualities, the degree of virtue they have acquired, their spiritual wants and infirmities; diversify his conduct according to his knowledge; lead the weak by the hand; carry the others in his arms, according to the language of the prophet, "He shall gather together the lambs, by the strength of his arm"(Isa 40:11). And, in a word, keep always near them, in order to assist them in the least anxiety or agitation that may happen to them.

Nothing deserves to be noticed more than the instruction given by the spirit of God in the council of Trent, to all pastors. That holy council, after having recommended to them, in the words of the apostle, to watch and labor without intermission in the duties of their ministry, declares to them that they are not to imagine that they can fulfill this duty if they forsake or

---

[221] *Epistola Joannis Papae III Ad Episcopos Germaniae et Galliae,* PL 72:16.

[222] *Ad pastorem,* PG 88:1165-1208 (1864) / Ladder, 249-265.

neglect to watch over the flocks committed to their care; that the sovereign judge will demand a strict account of the blood of their sheep at their hands:[223] it being certain that the pastor will be inexcusable, and that he will not be attended to, if the wolf shall have devoured his sheep, even without his knowledge. [224]

But the best means to learn what their vigilance ought to be, is to consult that of Jesus Christ, and to examine with what assiduity He applied Himself to the forming and preserving those whom He had received from His heavenly Father. He lived among them, supporting their weaknesses, commiserating their infirmities; He reprehended their faults, instructed them day and night, in public and in private; He concealed nothing from them that could be useful to them, as He Himself declares (John 15:15); and He never left them, except when He retired into solitude to pray for their salvation and for that of the world.

In the divine prayer that He poured forth to His heavenly Father before His passion nothing appears more conspicuous than the greatness of His solicitude and love. At the moment in which He was betrayed to His enemies, He seemed to forget Himself, when He said, "Let them go their way" (John 18:8), as if He only thought of the preservation of His disciples; though bound and suffering all the violence of His persecutors, He did not forget His apostle; He was moved with pity for his weakness, and by His grace raised him up after his fall; thus accomplishing to the end of His life the truth of these words: when He had loved His own, He loved them to the end (John 13:1).

Q. 11. How do you require that the superior should not have any care of temporal things?

A.—As the entire government of the monastery belongs to the superior, and as he should extend his care to everything in it, though he ought to apply himself chiefly to the care of souls, yet he is not to neglect the care of temporal things; but he ought to observe such order and regularity in his more important occupations, that he may find some time to attend to those of less consequence.

Although Saint Benedict requires that a superior should be always mindful of his duties, he moreover adds, that everything belonging to the monastery is under his command, and ought to be directed by his orders; but he admonishes him, at the same time, to apply himself with such

---

[223] Con. Trid. Ses. 6. c. 1. de refor.; Theodore Alois Buckley, *The Canons and Decrees of the Council of Trent* (London: Routledge, 1851), 47.

[224] Buckley, *Canons*, 47.

moderation and reserve to the care of transitory things, that the souls of whose salvation he must render an account to Jesus Christ may suffer no loss by that care. He anticipates the objection with which the greater part of superiors endeavor to palliate and excuse their immoderate application to exterior affairs, by declaring to them that the reason they may extract from the poverty and indigence of their monastery is not admissible; and that they should remember that it is written, "Seek ye first the kingdom of God, and His justice, and all other things shall be added to you" (Matt 6: 33). And that those who fear God, never want anything.

Saint Gregory says:

> A pastor ought to apply himself in such a manner to the care of temporal things, as not to neglect those which are interior; and on the other hand, he should not give himself so entirely to the care of interior things, as wholly to neglect those which are exterior. [225]

He adds:

> There are some who frequently conduct themselves as if they no longer remembered that they were raised to that superiority for the sanctification only of their brethren. They give themselves to secular affairs without reserve, and plunged in this erroneous and disorderly way, they are quite charmed when any occasion appears that may enable them to act; but when they are obliged to remain without motion, their minds are distracted with trouble and anxiety, day and night.

The same saint continues:

> Saint Paul, in order to prevent those who are in the service of Jesus Christ from engaging in worldly affairs, tells us that he who is engaged in the service of God, should not embarrass himself with secular affairs, so that being free, he may please God to whom he is consecrated. The consequence is that such employments are not of the number of those to which pastors should sacrifice their time. Pastors should, therefore, renounce them, for if they do not, they cannot avoid straying far from the path of truth. He tells them that if any difference should arise between them concerning the things of the world, they ought to make the less considerable persons in

---

[225] Gregorius Magnus, *Regulae Pastoralis Liber.* PL 77:27 (1849); Gregory, Pastoral, 68.

the Church judges in such cases, that thus, such only as have no spiritual or superior qualities may be employed in those affairs. As if he would say, that those who were not capable of interior things, should attend to such as are exterior and necessary. [226]

Now if Saint Gregory did not allow ecclesiastical superiors to engage in worldly affairs, without these conditions, though they are, by their condition, engaged in exterior solicitudes, what would he not have said to religious, who, by the nature of their profession, are separated from them? What would his sensations have been, if he saw monastic superiors attach themselves with ardor to them? Could he think that the liberty of frequently leaving their communities and forsaking their flocks like mercenaries for the purpose of appearing in the palaces of the great, in cities, and before every tribunal, were like anything else in effect, but a desertion, and an inexcusable contempt of their essential duties? Such was the opinion of the fathers in the council of Trent, as they expressly declared in these words:—But let them remember, that they cannot possibly fulfill that duty, if, hirelings, they forsake the flock committed to their care.[227]

They will tell us that necessary and important affairs compel them to act in that manner. But what proportion is there between the affair that the superior neglects, and the other to which he applies with so much earnestness? What comparison can he make between that temporal interest, and the value of immortal souls who cost no less a price than the blood and death of the Son of God? Is it not preferring the perishable goods of this life to the eternal riches of the next, the goods of the earth to those of heaven, and falling precisely into the misfortune which the holy council of Trent so much deplored when it said, It is exceedingly to be lamented, that there are in these times some persons, who being unmindful of their salvation, and preferring temporal things to eternal, human to divine, forsake the care of souls, etc..[228]

To this it will undoubtedly be answered, that the evil is not so great as it is represented, that the flock is not abandoned, and that the superior is careful to place it under the custody of proper substitutes, who will keep a strict watch over it during his absence. But why does he not rather invest them with the power of transacting his temporal affairs? Why does he divest himself of a duty, so important in itself and so strictly enjoined, and

---

[226] S. Gregorius, *Pastoralis*, PL 77:39 / Gregory, Pastoral, 70.

[227] Con. Trid. Ses. 6. c. 1. De refor.; Buckley, *Trent*, 47.

[228] Buckley, *Trent*, 47.

contrary to the spirit of this rule, the example of Jesus Christ, and that of the saints, retain that which contains nothing but abject and contemptible functions?

He would blush to say that he can find no person to whose care he might confide the success of such affairs, since it is evident, he can easily procure those who are capable of directing souls. It is a no less evident fact that for a hundred who may be found capable of transacting external business, scarcely one is found sufficiently qualified to be a proper director in the way of religious perfection. All things being thus considered, it is as evident as the light that it is nothing but anxiety, the want both of the knowledge and the spirit of his state, immortification, the love of the world, and the same avidity of its goods, as fills the hearts of those who are as yet of the world, that so easily allures this superior from his cloister and blinds him to that degree that he cannot perceive how dangerously he exposes his own salvation by ceasing to watch over that of his brethren.

Saint Bernard, speaking on a subject of the same nature, says, that if an Egyptian, an infidel, reposed his confidence in such a manner in a slave and a stranger, that as to the administration of his goods and affairs, he knew not what he had in his house (Gen 39:8), why will not a Christian have the same confidence in a Christian? It is a surprising thing that pastors can so easily procure substitutes to whom they commit the care of souls, and yet can find no person qualified to transact their temporal affairs. Truly it must be an erroneous way of appreciating the value of things, to have such a zealous solicitude for those of no value, and little or none for those of the highest importance.[229]

To speak properly, this is nothing else than to feel less pain at beholding the destruction of what belongs to Jesus Christ, than at that which belongs to ourselves. We are vigilant to sum up our daily losses, but no way attentive to what perishes in the flock of Christ. An exact account is required every day of servants, expenses are nicely estimated; while the number of sins committed by those of whom we are the guides is indifferently disregarded. Help is quickly procured to save an animal fallen into a pit; but a soul perishes, and no one is concerned.[230]

Pope Saint Gregory, in one of his letters, writes to a subdeacon that as it is his duty to prevent the monks from engaging in such affairs as induce them to appear in courts of justice, and enervate their application to the divine service, so, it is a no less important obligation for him to provide

---

[229] *De consideratione*, PL 182:786a (1854) / *Consideration*, 118.

[230] *De Consideratione*, PL 182:786b (1854) / *Consideration*, 119.

for their temporal cares, lest their minds being divided by a diversity of things, they may be induced to fulfill their ordinary duties with sloth and indifference. He commands the abbot, who is the subject of his letter, to commit the entire administration of his temporals to a person whom he nominates for that purpose and to whom he should pay a proportionate stipend. For it is a great advantage, as that great pope remarks, for those who serve God, to purchase the repose of their souls at some futile expense that thereby they may secure to themselves the advantage of their retirement, and moreover, preserve that disengagement and liberty which are so necessary in order to apply themselves in a proper manner to the things of God.[231]

But if some superiors be found who destroy by their absence, there are others who effect no less a ruin by their presence. They are among their brethren as if they were not. They are present in the monastery as to the body, but their minds and hearts are far from it, and it may be said that they have eyes and see not, ears and hear not, tongues and speak not. Their lives are so implicated in exterior business and affairs, or with their own slothfulness, that they can find no time either to watch over their brethren, to hear them in their interior wants, or to break to them the bread of life by pious instructions and exhortations.[232]

And if it should sometimes happen that they exhort or reprehend them, their words produce no effect, because as their lives are disorderly, they give nothing but bad example, so through their own fault they are contemned and gather nothing but confusion. There are others who imagine that they have fully complied with all the duties of their charge, when they have performed some superficial offices, and attended to an exterior inspection, by which they make their government become merely political. Being in their communities like a magistrate in a city, they content themselves with repressing disorders, and punishing the more grievous faults, thus persuading themselves that they have done sufficiently and that such a mode of conduct is a full accomplishment of all their duties. But they certainly deceive themselves if they think that their works are thus full, and that their ministry requires nothing more.

For, as Almighty God has charged them with the care of their brethren's salvation; as the brethren depend entirely upon them; and consequently, as

---

[231] Gregorius Magnus, Epistola LXIX. *Ad Petrum Subdiaconum Sicillae.* PL 77:525b (1849) / Gregory the Great, *Letters,* Book I: Ep. 69.

[232] *Liber Regulae Pastoralis,* PL 77:39a (1849) / Gregory, *Pastoral,* 69.

they are obliged to have an entire knowledge of their brethren, to penetrate into the bottom of their consciences, visit the folds of their hearts, in order to regulate all their dispositions and affections; so long as they content themselves with a simple exterior direction, and reduce their principal functions to that alone, their lives will be nothing but a frightful void. They will possess the appearance only, the sign and exterior of a true pastor. Nor shall they even escape the malediction, which the Lord fulminates by the mouth of His prophet, against those pastors who are not solicitous to fortify the weak, heal the sick, repair what has been broken, lead back what has gone astray, and who take no pains to seek those who were so unfortunate as to lose themselves (Ezek 34:4).

Q. 12.—*How shall superiors be able to assist their brethren in all these ways, if the brethren on their part are unwilling to seek even their advice, and if, as is usually the case, they have no confidence or respect for them?*

A.—I allow that the little confidence which is found in religious persons for their superiors is the cause why they derive no advantage from them, and that the superiors have as little to do with the direction of their inferiors as anyone else. But whatever may be the source of this evil, whether it proceeds from inferiors or superiors; or, what is most probable, whether both the one and the other are the cause, the superior is indispensably bound to employ all his care and to take the best method to heal them, which is that of acquiring their esteem, friendship and confidence.

For that purpose, he ought to exert himself according to the rules of Christian prudence and charity. Above all, he ought to evince the greatest love for his rule, and he should possess that love in effect. He ought to prove by his conduct that he has but one affair in this world, which is that of serving God, and laboring without intermission for the salvation of his brethren. He must, I say, make this truth become convincing, not by simple discourses, but by word and work united, by his example, by his vigilance, by his mildness, by his patience, by his prayers, by a separation from all persons and things which might oppose his design.

Should they, after this, by their obstinacy become inflexible to his efforts, if their malignity resist his care; if all the tenderness of the father is insufficient to soften the obduracy of the children, the testimony of his conscience will console him in their loss, which according to the words of the spirit of God, will not be imputed to him. "But if thou wilt declare to the wicked man, and he will not be converted from his wickedness, thou hast delivered thy soul "(Ezek 3:19).

But if the superior is not affected at the unhappy state of his brethren;

if he take no pains to change their evil dispositions, with which he beholds them animated; if because they have forsaken their duties he should also neglect his; if their insensibility make him become insensible also, if he become obdurate because they are so; if he neglect to apply a remedy to their evils, because they are indifferent about it themselves; in a word, if he does not exert every faculty to lead them back into the way of salvation, he may be assured that he becomes a partaker in their sins, that their iniquity shall be imputed to him, and that he becomes guilty of their death. Let him flatter himself with a false security, so long as he pleases, the misfortune will still be common, the master and the disciples shall find themselves crushed under the same ruins.[233]

We ought to beseech the divine goodness to enlighten the superiors, or rather that it would please our Lord to animate both their minds and hearts, that he may convince them how great the error is, or to speak more correctly, that there is no greater error than to imagine that they may refuse with impunity their solicitude, their time and their assiduity to those, for whose sake, Almighty God requires they should be ever ready to shed their blood, and to sacrifice their very lives.

Q. 13.—*We desire to be informed concerning the obligation by which a superior is bound to pray for those who are under his care, in what does it consist?*

A.—Although the duties of instructing the brethren, of edifying them by example, and of supporting them by vigilance, are essential to the state of a superior, yet they admit dispensations. But it is not so as to prayer; a superior is always in a condition to discharge that duty; and while he is able to raise his hands and eyes to heaven, for the graces which are necessary for his own salvation, he may implore at the same time the like mercy for his brethren, and thus satisfy the duty by which he is bound to pray for them.

First, this duty is founded on the weakness and inability of the pastor himself. For as he is obliged to answer for the salvation of his brethren, and as all his labors, cares, and assiduity are of no effect unless they receive strength, influence and efficacy from above, it cannot be doubted—unless we are willing to persuade ourselves that his ministry is a ministry of death—that he is obliged in a very particular manner to address himself to our Lord Jesus Christ without intermission, and to beseech him by continual prayers to vivify his words, animate his example, and bless his solicitude; in a word, that our Lord would please to be Himself the soul

---

[233] RB 2.8.

and life of his government, and make it an effectual instrument for the salvation of the souls committed to his care.

Secondly, the numerous duties, the diversity of cares and services which a superior is bound to employ and fulfill, in favor of his brethren, is another motive that enforces the necessity of continual prayer, and proves that they cannot be too fervent nor too constant. How shall he become the guide of the blind, the support of the weak, the physician of the sick, the consolation of the afflicted, if our Lord does not give him light, strength, sanctity and wisdom? Shall he find light within himself?—he is nothing but darkness; holiness?—he is nothing but sin; strength ?—he is weakness itself; wisdom?—he is nothing but folly; and can he think that Almighty God will open His treasures, communicate all His favors to him, and fill his soul with all those holy sentiments, if he, on his part, does not solicit the divine goodness, and endeavor to obtain them by fervent and continual prayer?

Thirdly, a superior is obliged to provide for all the wants of those persons who are under his care; all their infirmities are become his own, and their sufferings are so peculiarly his, that he may say with the apostle (2 Cor 11:29), he feels all their evils; with them he is sad, afflicted and languishing; hence, at every moment arise successive wants; every instant gives birth to new motives, and pressing reasons, which point out the necessity of fervent prayer, for the comfort, repose, advancement and perfection of his brethren.

In fine, the superior is the channel by which God communicates his graces to every member of the community; through his hands they pass. He is the true medium of the gifts of heaven. He is the reservoir (to use the expression of Saint Bernard[234]) which receives and is filled, and which afterwards diffuses the waters it contains. And as it is from Jesus Christ alone that he is to receive the bread which he is to break for those of whom our Lord has made him the father and pastor, so should he continually stretch out his hand to receive it, and be incessant in his petitions to retain it— prayer being a condition without which our endeavors are ineffectual before God (Matt 7:7).

It was in these sentiments that Saint Paul told the Colossians that he prayed to the Lord for them without intermission, beseeching Him to fill them with the knowledge of His holy will, to give them all wisdom and spiritual understanding, in order that they might conduct themselves in a manner worthy of God, please Him in all things, produce the fruits of every good work, and increase in his knowledge (Col 1:9).

---

[234] Sermo XVIII, in *Cantica*, PL 183:860 (1854) / Canticles, 1:176.

When Saint Basil says[235], that a superior is a man who represents Jesus Christ, and who performs the office of a mediator between God and men, he means no more than that such a person should, by his petitions, by his mediation, and by the favor he has acquired with God preserve the divine fear and charity of God in his disciples' hearts, either by taking care that they do not lose those heavenly gifts, or by exerting himself in assisting them to recover them, if they had the misfortune to lose them. This supposes an intercourse and a holy familiarity with God, and, consequently, fervent and continual prayer, without which, such a commerce cannot exist.

Saint Clement of Alexandria, speaking of the dispositions which we ought to have towards our superiors, says:

> Fear your superior's anger; weep when he sighs for you; respect him when he is appeased; anticipate him, when, by his prayers, he endeavors to preserve you from the punishment you have deserved; when he spends many nights in prayer for you, performing the duties of a mediator between God and you, and addressing continual supplications to the Father of mercies, to obtain of Him for you, all necessary graces.[236]

Saint Gregory of Nyssa, comparing a superior to Moses, says:

> If the superior truly imitates that holy legislator, he will reanimate those who are depressed with fear, which can never be the case unless he address his prayers to the Lord, for there are many who seem to be raised to the dignities of the Church for no other purpose than to keep good order in exterior things. They make little or no account of the interior which is invisible and is known to God alone. This was not the rule that Moses observed. To animate the dejected with confidence he convinced them that he cried to the Lord for them, though he spoke no words when doing so, to teach us that the desires which are formed in a pure heart are to be considered as a strong cry that ascends even to the throne of God much

---

[235] S. Basilius, Caput XXII, "De Obedientia uberius." In *Constitutiones Monasticae*, PG 31:1402 (1857).

[236] S. Clemens Alexandrinus, *Liber Quis Dives Salvetur*. PG 9:647 (1857) / Clement of Alexandria. *Who Is the Rich Man that Shall Be Saved?* In *Fathers of the Second Century: Hermas, Tatian, Athenagoras, Theophilus, and Clement of Alexandria*. A. Roberts, et al. eds. W. Wilson, trans. Vol. 2. (Buffalo, NY: Christian 1885), 603.

more effectively than those which might be uttered with the usual organs of the voice.[237]

Saint John Climacus says, that the prayers of the superior are the helmet that covers the solitaries' head.[238] He says in another place that those superiors who are friends of God, by keeping their minds and hearts constantly united to Him, may, by the force of their prayers, reconcile to Him, not only those of His servants who have failed in their duty, but also such as have lived in real enmity with, and separation from Him. It is profitable, says the same saint, to live under superiors who are the friends of God, there being nothing better qualified to assist us in the practice of virtue than the concurring help of those whom He loves, to whose prayers He can refuse nothing; and He never fails to pour down abundant graces on those who serve Him, being moved thereto by the prayers of their pastors.[239]

Saint Bernard teaches us that a pastor ought to guide his flock by word, by example, and by prayer, but that prayer is the most excellent. He says that action is the virtue of the word, but that prayer obtains grace and efficacy both for the action and for the word.[240]

The conclusion of all these truths is, therefore, that the functions of superiors are replete with dangers and difficulties. This was the reason why the saints avoided as much as possible the care and direction of souls. Some refused it when it was offered them; others forsook it after having accepted the charge. Moreover, all those who accepted it, consented only with tears, and for fear of offending God by opposing His will.

Nor is there any superior but should tremble on considering the extent of his duties, for although these duties are diversified, and God does not require an equal perfection of every pastor, yet they ought to be adorned with an eminent, or at least an advanced piety, and with superior virtue in order to conduct themselves as worthy ministers and faithful stewards, and to be thereby qualified to fill, in a holy manner, the place given them by Jesus Christ among men. It was this consideration that induced Saint John Chrysostom to pronounce this terrible expression: It is an astonishing thing, if any superior be possibly saved.[241]

---

[237] S. Gregorius Nyssenus, *De Vita Moysis*, PG 44:298; Gregory of Nyssa, *The Life of Moses*, Abraham J. Malherbe and Everett Ferguson, trans, intro. and notes (NY: Paulist, 1978).

[238] *Scala*, PG 88:678 (1864). / *Ladder*, 68.2.

[239] *Ad pastorem*, PG 88:1171(1860); *Ladder*, 251.

[240] Epistola CCI, PL 182:370 (1854). / Bernard, *Works*, 2:611.

[241] "Miror an fieri possit ut aliquis ex rectoribus sit salvus."–Hom. 34, in Ep. Ad hebr./

10 | OF THE CHARITY THAT THE BRETHREN SHOULD HAVE FOR ONE ANOTHER—CONTENTS:

"Oh! how great the danger! What should one say to those wretched men, who throw themselves upon so great an abyss of punishments? Thou hast to give account of all over whom thou rulest, women and children and men; into so great a fire dost thou put thy head. I marvel if any of the rulers can be saved, when in the face of such a threat, and of the present indifference, I see some still even running on, and casting themselves upon so great a burden of authority. " John Chrysostom. Saint Chrysostom: *Homilies on the Gospel of St. John and Epistle to the Hebrews* (NPNF1/14:519).

10

OF THE CHARITY THAT THE BRETHREN SHOULD HAVE FOR ONE ANOTHER

QUESTION 1 —*What should the brethren do in order to give one another sufficient proofs of their mutual charity*

ANSWER.—Fraternal charity is the most important commandment next to that of loving God. It is the mark by which, according to the words of Jesus Christ, His disciples are to be distinguished from those who do not belong to Him (John 13:35). Now, as religious persons should be the first among His disciples, and not in rank and dignity but in piety and devotion, their charity should, of course, be eminent. Again, as our Lord has demonstrated that he has a particular love for religious brethren, as they have received the effusions of His special graces, as they are men who are more immediately according to His own heart than other Christians are, in short, as they more exactly represent, and more effectually follow our divine Lord, they are consequently most worthy of our particular esteem and love.

Saint Basil, in order to give us a just idea of that charity which ought to reign among religious persons, says, that the religious state is a way of life, entirely spiritual; that it is the profession of an indissoluble union; that religious souls are linked together by a spiritual alliance, which was formed in the presence of the Holy Spirit of which He was both the mediator and witness; and that this union ought to be more close than that which is found among the members of the natural body. The saints gave monasteries the epithet of heavens because they considered them as the abodes of concord and peace; and because their inhabitants lead the lives of angels, being united to God by the bonds of a perfect and unalterable charity.[242]

Nevertheless, though the state in which you live does not furnish you with the same means of demonstrating your charity as those which men in worldly society enjoy, yet it presents you with others which are peculiar to yourselves. In proportion as your sphere is more limited, so should your zeal be more pure, for though confined, yet your love should be more extensive and more perfect than that of other men.

The means you possess of exercising your charity to one another may be reduced to some particular practices, namely: to prayer, and to a mutual demonstration of meekness, tenderness, affection, and to those marks of deference allowed by the rules and constitutions of the monastery.

Although the duty of edifying our neighbor is general, for Jesus Christ addressed His words to all men when He pronounced a woe to those who give scandal (Matt 18:6). This duty, nevertheless, binds religious persons in a more particular manner; and they, more strictly than any other, are obliged to become models of edification and good example.

First, their charity being wholly concentrated within the limited sphere of their state, and not being able to extend itself to that multiplicity of action, to which pious persons in the world may apply themselves, it ought to be more ardent and pure within their enclosure, with so much the more force, as it is not allowed to burn without. But, as the occasions so common in society, which furnish such frequent exercise for the charity of the faithful who live in the world, never present themselves in the cloister, because this state forms an asylum, in which its members live secured from such accidents as require those succours; and, as all wants are anticipated by the good order of the house, it necessarily follows that the members of the cloister ought to reduce all their affections for one another to a reciprocal desire of the real goods and solid advantages, which they shall effectually perform by laboring constantly and assiduously for the salvation of each other.

And because they are bound to keep a strict silence, and are thus unable to advise or exhort, all communication of that kind being prohibited to them, it follows that they are bound to do that by action, which they cannot effect by word. Their conduct therefore ought to be so regular, so exact, and holy, that their brethren may find in it, not only sufficient matter of instruction, but moreover, sufficient light to direct, and stimulus to animate

---

[242] S. Basilius. *Constitutione Monasticae*, Caput XXI, PG 31:1394.

them in the exercise of their duties. Each individual ought to feel supported and consoled by the sole view of contributing to the good of the whole body, so, that they who are already advanced in the way of perfection, and even such as only begin to walk in it, may be animated with new vigor on beholding those who are going before them. And those who have unhappily strayed from it, may be excited to re-enter the path with more zeal and fervor.

Secondly, true religious ought to be united by such close and firm bonds, that it might seem, as if in them alone, these words of Jesus Christ are most exactly verified: "The charity which thou hast given me, 1 have given to them, that they may be one as we are one" (John 17:22).

They have only one mind, says Saint Basil, and one heart. Let us add, the same affection, the same affair, which is that of fighting without intermission against the enemies of God's name and glory. They are therefore engaged in the same labors, exposed to the same dangers. Each individual, while he continually beholds his brother's conduct, is himself considered by him, of whose actions he is a constant witness. Too, as the weakness and timidity of one member may become the cause of an universal enervation and loss, so, on the contrary, many may find strength and courage in the constancy and fidelity of one individual, as their defense ought to be mutual and continual. Be therefore united in charity, assist one another mutually; let the strong support the weak; let those who stand firm stretch out their hands to assist those who are wavering; that thus all uniting in the same effort, all may gain the same victory, acquire the same merit, win the same prize; and thus terminate their combats with equal success. Yes, be persuaded therefore that he who by his example, does not encourage his brethren in this warfare, betrays the cause of his master, separates himself from their society, and disclaims having any participation in their future rewards.

Q. 2.—Are we therefore to conclude that, to fail in giving good example to our brethren is a great crime?

A.—As the giving good example is one of the most effectual means by which religious persons can assist each other and mutually contribute to the advancement of the great work of their salvation, it follows that he who refuses to assist his brethren in a manner so necessary and profitable fails in an essential point of his duty. He clearly evinces that he has no due charity for them, that their salvation is to him a matter of indifference, and that he makes no account of this great truth which the Holy Spirit teaches by the mouth of the wise man, that God has given to each individual the care of his neighbor (Ecclesiastic. 17:12). Such a person ought to reflect that Jesus Christ will demand of him an account of the souls of his brethren, and that he shall be answerable for all the faults they shall have committed, since they might have avoided them if he had the charity to enlighten, strengthen, and guide them by his good example.

Consider, my brethren, that religious persons are vessels of election, that God has placed them in His house in order that by their sanctity they may become its ornament, its honor and principal beauty; that they are formed by His hand for the edification of His Church, so that—notwithstanding the reigning corruption of the age—the purity of their manners and the innocence of their lives may announce to the world the sublimity and eternity of His divine truths. Hence a religious can find no medium between good and evil, nor can he ever stand balanced between merit and demerit.

He no sooner ceases to build than he begins to pull down, because he begins to stray from the will of God. And being no longer what our Lord requires he should be, his life soon exhibits a chain of actions in which nothing can be found worthy of the excellency of his state. Hence, those who are witnesses of his conduct are of course scandalized. They behold him like a tree without fruit, a fire without heat, a lamp without light, and it cannot be doubted but that he becomes an object of this terrible menace, fulminated by Jesus Christ against those who give bad example: "If anyone scandalize any of these little ones, who believe in me, it were better for him to have a millstone tied to his neck, and be cast into the depth of the sea" (Matt 18:6).

There is nothing more certain than that the reason why the lives of some religious are not exemplary is because they are not studious to acquire the virtues and other qualities which make their state respectable and recommendable, so the opposite vices reign in their conduct. For if they give no example of penance, mortification, or modesty, it is because they are neither penitent, mortified nor modest. If they give no edification by silence or manual labor, it is because they are neither silent, nor regular nor fervent. In fine, if their actions are dead, if they exhibit nothing that can inspire the spectators with the love of virtue, their irregularities, their defects and imperfections are, undoubtedly, the source from whence those evils spring. And it may be said that since a man of such a character is not a subject of edification for his brethren, he is on that very account a rock of scandal.

Also, it frequently happens that his conduct is so much the more dangerous as it is not deformed with any of those more criminal excesses, whose frightful aspect chill the affections; consequently such a

person more easily allures his brethren to imitation. It is a poison whose operation is slow, but whose effect, though lingering and inert, is still certain, and never fails in due time to give a deadly blow. [243]

Such is the evil into which he falls who lives in a disorderly manner, and neglects to give good example. There are alas! too many who confide in the innocence of their lives, while they are guilty before God of the ruin of their brethren, and of a great number of other evils of which they have no idea.

Q. 3.—*Are we also obliged to pray for our brethren?*

A.—As you must conclude from what has been already said, the precept of Jesus Christ imposes a strict obligation on you to love your brethren as you love yourselves, and the love you have for yourselves is the measure and rule of that by which you ought to love them. So, in like manner, you may with equal facility deduce the duty of praying for one another from the necessity, power and efficacy of prayer, and from the great influence and connection it has with the great work of our eternal salvation. Taught by experience and the doctrine of the saints we learn that prayer is the channel through which all the blessings of heaven are communicated to our souls. By it we obtain a constant fidelity to our duties, and final perseverance.

Consequently, as it is a powerful means to obtain all good for ourselves, it cannot be less productive when employed in favor of our brethren. It is therefore a duty to pray for them, and unless we comply with it, we cannot pretend to love our brethren in the manner our Lord commands us to love them. Without it our charity for them would be different from the love we feel towards ourselves, and of course not fraternal.

The wants, therefore, of your brethren must become your own. You must be affected with their various indispositions and misfortunes in the same manner as if they were your own. You must sigh over their miseries before God; and offer Him a tribute of thanks for the good things they receive from His munificence; and make the incense of your prayers ascend with mutual concord, each individual considering the whole as a body of which he is a member.

Do not fear that in praying for your brethren your time is lost for yourselves by obtaining favors for them. On the contrary, you ought to be convinced that your affairs never succeed better with your heavenly Father than when you are mediating those of your brethren. And as Saint Gregory says, he who prays for others with assiduous solicitude, performs the greatest and most useful act of charity to himself; for the

---

[243] Augustinus, Sermo XLVI, De Pastoribus in Ezechiel, PL 38:274 (1841).

more his piety intercedes for his neighbor, so much the more worthy does he become, and in proportion, deserves that the Almighty should quickly hear his petitions when he implores the divine assistance in his own exigencies.[244]

Remember, my brethren, what Saint Cyprian teaches us on this subject. The God of Peace, and the Doctor of Concord, says that great saint, who taught us the nature of unity, was pleased to ordain that one should pray for the rest, as He Himself bore all men in Himself.[245] The three children, says he, observed the same rule of praying together in the fiery furnace, being united in the same prayer and with the same spirit. This is what the holy scripture teaches us, and in pointing out the manner in which they prayed it exhibits an example for our imitation: then, these three, says the inspired writer, blessed God, and sang His praises with one mouth (Dan 3:51). They magnified the Lord with mutual hearts and tongues, though Jesus Christ had not yet taught them how to pray; therefore, their prayer was most earnest and effectual, and deserved to be heard because it was charitable, simple and spiritual. In the same manner the apostles and disciples of our Lord, after His ascension, prayed unanimously (Acts 1:14); for we read, that they persevered with Mary the Mother of Jesus, with His brethren and the devout women in pious and fervent prayer. "The Lord, who makes those of one mind, dwell in the same house" (Ps 67:7), will never admit into His eternal dwellings any, but such as have been united here in the same prayer[246]

Now, if that great saint spoke in this manner to all Christians, what would he not have said to monks, whom the Lord has assembled in the same house, for no other purpose, than to reproduce that holy and perfect union, which flourished with such beauty amongst the primitive Christians? You are united, my brethren, in your exercises, in your rules, in your occupations; days and nights behold you in an amiable fraternity. No one amongst you claims or possesses anything as his own, everything is common, but should we not infer from these practices that we ought to be united in our hearts, wills, and minds? Nevertheless be assured that this union will never exist, or at least can never be perfect, unless it is found in your prayers; and that

---

[244] S. Gregorius Magnus, *Moralium Libri, sive Expositio in B. Job,* PL 76:761 / Saint Gregory the Great. Morals on the Book of Job , Vol. 3. (Oxford; Parker, 1850), 675-676.

[245] S.Cyprianus, *De oratione Dominica,* PL 4:524(1844) / St. Cyprian, On the Lord's Prayer. In *Tertullian, Cyprian, and Origen.* J. Behr, ed., A. Stewart-Sykes, trans (Crestwood, NY: St Vladimir's Seminary Press, 2004), 69.

[246] Cyprianus, *De oratione,* PL 4:524(1844) / Cyprian, *Prayer,* 70.

you are solicitous to recommend your brethren to our Lord, as you are to implore His mercy for yourselves.

Hence, do not imagine, that praying for your brethren, is a simple counsel, or a commandment of little or no importance; but be convinced that you are the persons to whom the beloved disciple of Christ addresses the following words: "For he who does not love his brethren whom he sees, how can he love God whom he sees not (1 John 4:20)?"

Now it is certain that you do not love them if you refuse them the assistance of your prayers, which is one of the most essential proofs you can give them of your love.

Q. 4.—In what manner are we to fulfill the other duties of charity which we owe to our brethren ?

To prayer and good example you must add the exterior offices of charity, because these latter are the bonds which keep all hearts and wills united. By them that union of charity which should ever exist among you is preserved. They are so many testimonies and proofs of the love you have for one another.[247] Religious persons enlighten one another by good example; they strengthen and consolidate their society by prayer and exterior offices of charity. Being thus united, they are, as it were, blended into one body, without which they are nothing better than a collection of different members and parts, among whom there is neither relation, nor union.

Every individual in a monastery ought to be solicitous to demonstrate the existence of this pure charity in his heart by all possible means, and never lose any occasion by which he might convince his brethren that he loves them.[248] They who are more immediately commissioned to serve the community, ought to perform their duties with such diligence and exactitude, that the goodness and affection of their hearts may appear in their actions.

If they are appointed to attend on the sick, they ought to consider Jesus Christ in their persons, and that He continues to suffer in them what He cannot now suffer in Himself; and that by the pains, anguishes, and other circumstances of His infirm members, He is completing what might appear to be still wanting to His own sufferings.[249] Hence, animated with these sentiments, they should serve them with great fervor, support their weakness, and assist and comfort them in their infirmities, whether of

---

[247] "Glutinum animarum societas fidelium." S. August.

[248] *RB* 72.8

[249] *RB* 36.

body or mind, as they desire that Jesus Christ would assist, support and comfort themselves.

But here let the sick also remember, that our Lord is to be considered no less in those who serve them, than in the sick themselves. For if He says of these, "I have been sick and you visited me" (Matt 25:36), He says also of those, "He who abides in charity, remains in God, and God in him" (I John 4:16); thus you should all serve one another with an equal attention and respect; if they who attend, esteem themselves happy to serve their brethren who want assistance, these latter ought to believe themselves unworthy to be served by them.

As to those who have no particular employment, and of course, no immediate occasions of exhibiting this charity of which we speak, they ought to live in such a perfectly uniform peace that this amiable virtue may never suffer the least injury. Let every individual consider his brother as his superior, always acquiesce to his sentiments, and renounce his own will, in order to comply with that of his brother, and let all mutually anticipate each other with marks of esteem and respect.[250] Let the one undertake the most painful and difficult part of the work, so that he may thereby make it more light and easy for his brother; let him be content to appear guilty, that the other may be esteemed innocent. In fine, let him partake as, Saint Basil writes, in the prosperity and adversity of his brother; and let the different circumstances in which he beholds him excite in his heart sentiments of pleasure or of pain.[251]

Q. 5. —Will you allow no restriction to these principles, and are the ancient religious obliged to obey the younger?

A.—Undoubtedly, my brethren, I do not. I maintain that this obligation is universal, for charity is the foundation and cement of religious communities. By it they are formed, and by it alone they are preserved. By charity the members of a house live according to God, in peace and concord, and by it they are qualified to carry the yoke of the Lord [252]with the same mind, with the same heart, and with the same will—being convinced that the submission and respect with which they ought to be actuated for each other are the basis on which this charity stands. Thus, you shall be more effectually qualified to anticipate or remove everything that might trouble its order or enervate its strength. This conviction will, moreover, serve as a

---

[250] *RB* 72.

[251] *Brevius*, Interrogatio CLXXV, PG 31:1198 (1857) / Anna M. Silvas, *The Asketikon of St. Basil the Great,* (Oxford: Oxford University Press, 2005), 368-369.

[252] "Humero uno." Soph. 3:9.

powerful incentive to make a profitable use of every occasion in which you may give evident proofs of your charity, and exert, in favor of one another, a prompt and exact obedience.

This is a truth of which all those who are called by God to the monastic state ought to be seriously convinced, but more especially such as live under the same discipline, and are consecrated to God by the same vows. Obliged to tend to the highest perfection, they ought to obey one another so fully, so extensively, and so cordially, that at the least signal by which they discover each other's desire, they should fly to the execution with the same velocity, and perform the thing required with the same punctuality, as if they had received an order from their first superior. Moreover, this should be observed with so much exactitude that even the more ancient ought to submit to the younger brethren without any exception which they might deduce from their age, or their length of time in religion.

Q. 6.—Is this doctrine entirely conformable to Saint Benedict's rule?

A.—This objection, I allow, my brethren, may find admittance into the minds of persons who only consider our state in a superficial manner, without entering into, or examining its nature and substance. For we allow that it may derive some apparent solidity from several passages of our rule, when it is commanded that the more ancient religious shall love the younger; and that these latter shall honor and obey their ancients with every mark of charity and submission. "Let the younger brethren honor the more ancient, and let the more ancient love the younger; let all, both old and young, love one another; let the young obey the ancient with all charity and care."[253] But, it is necessary that you should know how unfounded such an objection is, and with what facility it may be removed.

In the first place, if we undertook to combat these two articles, we would begin by saying that the more ancient ought to love the younger with a pure and sincere charity, yet does it therefore follow, that they ought not to condescend to the lawful requests of the younger brethren, with a religious promptitude and respect; and, more especially, when they feel prompted to do so by their humility and example?

No: neither is there reason to believe that Saint Benedict did intend to inculcate anything of this nature by the passages we have cited, since he enjoins that the brethren shall be careful to anticipate one another with mutual demonstrations of honor; that they shall support, with patience, their imperfections, whether of body or mind; that they shall obey one

---

[253] *RB* 63:10 and 71:4.

another with care and emulation, and no one among them shall prefer his own pleasure and will, but on the contrary, always sacrifice whatever is agreeable to himself, in order to do that which is pleasing to his brethren[254].

If it should be insisted on that the more ancient ought not to obey the younger, because it is said that the younger are bound to honor them, it can be replied, that those who make this objection do not seem to reflect that, although men are bound to give divine homage, respect and adoration to the Son of God, yet He came not to be served, but to serve, according to His own divine expression.

Secondly, Saint Benedict did not suppose that all perfection is to be found in the letter of his rule, as he himself declares in the last chapter—

> We have written this rule, that by observing it in our monasteries, we may appear to have, in some degree, either honesty of manners, or that we are at least resolved on a virtuous way of life, but for those who aspire to a higher perfection, they have the precepts of the holy fathers, the observance of which leads a man to the highest degree of perfection, for what page or chapter of the Old or New Testament is not the truest guide of a human life? [255]

It is delightful to behold such order in a religious community, where everything depends on the superior, and moves according to the motion of his will, where the ancients love the younger religious, and where these latter obey the ancients with fervor and respect; but it is a more eminent perfection when the ancients serve the younger with deference, and teach them by their humility, as nothing is so estimable among persons consecrated to God by religious vows, as docility and obedience. Hence, if we have changed anything in the rule, it is certainly a mutation that neither enervates or weakens it, but rather serves to enfold and perfect it, according to the spirit of its holy author (Rom 3:31). Thirdly, the same saint, in the part of his rule to which I have just called your attention, proposes to his disciples the practice of the instructions contained in the holy scriptures.

Now there is nothing more strongly inculcated by the word of God than that mutual submission which Christians owe to one another. Saint Paul, writing to the Philippians, exhorts them to consider each one of

---

[254] *RB* 72.7.

[255] *RB.*73:1-3.

their brethren as a superior, that is, to obey one another with the same humility, charity and sincerity, as inferiors obey their superiors (Phil 2: 3). But nothing can be more clear and decisive than the words of Jesus Christ Himself, expressed in His gospel, where He tells us that he who desires to be greatest must become the least and the servant of all, and that he who would be the first, must place himself in the lowest place (Matt 20:26).

And in order that He might evince the truth of His words by His example, He adds, that He came not to be served, but to serve (Matt 20: 28).

Fourthly, we find that Saint Benedict advises, and even invites those who desire to embrace a life more perfect than that which he established by his rule, to follow the institutions of the holy fathers who preceded him, and, in particular those of Saint Basil. Give ear to his words, which we have already cited,[256] "Whoever aspires to perfection, ought to follow the documents of the holy fathers, particularly the rule of Saint Basil," etc. Now Saint Basil informs us that the brethren in his time observed an equal and mutual charity, deference and submission, and that no one sought any exception in consequence of age, or of any other prerogative. They are, says that holy doctor,[257] equally the servants and masters of one another, and they, nevertheless, enjoy an invincible liberty. They mutually give demonstrations of a perfect submission, which is neither the effect of necessity, misfortune, nor violence— qualities that never fail to produce pain and affliction— but proceeds from a free choice, and is to them an inexhaustible source of joy, because divine charity animates them to sacrifice their liberty by making themselves the servants of one another, and as they perform it from the choice of their free will, they may be said to enjoy a perfect liberty.

He says in another place that the distinction of those who command ought not to be a motive to excuse anyone who is able to obey, since Moses did not resist the order of Jethro, his father-in-law (Exod. 18:24).[258]

The same saint, in the 64th question, having interrogated himself— How are we to obey one another?—answers: in the same manner as a servant is bound to obey his master, according to our Lord's expression,

---

[256] RB 73:2-6.

[257] S. Basilius, *Constitutiones*, PG 31:1382, 1383, 1386 (1857).

[258] *Brevius*, Interrogatio CXIV, PG 31:1159-1160 (1857); cf. St. Basil, Question 13, *The Rule of St. Basil in Latin and English*, trans. Anna M. Silvas (Collegeville: Liturgical, 2013), 115.

in which He says, "Let him who desires to be first among you become the servant of all" (Matt 20:26). This sentiment he corroborates by other passages of the gospel, and of Saint Paul's epistles (Gal 5:13),to which we have alluded in the foregoing pages.

Let us moreover add, my brethren, though it were true that Saint Benedict had really established this independence, such as it is pretended to be, in favor of the ancient religious, the reasons which at present require a suppression of that article are so strong that it would be improper to blame those who do not observe it; and it is reasonable to believe, that if Saint Benedict lived in our times, he would annul it himself.

We learn from Saint Bernard that if the constitutions which have been formed for the purpose of maintaining charity and good order in religious communities should produce a contrary effect in the course of time, they are then to be considered as having lost their strength and authority, and ought no longer to be observed.[259]

Now, of all the abuses which found entrance into the cloister, there is no one greater than that which is found to spring from the exemptions and privileges claimed by the ancient members. The number of years they have spent since their profession is become a title to withdraw themselves from the laws of subordination and dependence to which their brethren are subject. They persuade themselves that they have sufficient authority and capacity to examine, judge, and censure all things. And it may be said, that there are as many superiors in monasteries as there are ancients—by which disorder is introduced, piety is banished from them, their discipline is ruined, and the source of irregularity and scandal set wide open.

Hence, is there anything more reasonable—in order to prevent so great an evil from gaining any entrance into the cloister—than to endeavor to remove from the ancients, as much as possible, every thought, every idea, and, if possible, even all remembrance of their seniority? They should live with their brethren in an entire and perfect equality, being convinced that every distinction is dangerous, that exemptions are always to be feared, that the heart of man is neither sufficiently simple, nor sufficiently upright, to make a good use of them; that a man may go astray on every road; that in the way of humility alone security is to be found; and that to submit without distinction to the great and to the little, to the young and to the old, is the peculiar virtue of Jesus Christ and of His saints; and ought, consequently, to be that of monks.

But, after all, why do the ancients claim such an exemption from this

---

[259] *De praecepto,* PL 182:863, 864 (1854). / Treatises I, 108.

obedience? If it be alleged that it derogates from their age and dignity, it is proper to reflect, that as their state is nothing else but a public profession of humility, so nothing can be more in harmony with the profession than that which affords them the means of frequently humbling and abasing themselves; and that there is no time nor age which can exempt them from the obligation of demonstrating, by their actions and conduct, what they really are by their state and profession.

If it be objected that this submission is contrary to the order of nature, I answer that every person is well informed how, on many occasions, the law of grace suspends or annuls the law of nature; that grace wrests children from the embraces of their parents, separates husbands from their wives, that it subjects aged persons to the authority of young superiors, places fathers under the government of their children—in a word, how can anyone maintain such exemptions? where can they find any reasons to defend them? since it is written of the Son of God: He was subject to them (Luke 2:51).

Neither can it be proved that this deference can inflate the minds of the younger brethren, or become the cause of making them arrogant, or less submissive to the ancients. Such an idea is without any foundation, since, on the contrary, it is more reasonable to conclude that the good example of the former will excite them to become perfectly fervent and exact in the duties of obedience and submission. In proportion as they behold their fathers humble, so will they consider them worthy of veneration and respect. And in the same measure as they shall behold them adorned with these beautiful virtues, so will they study to give them proofs of the same, anticipating them with all attention, and executing their orders with promptitude so soon as they discover, by the least sign, the will of their respectable seniors. In effect, moreover, nothing is better qualified to recommend the virtue of obedience— to those who are young in its practice—than to behold the ancients renouncing every exemption to which they might have any claim by reason of their age and professional rank, in order to enjoy the advantages, merit and blessings, which result from the practice of that virtue.

All that has been said proves in an incontestable manner,

First, that the submission and obedience of the ancient to the younger religious contains nothing contrary to the rule of Saint Benedict.

Secondly, that it is according to his spirit, that he approves it, that he counsels it.

Thirdly, that it is authorized by the example of Jesus Christ, and by the precept of the apostle.

Fourthly, that this mode of conduct, so far from being unjust in any manner, is, on the contrary, the most perfect, the most eminent, and the most holy.

Fifthly, that it obviates many evils, and produces many advantages.

Sixthly, that by establishing a perfect obedience in the cloister, it cuts off all matter of disputes, and, at the same time, maintains therein a constant peace. In brief, that there can be found no just nor lawful reasons either to oppose or condemn it.

Remark, my brethren, that in all this discourse we understand the private religious only, not those who fill any office, nor possess any authority in the house, for everyone allows that their commands are to be obeyed at all times, and in every place, with attention and exactitude.

Q. 7.—By what means can we fulfill these duties?

A.—There are two principal ones, the first is to observe this precept of Saint Benedict. [260]To declare not only in words that we are inferior to, and more miserable than all others, but also to be interiorly convinced that such is really the case. The religious who is convinced of his own nothingness, who considers himself as a useless member, who, in the sincerity of his heart, applies to himself those words of the prophet, "I am a worm and no man; the contempt of men, and the outcast of the people" (Ps 21:7), will believe himself much inferior to his brethren in all things. He will account himself unworthy of their society, and will find no difficulty in fulfilling all the duties of charity, respect, submission and deference, in the manner to which he is obliged by his profession.

The second is, to observe that rigorous silence with your brethren, which Saint Benedict's rule prescribes.[261]

The reason why mutual civility and respect sometimes decay amongst religious men is because they give offence to each other in conversation. Diversity of sentiments disunite them. Human friendships and familiarities, which are the ruin of -true charity, are the cause of mutual disesteem, for by these frequent communications they discover the defects of one another, which produce a dangerous contempt and disrespect.

Silence prevents all these inconveniences. By it you shall be enabled to avoid every occasion in which charity might be wounded. The privation of useless conversation, or the limited communication you are allowed to have with one another, destroys or removes the imperfections of each

---

[260] *RB* 7 51

[261] *RB* 6.3.

individual, and thus you will always seem to be quite new men, and appearing with such ornaments as make you more commendable, you will constantly esteem your brethren as men perfect in every religious virtue.

But it is of the greatest importance, my brethren, in the practice of all these things, to have nothing but the glory, honor, and love of God in view, to have no desire but that of pleasing Him, and of doing His holy will. And, as Saint Gregory says, your love for your brethren must emanate to you from the heart of God, as from its source.[262]

---

[262] S. Gregorius Magnus, *Moralium Libri, sive Expositio in Librum B. Job.* In Opera Omnia, Vol 1. 1902, PL 75:780 (1849) / Saint Gregory the Great. *Morals on the Book of Job.* Vol.1 (Oxford: Parker, 1844), 383.

11 | ON PRAYER—CONTENTS:

11

ON PRAYER

QUESTION 1.—In what manner ought we to pray?

ANSWER.—Prayer, according to the opinion of the holy fathers, is the strength and fortress of religious souls. By it they are qualified to resist and surmount the efforts of their enemies. By prayer they keep close to God, solicit His mercy, and obtain the graces and helps without which they cannot ascend to the summit of perfection to which they are bound to aspire with continual ardor. Hence, the religious who neglects prayer withdraws himself from the care of his salvation. He rejects the most powerful means which were put into his hands by his heavenly King for his own defense and preservation. He is a soldier who throws down his arms in the middle of the combat, of whom nothing may be expected, but inevitable destruction.

The first precept given by Saint Anthony to his disciples was to pray without intermission. [263]Saint Benedict enjoins assiduous prayer;[264] and that his disciples should never undertake anything without previously asking its accomplishment of God by fervent prayer.

Saint John Climacus says that prayer is the source of all virtues, the canal through which all the graces and gifts that we receive from the divine goodness flow, an imperceptible advancement in the way of virtue, the food of the soul, the light that illuminates the mind, the conqueror of despair, the riches of solitaries, the treasure of anchorites.[265]

Saint Ephrem teaches, that a solitary ought to pray day and night

---

[263] S. Antonius Magnus Abbas, Regulae ac Praecepta S.P.N. Antonii ac Filios Suos Monachos. In S.S. Patrum Aegyptiorum, Opera Omnia, PG 40:1067 (1863)

[264] RB 4:56.

[265] Scala, PG 88:1130 (1864). / Ladder, 233.1.

without intermission; that every virtue is formed and preserved by prayer; that it is the guardian of temperance, and conqueror of anger; that it pulls down the haughty swelling of pride, represses the motions of envy, effaces the remembrance of injuries, and makes men become like angels.[266] It is related that Saint Ephrem said that a true solitary either prayed or sang psalms continually.[267]

Cassian requires that the soul of a religious should be constantly united to God and be never separated from Him; that he ought to consider as a loss and as hurtful everything that might distract him for a single moment.[268] He says that the end of a solitary, and his greatest perfection, consists in never interrupting his prayer, in possessing on earth as much as human weakness will allow, an undisturbed tranquility of soul, and an inviolable purity of heart.[269]

If these and such like instructions were properly attended to, the cloister would be at present—as well as formerly—the edification of the Church. Monasteries would preserve their primitive sanctity and the greater part of monks would not be immersed in that frightful dissipation by which they have justly drawn down on themselves the anger of God and the contempt of men.

Remember, therefore, my brethren, to observe this precept of the Holy Spirit: that we must always pray and not faint (Luke 18:1). Be particularly careful to purify yourselves by prayer. Let this exercise be one of your principal occupations and let nothing deter you from attending to an obligation so essential, and so forcibly commanded by your rules.

But be no less careful not to make your prayers consist of a barren and speculatory mode of prayer, destitute of the interior spirit from which alone its strength is derived, and without which they are neither agreeable nor acceptable before God, to whom they are offered. Do not imagine that prayer is a simple production of the mind, an arrangement of spiritual thoughts, or a discourse on some subject of piety. Do not imitate those who imagine that they have prayed well, when, being prostrate at the foot of the altar, they have reasoned on some truths of religion, and have

---

[266] S. Ephraem Syrus, De Oratione. In Opera Omnia (Antwerp, Keebergium, 1619), 29.

[267] Vita Sancti Ephraem, Syri, Diaconi Addis. In Vitae Patrum sive Historiae Eremiticae Libri Decem, PL 73:321-324.

[268] Collationes, PL 49:497 (1846) / Conferences 1.1.13 (NPNF2 /11:300).

[269] Collationes, PL 49:771 (1846) / Conferences 1.9. 2 (NPNF2/11:387).

carefully observed the rules laid down by those authors who have written on this subject.

Rather let your prayer be the cry of your hearts. Let it proceed from the inward affections and fervor of your souls, or better, let the divine spirit of love infuse it therein, by His heavenly operations. Let Him open your interior mouths, give motion to your tongues, and put the words on your lips, since His expressions only are worthy to be heard by the majesty of God. Endeavor, as much as possible, that your prayers be inflamed with the sacred fire of which the prophet speaks, when he says: "My heart became warm within me, and in my meditation a fire shall break out" (Ps 38:4).

Banish from your souls all tepidity, distraction, languor, and sloth. Never present yourselves before the Lord but in all the strength and vigor of your souls, so that your prayers may not only be such as are agreeable to the greatness of Him to whom you offer them, but also conformable to the excellency of your state. Be convinced, too, that the ordinary manner of praying is not supportable in those who have promised Almighty God to lead a life of special purity and sanctity.

But if you are obliged to offer up to God the sacrifice of frequent and fervent prayer, to prepare yourselves in a proper manner for an action so holy there is another command no less positive, for the same divine spirit who enjoins the duty of assiduous prayer,[270] commands you at the same time, to bring to it the necessary preparations.[271] The saints have not been indifferent on this point, but have left us many great and useful instructions on the subject, because they knew how much the divine majesty is offended by the indiscreet and presumptuous prayers of men.

Saint Basil teaches that we ought to begin our prayers by renouncing ourselves, by forsaking all created things, husband, wife, children and all worldly affairs; that we must raise ourselves to the heavenly regions above, and soar high above all creatures visible and invisible. . . .That we ought to be so disposed as not to be condemned at the tribunal of our own conscience.[272]

Being about to appear in the presence of our King and our God, says Saint John Climacus, to converse with Him in prayer, let us always be solicitous to prepare for that important exercise in a proper manner:

---

[270] "Let nothing hinder thee from praying always." Ecclesiastic. 18:22.

[271] "Before prayer prepare thy soul: and be not like a man that tempteth God." Ecclesiastic. 18:23.

[272] *Constitutiones*, PG 31:1327 (1857).

Lest beholding us as yet afar off, not clothed with the garments which are necessary to appear in His presence, He should command the ministers of His justice to bind us hands and feet, to rend in pieces our petitions, and to cast us forth from His presence filled with confusion, in the same manner as the officers of earthly monarchs are accustomed to do in their courts of justice. . .[273] Prepare yourselves—by the continual supplications and desires of your hearts—for this interior and exterior conversation with God, in which you offer Him your petitions and solicitations; and your endeavors will be rewarded with a great advancement in the way of virtue in a little time.[274]

Saint Augustine says that he who applies himself to prayer without taking any care to correct his vices and defects, does not pray in effect.[275]

Saint Gregory assures us that he who takes no care to regulate his life, but nourishes his evil habits, provokes the Lord to anger rather than to mercy by his prayers—and that he alone whose conscience is undefiled can pray with confidence (1 John 3:21).[276]

According to Saint Isidore, there are two things which impede the good effect of prayer; the first is, when he who prays continues in the way of sin, and the second, when he refuses to forgive those who offend him.[277]

Cassian tells us that a religious who desires to pray with all the purity and fervor to which his state obliges him, ought in the first place to cut off all carnal solicitude, separate himself from all cares; and so far from seeking information concerning anything, he ought to forget all the past; that he must avoid all detraction and even much speaking; that he must renounce all railing and dissipation, tear out of his heart the smallest roots of anger and sadness; mortify all the concupiscence of the flesh, destroy the principle of covetousness; and having burst all the links of carnal attachments, he may then begin to purify the place where the edifice is to stand, and lay the foundation of a profound humility. On this foundation— as on a firm basis—all the other virtues are to be erected; but the work must be carried on with care and attention, that he who labors therein

---

[273] *Scala*, PG 88:1130 (1864) / *Ladder*, 234.3.

[274] *Scala*, PG 88:1135 (1864) / *Ladder*, 237.

[275] *In Psalmum XLIX Enarratio.* PL 37:564-585; Augustine. *Expositions on the Book of Psalms.* (NPNF1/ 8:177).

[276] S. Gregorius Magnus, *Moralium.* PL 76:42,43 (1849).

[277] S. Isidore of Seville, DE SUMMO BONO, lib III, Jean Aleaume, ed. (Paris: Roigny, 1538), 67.

may gradually ascend to the contemplation of God, and the meditation of heavenly things. . . .[278]

Let us be attentive, says the holy abbot Isaac, to purify our hearts before the time of prayer, that nothing may be found in them that might impede us in that holy exercise.

From all this you may easily gather, that there are two principal preparations, the one remote and general, the other immediate and particular. The first is effected by the amendment of our morals, the regularity of our actions, the sanctity of our lives, the purity of intentions by which we seek only the love, honor and glory of God in all we do, and carefully avoid everything that might displease or offend His Divine Majesty.

The second consists in separating ourselves from the consideration of all created objects during the time of prayer, expelling from the senses, from the imagination, from the memory, the understanding, and will, and from all the affections of the heart everything that is not God. Thus considering the actions which at other times are commanded, as being improper at the time of prayer, we may be properly qualified to attend to God, and that He alone may be purely the object of our employment. By this twofold preparation, a religious may acquire the two conditions of which Cassian speaks, and which are so essential to prayer, that they communicate to it all its vigor, and make it ascend as a sweet scented sacrifice before the throne of God.[279]

Q. 2.— What do you understand by those two conditions?

A. I understand purity of heart and fervor—persuaded that these two conditions are so necessary to prayer, that the want of them cannot be supplied by anything else, and that the saints preferred them to every other condition. They teach us that by these, as by so many wings, men may raise themselves even to the throne of God, find a favorable access to Him, and obtain of Him everything they ask, because the Lord can refuse nothing to those who present themselves before Him accompanied with these dispositions.

It was this consideration that made Saint Augustine say, "Prayer, when pure and holy, penetrates the heavens, and never returns without having obtained its requests."[280] And again, "So great is the efficacy of prayer when pure, that it surmounts every difficulty. Like a faithful messenger, it

---

[278] *Collationes*, PL 49:771 (1846) / *Conferences* 1.9. 2 (NPNF2/ 11:387).

[279] *Collationes*, PL 49:773 (1846) / Conferences 1.9. 3 (NPNF2/ 11:388).

[280] "Oratio si pura est, si casta fuerit, coelos penetrat, vacua non redebit." S. Aug. in Serm.

accomplishes everything commanded, and makes to itself passages where flesh can find no entrance."

We read that the ancient monks of Egypt said a great number of prayers, but which indeed were short, so that being less exposed to distractions, they might more easily preserve their purity and fervor.

Saint Benedict enjoins that prayer must be performed with purity and fervor. He requires that it should be short when done in common, lest the weakness and instability of the human mind should tarnish the beauty of an action so holy.[281]

Saint Ephrem gives the following rules for prayer:

> Be vigilant, that you may secure your mind from wandering. Let fear and trembling accompany you, when you are going to appear in the presence of the Majesty of God. Expel from your mind all earthly thoughts and cares. Be like a heavenly spirit in the time of prayer, and employ all possible means to make it ascend on high, irreprehensible, pure and holy.[282]

Prayer is a holy familiarity, a sacred union formed between God and His creature. In prayer He communicates Himself to those souls whom He loves. In prayer He speaks to them with the tenderness of a friend and the affection of a spouse. In those delightful moments He pours into their hearts His choicest gifts, convinces them that He can refuse them nothing, and that He takes a particular satisfaction in making them feel, by the ineffable effusions of His confidence and love, the effect and accomplishment of these words of the prophet: "My delight is to be with the children of men" (Prov 8:31).

But He requires that there should be no witnesses of this intimate commerce. He requires that all creatures should be dismissed, and that He be given possession of every power of the soul. He is pleased only when alone with those whom He favors with these tender demonstrations of His infinite goodness, and everything that He finds in them distinct from Himself is to Him an object of displeasure.

"Be ye alone," cries out Saint Bernard,[283] speaking to those who are the particular friends of God. "Do you not know that your spouse is quite

---

[281] RB 20;1-2.

[282] S. Ephraem Syrus, *De Agone, sive de luctamine spirituali.* In *Opera Omnia* (Antwerp, Keebergium, 1619), 372d.

[283] Sermo XL, *Sermones in Cantica,* PL 183:983d (1854). / "Remain alone, and amongst all preserve thyself for Him alone, Who has chosen thee from amongst all." *Canticles,* 466.

bashful, that He will never allow you to enjoy His presence until you are entirely alone, and separated from every other company." This purity is a duty, to which every Christian ought to attend, but it is so, in a particular manner for religious persons. Selected from the midst of the world, and led by the hand of God into solitude, they ought to live in such an exact disengagement, that their divine benefactor may effect without opposition the work He has begun in them, that by perfecting their purity, and filling their hearts, He may transform their souls into a real paradise.

Fervor, which is the second condition of prayer, is no less important and necessary than the first. It is inseparably united to purity, for prayer can never be pure without being fervent.

The reason why we pray without fervor is that our souls being weighed down by the thoughts, affections, and solicitudes of created things—the holy activity which should animate them being, of course, enervated—they find it impossible to elevate themselves to the consideration of heavenly things. Engaged in the base employments of the earth, they are unable to ascend to those sublime reflections which belong to their heavenly country. And when it happens that they make some efforts to disengage themselves, they exert themselves only with indifference, distraction, and tepidity.

If, then, my brethren, you really desire that your prayer should be fervent, labor in earnest to make your hearts pure. Let them be employed in no affairs, occupied with no cares but such as are pleasing to God. Let them give admittance to nothing but what may serve as a means to assist them in advancing in the way that leads to the enjoyment of that holy and tremendous Majesty, and pluck out of their inmost recesses every plant that has not been sown there by His adorable hand.

Thus it is that acceptable prayer will be formed in your breasts, and shall dart forth with unimpeded ardor and rapidity. Being thus purified and free, it shall ascend—repelling all opposition that might obstruct or weaken its flight—to attract the attention of the Most High. That cloud of which the prophet speaks (Lam 3:44), will not oppose its passage, nor prevent its access to the throne of Him to whom it is directed; and the angels, your guardians and protectors, will not fail to present it before the Lord as a sacrifice of praise, and an offering of benediction.

But above all, be convinced that languor disfigures the beauty of prayer, that it enervates its strength, destroys its charms and merit; and that he who prays without fervor, evidently demonstrates that the success of his petitions is to him a matter of indifference.

To these two conditions the holy fathers add a third, which is compunction of heart. And indeed this latter may be considered as a necessary effect and

consequence of the two former, for it is not possible that those who are united to God by pure and fervent prayer—that is, by a plenitude of gratitude and love—can be so, without being at the same time penetrated with a lively sorrow when they consider that this divine goodness, so worthy to be loved, is daily outraged by the malice of men; and more particularly, when they reflect that they themselves have the misfortune to be of the unhappy number of those who have offended Him.

It is, I say, impossible to contain the grief that a serious consideration of the innumerable multitude who combat against the amiable Creator who gave them existence must produce. No, torrents of tears must spring and flow from their eyes, as from so many fountains. Some of those unhappy mortals declare an open war against Him by unconcealed crimes and public excesses. Others, though they sin more privately, yet provoke Him with no less ingratitude and outrage. And it is certain, my brethren, that those souls who receive particular graces from our Lord and who are animated by His Holy Spirit, cannot behold—without sorrow and affliction—so many souls deprived of the merits of His death, that they live as if they knew Him not, and as if every idea of His sufferings were effaced from their memory.

Such ought to be the sentiments of the true disciples of Christ, and of all who are inflamed with a zeal for His glory; but it is peculiarly that of monks, for it forms their distinguishing mark, and special character. Their profession is a state of compunction, and continual mourning. Their life is a continual sacrifice of tears, which they offer up to God for the sins of the world as well as for their own.

In this they have been prefigured by those men who mourned over the abominations of the people, who were signed by the prophet with the letter of mercy by the command of God, who by that mark was pleased to distinguish them from others who were to be the victims of His avenging justice. Mark the letter Thau, says the spirit of God, on the foreheads of those men who grieve and afflict themselves, for the abominations which are committed in Jerusalem. Kill, without mercy, the old and young, virgins, women and children—but those on whom thou shalt see the letter Thau, do not kill, and begin from my sanctuary (Ezek 9:4-6).

This is the reason, my brethren, why the ancients so earnestly recommended to all monks to begin and continue their prayers with compunction of heart; that it should be their inseparable companion in all their actions, and in every circumstance of their lives; and that they should be particularly careful to purify their prayers with tears of compunction.

Saint Ephrem cries out, in the person of all monks: "Give me, O Lord! a fountain of tears; give me light and strength so that I may pour out unceasingly rivulets of tears, and that I may wash and purify my heart in pure and holy prayer."[284]

Saint Anthony exhorted his disciples to lament and grieve, day and night, for their past sins. "Let the oil with which you light your lamp," says he, "be the tears of your hearts. Retire into yourselves, that your prayers may be seasoned with your tears."[285]

Saint Macarius said that the glory of a solitary consists in watching and prayers, accompanied with tears.[286]

Saint Benedict requires that the prayers of his children should not consist in much speaking, but in purity of heart, and in tears of compunction.[287]

Saint John Climacus says that our grief and sadness are so many voices which cry without intermission in the ears of the Lord, that the tears which are produced by the fear of His justice, are so many potent mediators before Him. . . . When you are at prayer, tremble before the Lord, like a criminal before his judge. He cannot refuse to hear the petitions of a soul who appears before Him like an afflicted desolate widow, who by her assiduous and fervent prayers endeavors to importune His goodness, though He should be incapable of being importuned.[288]

Such are the three conditions which ought to accompany the prayers of a religious. These are the three dispositions which the Lord requires in him. It is in these as in a sacred brine of purity, fervor, and compunction that his prayer shall find beauty, dignity and efficacy. These are the three fruits which grow only in the desert. The world cannot produce them. These are the riches which monks gather in their solitude, and which are multiplied and conserved in silence and repose.

Do not imagine, my brethren, that when the Lord declared, by His prophet, that He would transform the barren land into pools of water, that He would make fountains spring up in the most desert plains, and that the verdure of the rush and reed should appear in the caves and dens of dragons (Isa 35:7), do not imagine, I say, that He would point out by these words the ordinary rules of His conduct in the government of souls. No,

---

[284] S. Ephraem, Syri, *De Compunctione.* In *Opera Omnia,* (Antwerp, Keerbergium, 1619), 118.

[285] S. Antonius Magnus Abbas, "Regulae ac Praecepta S. Antonii ac Filios Suos Monachos." In *S.S. Patrum Aegyptiorum,* PG 40:1069 (1858).

[286] "Epistola ad Monachos. "In *Macarii Aegyptii et Macarii Alexandrini Opera Quae Supersunt Omnia,* 1860. PG 34:443.

[287] RB 20:3

[288] *Scala,* PG 88:803 (1864). / *Ladder,* 112.11.

such was not His design. On the contrary, He signified thereby that He is superior to these rules, that He exempts himself from the observance of His own orders, and that He effects, extraordinarily—by the power of His grace—whatever change He pleases to produce in the hearts and wills of His creatures.

But when He tells us, that briars and thorns do not produce figs or grapes (Luke 6:44), He then points out His ordinary providence, and the usual mode He observes in the government of the world: namely, that purity is not found in corruption, that the love of Jesus cannot dwell in the heart in which the love of the world reigns triumphant; and that it is vain to seek the spirit of penance and compunction in the tumult and dissipation of temporal things. This is well signified by the wise answer made by the levites to the people of Babylon: How can we sing a canticle of the Lord in a strange land (Ps 136:4)? In a word, my brethren, there is no pure or real sacrifice offered to the God of Israel in the tabernacle of Moloch or Rempham.

Q. 3.—Are we therefore to conclude, that worldly people cannot pray with that purity which Almighty God requires?

A.—There are many in the world who make long prayers, but very few who really pray. Those persons who are engaged in the world, by a true vocation, or who, having chosen that way by their own free will and inclination, but have since that time repaired the errors of their first steps, are now conformed, and subject to the divine will; who walk in the presence of God, and nourishing His fear and love in their souls, live in the world as if they were not of the world, exempt from the influence of its maxims, undefiled with its spirit and works, such persons as these are undoubtedly qualified to present their prayers to God with the same characters of purity and sanctity as should distinguish their lives.

But as to those, who do not live in this disengagement, who, instead of observing the precept of the apostle, Be not conformed to this world (Rom 12:2), make the affairs, commerce, or pleasures of the world their principal occupation, they are to be ranked with those, who, indeed, may recite long prayers, but have little or nothing of the qualities necessary for praying well. For by their actions they remove themselves from the heavenly goods, which, in their prayers, they seem to desire, as Saint Gregory speaks. [289]They sometimes shed tears in the time of prayer, but, when they retire from that holy exercise if attacked by a temptation of pride, they immediately admit that enemy into their souls, and follow the motions he imparts. If avarice

---

[289] S. Gregorius Magnus, *Moralium*, PL 76:700(1849).

solicits their attention, they are inflamed with the desire to satisfy it. [290]If moved by impurity, they conceive unlawful desires. If they meet anything that irritates them, the fire of anger begins to rage, and quickly consumes all their meekness. [291]

In a word, says that great saint, they weep at the moment they are praying, but if they meet anything that excites their passions, you may behold them acting as if they had lost all remembrance of their tears.[292] In brief, my brethren, when he that prays does not become better, if he can discover nothing in his conduct that may furnish him with motives to prove the sincerity of his prayers, he ought to be convinced that his supplications are nothing better than mere illusions and the effects of a duped imagination. To what purpose, says the Holy Spirit by the mouth of the wise man, are the fasts of a man who continues to offend God? What advantage can he derive from his humiliations, and who will hear his prayer (Isa 35:7)?

Q. 4.—Recapitulate in a few words, what you have just taught us, concerning prayer: how may we easily reduce it to practice ?

A.—Before all things, my brethren, let your conduct be regulated according to the designs of God, and according to that exact piety to which you are obliged by your holy state, as we have already said. When you are about to present yourselves before God in prayer, expel everything from His temple that ought not to be there, and which have no connection with an action so sublime, imitating therein the example of our Lord, who would not allow anything profane to be in His Father's house, because it was a house of prayer.

And to speak more clearly, separate yourselves from all affection to creatures—and as much as possible from their sight—so that God alone may be your only object. Always begin your prayer by profoundly acknowledging your own nothingness, having a lively faith in this promise of the Holy Spirit— The prayer of the humble shall pierce the clouds (Ecclesiastic. 35:21). Let your hearts be fed with some words of the sacred writings, which are proper either to express your wants, or are connected with, and contain the mysteries or truth you are about to adore—such was the advise of Saint Basil. [293]

But that I may proceed with more order, let me tell you, first, whether

---

[290] B. Rabanus Maurus, Fuldensis Abbatis et Moguntini Archiepiscopi. *Ennarationum in Librum Numerorum.* In Opera Omnia, Vol 2. 1851. PL 108:736.

[291] S. Gregorius Magnus, *Moralium*, PL 76:700 (1849).

[292] S. Gregorius Magnus, *Moralium*, PL 76:701 (1849)

[293] "Quod precatio omnibus est anteponenda." *Constitutiones*, PG 31:1327 (1857).

you propose for the subject of your prayer some divine truths, or mysteries of faith, consider them attentively, reflect on them seriously, enter their sacred and awful region, as far as you possibly can.

Secondly, endeavor that they may penetrate into the inmost recesses of your hearts, that you may inflame your zeal, animate your piety, and produce holy affections in your soul.

Thirdly, if your miseries and wants form the subject of your reflections, examine them with proper application; enter into yourselves, judge yourselves severely, and show your necessities and wounds to your heavenly physician, that He may be moved to show you mercy.

Fourthly, in order that your prayers may not be confined to simple emotions and pious affections, be careful to make firm resolutions suitable to your wants, and proportionate to the proper amendment of your lives, in a word, such as may afterwards serve as a rule to direct you in the measures you are to adopt for avoiding your accustomed imperfections, and for the more secure advancement of your soul in the way of perfect virtue.

Fifthly, return thanks to God, for, though you are so unworthy of any favor, He has been pleased to admit you into His divine presence. Finally, that you may be better qualified to reduce all these things to practice, be attentive to lay up in your minds those passages of your lectures which made the most sensible impression on your souls, to which you must join such reflections as are best suited to animate your piety.

Here, my brethren, you have a short but a useful and holy method of prayer, the use of which will be very profitable to your souls. But if it happen that you find it difficult or inconvenient, if you do not extract the profit and utility of which it is productive, do not adopt it with such adhesion as to conclude that you ought not to pray in any other manner, for the spirit of God is free. He is not bound to the rules and practices of men. He communicates Himself to devout souls, and inspires them as He pleases.

Hence, when you are in the presence of God, prostrate at the foot of His altar in prayer, give yourselves up without reserve to the motions of the Divine Spirit. Place an unlimited confidence in Him, and be assured that He who—by a continual protection—conserves the life of your body, will not refuse you the gift of prayer, without which the life of your soul must perish.

Place the direction of the interior man in His hands, without reserve, and follow the impulse of this Holy Spirit with perfect simplicity of heart, whether He moves you to meditate on some mysteries of faith, or excite you to expose your spiritual miseries and wants; whether He touches the springs of compunction, and by a retrospective view of your past sins, makes you pour forth abundance of tears, or elevates your souls to a contemplation of His infinite beauty and excellence, or moves you to adore Him in profound silence, or attracts you to a perfect union, by the bonds of love; whether He illuminates you with the splendid rays of celestial light, or makes the source of heavenly affections flow; whether He forms in your soul holy resolutions, for your future direction and particular conduct, or suffers you to remain in His presence, awaiting and reposing in a holy inaction, until it shall please Him to effect in you, according to His good pleasure, the different operations He usually accomplishes in the souls He loves.

Do not employ long discourses, lest this seeking after studied phrases should fill your mind with vain imaginations, or pernicious dissipations. Fear all sorts of distractions, though they are not imputed when involuntary; and consider as a real evil everything that disturbs the eye of your intention, during these precious moments, or that might deprive you, even for an instant, of the enjoyment of this infinite beauty in whose presence you should always live.

I need not proceed to other more extensive rules for the faithful discharge of this important duty; for there is no subject on which so many authors have written, as on this of prayer; it may be said, that, as it is exclusively a divine operation, the manner of performing it is more effectually learned by the unction of divine grace, than by the instruction of men; and that in the school where it is taught, the Holy Spirit is the chief master and doctor, as He is the true source and principle from whom it flows.

Q. 5.—*By what means can it be effected, that being so weak and feeble as we really are, we may nevertheless keep ourselves in the presence of God, and live in continual prayer?*

A.—When the saints taught us that the prayer of a religious ought to be continual, and that he ought to be indefatigable in that holy exercise, they did not intend to inculcate that he is obliged to contemplate God in such an uninterrupted manner, or with an attention so actual, that he should never apply himself to any other object. They know that a state so invariable, and an immobility so constant, are more properly those of the heavenly spirits than of weak and imperfect men here below; and, moreover, that in our state, there are many occupations appointed by God which require an application so entire, that the brethren must leave those more immediate entertainments with God—in order to attend to them—by which they inevitably lose His presence for some time, so that they cannot consider

Him as in Himself, if I may be allowed the expression, as they did before, but only through the medium of creatures.

Hence, my brethren, we may infer that the saints were persuaded that a religious may fulfill the duty of praying without interruption by making the divine will the rule of all his actions, by keeping his heart inflamed with the love of God, by observing the rule of conduct He has given him in all things, by having only one desire, namely, that of pleasing Him, by making the greater glory of his creator the end of all he does, and by never undertaking anything without imploring, by earnest prayer, that our Lord would be pleased to sanctify it with His heavenly benediction, as Saint Benedict admonishes.[294] Where a religious is faithful to this exactitude, and lives in this piety, it may be said that all his ways are holy, that his life is nothing but a sacrifice of praise, that he is in continual prayer; and if amidst his various occupations, he sometimes lose the sensible presence of God, yet he always reserves it, in the fidelity and perfect dispositions of his heart.

Saint Augustine says that there is no tongue capable of praising God the whole day without ceasing; but that we praise Him by doing well what we do. And that we are to make our prayer become continual by the innocence of our lives and actions. [295]He tells us in another place that our desire is our prayer, that if our desire is uninterrupted, our prayer is continual; that the command of the apostle which enjoins continual prayer (1 Thess. 5:17) is not vain; and as it is not possible to be kneeling, prostrate, or raising our hands to heaven without intermission, so there is another means, by the use of which our prayer may be continual. This means is desire. If you perform everything you do in the desire of obtaining eternal bliss; you may be assured that if you do not interrupt your desire, you do not cease to pray. [296]

Hence, you see what Saint Augustine says, speaking to Christians in general; and Saint Basil, addressing himself to religious in a particular manner, says:

> There is no time but is proper for prayer. During our works we ought to recite our vocal prayers; and if that is not possible, it ought to be done mentally, and we ought to glorify the Lord in psalms, hymns and spiritual canticles. To these we must add thanksgiving for the benefits and grac-

---

[294] RB Prologue 4.

[295] S. Augustinus, *Enarrationes in Psalmos*. PL 36:341(1845).

[296] S. Augustinus. *Enarrationes*. PL 36:404 (1845)

es we have received, particularly for giving us strength to act, light and understanding to know our duties; and conclude by imploring the assistance of His grace, so that being continually fortified and enlightened, we may study to please Him, and do His holy will in all our actions. In this manner, we shall arm ourselves against the dissipations and wanderings to which our minds are so naturally exposed. Our Lord will graciously hear our petitions when we beseech Him to bless and direct the works of our hands; and the fidelity, by which we shall offer Him a just tribute of thanksgiving, for the success of our undertakings, will not be less agreeable to Him, nor less profitable to ourselves. Without adopting these measures, it would be impossible to reconcile the apostolic precept of praying always (1 Thess. 5:17) with our occupations by which we are obliged to labor day and night.[297]

Saint John Climacus makes the continual prayer of a solitary consist in making God the object, end, and rule of all his exercises, of all his thoughts, of all his steps, and of all his motions; and, in a word, of doing all his actions in the divine presence, with interior fervor of soul.[298]

Cassian says:

We shall fulfill the Apostle's precept by establishing our soul in peace, by disengaging ourselves from all our carnal passions, and by invariably keeping our hearts united to God. Pray without ceasing, and elevate your pure hands to heaven, at all times and in every place. When our souls, says he, are purified and transformed into pure spiritual beings, like the angels, everything we then hear, see, speak, do, and understand, becomes a most pure and a most perfect prayer. In another place, he says, Our prayer shall be continual, when we desire nothing, speak nothing, and hope for nothing but God, and God alone.[299]

Q. 6.—*Is it necessary to avoid willful distractions with so much care ?*

A.—The holy abbot Moses says:

So soon as a solitary perceives that he is separated from God by any distraction, he ought to be instantly afflicted at the accident, and give himself

---

[297] S. Basilius, *Fusius*, PG 31:1010 (1857).

[298] *Scala*, PG 88:1114 (1860). / *Ladder*, 230.66

[299] *Collationes*, PL 49:775 (1846) / *Conferences* 1.9. 5 (NPNF2/11:388)

up to sighs and tears. He should remember that he strays from his sovereign Good as often as he removes his thoughts from that divine object, and believe that he commits a spiritual fornication when he ceases to contemplate his Redeemer, though only for an instant, in order that perceiving his separation and misfortune, he may immediately recall his heart from his wanderings, and turn all his thoughts to his divine spouse, fixing them so firmly on Him, that he may be never more separated from Him.[300]

We learn from Saint Basil that the straying and dissipation of the soul spring from the little care we take to employ it in the pursuit of necessary affairs, that sloth and inertia are produced from an unfaithful attention to the presence of God, who examines the heart and reins. [301] He says in another place, if they who appear in the presence of princes and magistrates, remain standing, and speak to them with much fear and bashfulness, with how much more ought we not to appear in the presence of the Lord of heaven and earth, and with what care ought we not to keep our minds attentive to Him alone?[302]

We read in an epistle of Saint Macarius, that distractions dissipate the soul, as worms reduce clothes to dust and rottenness.[303]

Who is the man, says Saint Augustine, who having begun to speak to his friend, and seeing him unwilling to answer, or absolutely leaving his company for the purpose of entertaining himself with another, that would not find it difficult to endure such treatment? and where shall a judge be found who would have patience, if, after you requested an audience, you should leave him on his seat, and turn away to discourse with one of your friends? Nevertheless, God bears patiently the inconsistency of those souls, who while they pray, allow themselves to be carried away by a thousand thoughts, for, independently of wicked thoughts, by which He is outraged, those which are useless deserve to be considered as injurious to the Majesty of Him to whom you speak, for when you read, God speaks to you, and when you pray, you speak to God. [304]

Saint John Climachus says that as an earthly monarch would be offended with one of his servants who in his presence would turn away from him and entertain himself with the enemies of his prince, so Almighty God is much

---

[300] *Collationes,* PL 49: 826 (1846) / *Conferences* 1.10.6 (NPNF2/11:403)

[301] S. Basilius, *Brevius,* PG 31:1098 (1857).

[302] S. Basilius, *Constitutiones,* PG 31:1326 (1857).

[303] S. Macarius, *Epistola Suppositicia.* PG 34:446 (1860).

[304] Saint Augustine: *Expositions on the Book of Psalms* (NPNF1/8:412).

provoked against the soul—who being in His presence by prayer—willfully turns away from Him to entertain herself with her own bad or indifferent thoughts.[305]

Saint Gregory tells us that however great may be the attention of the children of God in prayer, the devil is no less active in his endeavors to distract them, and he considers it as much gain, when he succeeds in distracting them, even for an instant.[306] The same father says another thing very remarkable: Almighty God, who does not consider those idle thoughts as an inconsiderable evil, punishes such wanderings of the heart by forsaking it.[307]

Were you penetrated with these sentiments, my brethren, as you ought to be, you would be far from considering willful distractions as transitory failings and indifferent accidents of little consequence. On the contrary, you would avoid them with all possible care and attention. You would close up every door and avenue of your souls against them; you would consider them as so many dangerous rocks to be dreaded in the course of your navigation, and you would not have any but such as might be the mere effect of your frailty and weakness.

In effect, what is it to be voluntarily distracted in the time of prayer? It is nothing less than to leave the Creator, and to go after the creature. It is forsaking the sweet entertainment of the best of friends and contenting one's self with the illusory discourse of an enemy. And what is still more criminal, it is always found that this never takes place but from a secret preference, by which the Lord is rejected and the servant placed on the throne of our affections. For, notwithstanding whatever may be said, we never leave the presence and company of God, but when allured by something that appears more pleasing in the creature—which then makes it appear better and more agreeable. And by this we willingly persuade ourselves we shall find in its enjoyment what we cannot find in our God.

But remember, my brethren, that distractions may be considered in a twofold sense. Some are involuntary and surprise the elect, even in the fervor of their prayers, and at the time they are most solicitous to keep themselves in the presence of God. These spring either from the weakness of nature, the envy and suggestions of the devil, or from a secret dispensation of God, who,

---

[305] *Scala*, PG 88:1138d (1864) / *Ladder*, 239.54.

[306] S. Gregorius, *Moralium*. Liber II, Caput XLVI, PL 75:588-590 (1849) / Saint Gregory the Great. *Morals on the Book of Job.* (Vol. 1.; Oxford: Parker, 1844), 113-115.

[307] S. Gregorius Magnus, *Moralium*, Liber XIX. Caput V, PL 76:100(1849) / Saint Gregory the Great. Morals, 394-395.

to humble, or to exercise those who serve Him, permits them to struggle under the weight of these infirmities.

Though, in all such occurrences, they are frequently exempt from sin, yet those holy souls who desire to live for Jesus alone, who consider everything as lost that cannot contribute to promote the glory of His holy name, and who also know that these distractions necessarily produce many bad effects when they are neglected, are afflicted at the misfortune and do all in their power, by sighs and tears, to satisfy for the faults they have not committed.

This made Saint Augustine say, when speaking of those involuntary wanderings of the mind:

> What, then, shall we despair of salvation, and believe that those who in the time of prayer fall into some distractions, are therefore lost? If we admit such a thought, my brethren, I cannot perceive what hopes we have left; but since we ought to hope in God, let us say to him, rejoice, O Lord, the heart of thy servant, because to thee I have raised my soul (Ps.85.4).[308]

Saint Jerome, penetrated with sorrow, cries out on the same subject:

> If I had no faith I would not pray at all; but if I had a true faith, I would take care to purify this heart by which God is seen. I would strike my breast. I would water my face with my tears. My whole body would be seized with a holy awe. Paleness would be imprinted on my countenance. I would cast myself at the feet of my God, I would bathe them with my tears, I would wipe them with my hair, I would cleave fast to the foot of the cross, and would not leave it until I had obtained the pardon of my sins. But now it frequently happens, that during my prayer, I am walking in galleries, or counting the interest of my revenues, or, that allowing myself to be hurried away with immodest thoughts, I entertain such things in my mind as I cannot utter without blushing. In such conduct, where is my faith? Was it in this manner that Jonas prayed in the whale's belly, or the three children in the furnace, or Daniel in the lions' den, or the good thief on the cross?[309]

Saint Gregory says that the hearts of those who belong to God are in a continual solicitude, and that they are most sensibly afflicted by the least

---

[308] Saint Augustine: *Expositions on the Book of Psalms* (NPNF1/8:412).

[309] *Dialogus Contra Luciferianos*, PL 23:170A (1845).

of these agitations. [310]Who can sufficiently understand, cries out this saint, how many faults are committed by those inconstant wandering thoughts to which we consent?[311] We may avoid with care the sinful actions to which we feel impelled, but nothing is more difficult than to preserve our hearts from evil thoughts. Nevertheless, it is written, "Woe to you who entertain useless thoughts."[312] Behold here a subject for the most reasonable fear.

Now, as to those distractions of which we are the voluntary cause, they can be considered as nothing less than the effects of the hardness and insensibility of our hearts, of the little respect we have for the divine Majesty, and of our surprising indifference for our salvation. They are more dangerous than we esteem them to be. They carry along with them a hidden poison, and unless we immediately banish them by proper remedies, they will infect our souls. They are never alone. They may be compared to those circles which are formed in the water, and which being multiplied produce an infinity of others by successive agitation.

They appear in crowds, and beginning their operations by enveloping the understanding in darkness, soon gain the will and enervate its powers. They weaken the foundation of the spirit, make it become slothful in prayer, impede its access to God, and make it lose the possession of its sovereign good so soon as it begins to enjoy Him.

They produce inattention during the divine office, fill the soul with a multitude of unprofitable things, and by an almost inevitable consequence, plunge it into discouragement, and next into a disgust for its state. In fine, they derange the whole order of the life of him who becomes their voluntary slave, they lead him to the gates of despair. And after having, by a variety of relapses, produced in him all the interior vices of the mind, they extend beyond all limits, and precipitate him into every excess.

Behold the usual effects which are produced by distractions in those who entertain them, or who either are well pleased with them, or neglect to apply proper remedies to them. Behold the ravages which they effect in those ungrateful souls who lose, without regret or pain, the company of that infinite beauty whose only aspect should form the essence and perfection of all their happiness and joy. As they willingly turn away from the God of peace, it is but just that they should remain in trouble and confusion until

---

[310] S. Gregorius Magnus, *Moralium,* Liber II, Caput XLVI. PL 75:589 (1849).

[311] S. Gregorius Magnus, *Moralium,* PL 76:305 (1849) / Saint Gregory the Great. *Morals* (Oxford; Parker, 1850), 3:74.

[312] Mich 2:1.[Vulgate: "Vae qui cogitatis inutile."]

they are finally punished by an eternal dereliction of God, and of His divine enjoyments.[313]

As to those who are not led by these voluntary distractions into such dreadful excesses, their case is not much better. Some live in insensibility, without any reflection. They follow the vanity of their thoughts like so many fools. Others are the victims of anxiety and the sport of their imaginations. Their souls are like barren ground on which neither rain nor dew ever falls. The heavens are to them as brass; all their ways are strewed over with briars, and thorns.[314] They change their position every moment, without ever being able to find any situation that pleases them. In fine, they pass their whole lives, and finish their career, seeking apart from God that repose, which all creatures united together cannot procure them, because it is to be found only in God alone.

I earnestly desire that these examples— so deplorable and at the same time so useful—may make you more diligent in repelling everything that might separate you from God. Say to creatures, my brethren, that whatever goodness or beauty they possess, they are indebted for it to Him whose beauty infinitely surpasses all His works, and who, consequently, deserves to be loved above all;[315] or rather, cry out with the prophet, they who separate themselves from Thee shall perish: Thou hast destroyed those who have removed their affections from Thee, and placed them on creatures; but as to my part, I have known no other happiness but that of being united to Thee by the inseparable bonds of hope and love (Ps 72:27).

If this duty of being inviolably attached to God, that is to say, of never losing Him willfully, and with determination, should appear of too great extent, you ought to remember, that He has given you powerful means to facilitate its accomplishment. He has separated you from the world, which is the source and principle of dissipation. He has closed you up in the bosom of solitude, as within the walls of a strong fortress, so that you might be secured from everything that could withdraw you from His law, from His power and from His love. He has given you the law of silence, lest you should unhappily lose, even in the company of your brethren, what you have gained by renouncing the society of other men.

He has regulated every instant of your time, filling up your lives with holy exercises and employments, every one of which, like a voice, in an

---

[313] S. Augustinus, *Sermones de Diversis*, Sermo CCLII., PL 39:2211 (1845).

[314] "Contritio et infelicitas in viis eorum." Ps. 13:3 [Vulgate].

[315] S. Augustinus. *Sermo CLVIII, Sermones de Scripturis*. PL 39:866.

eloquent manner, speaks of Him to your eyes and hearts. Finally, He has given you superiors, invested with His own authority, who continually watch over you, and who are constantly attentive to prompt you, lest you should close your eyes in that sleep and forgetfulness of which the prophet speaks, when he says, "My soul slept through weariness "(Ps 118:28)?

Remember, my brethren, that all these advantages will become unprofitable, and that you will find the world, with its dissipation, within the walls of your solitude, if you have the least part with anything that passes in it. If you do not carefully efface from your minds its sentiments, its inclinations, its maxims, and even the very remembrance of it; and if you do not confine yourselves within the narrow limits of your state. You know that the people of God, after having been delivered from the slavery of Egypt, and conducted through the Red Sea by astonishing signs and wonders, found destruction in the desert, where they ought to have found a secure asylum (1 Cor 10:5), and that amongst so many thousand souls, two only were found, according to the judgment of God, worthy to enjoy the effects of His promises.

12 | OF PENANCE, OF HUMILIATIONS:

QUESTION 1.—By what means can a religious live in the practice of humiliations?   208

Q. 2.—If the religious have already acquired a great degree of perfection, how can a superior humble them without such means as are opposite to candor and truth?   208

Q. 3.—As the custom of exercising religious persons in this humiliating and sensible way is now so little attended to, so far from being profitable, would there not be danger in attempting to reduce it to practice?   209

Q. 4.—What can be said to those who allow that though this practice was indeed established among the ancient fathers of the east, yet maintain that the spirit by which it was directed was violent and passionate and that they did not observe the rules of decency and moderation, and suffered themselves to be easily hurried away into excess, that at present those humiliations do no longer exist, because the religious of the west, being more prudent and reserved, and not being able to conform to such a mode of conduct, have unanimously rejected it?   212

Q. 5.—Have we not sufficient reason to doubt of those humiliations, since it does not appear that the practice of them is founded on the testimony of holy scripture nor on the example of Jesus Christ?   217

Q. 6.—Do we not find it in the writings of the saints that a superior ought not to reprehend his brethren with too great severity and violence, and that with all his corrections ought to be accompanied with exterior moderation and mildness?   221

Q. 7.—Does not Saint Teresa combat your opinion, when speaking of her spiritual daughters she says, I would be much pleased if they would be satisfied when the rule is observed, in which there is sufficient work, and that mildness should be observed in all the rest, but particularly in what regards mortifications?   224

Q. 8.—Ought not the humility of a religious who earnestly seeks to be humbled, be considered as doubtful, and as proceeding from affectation? Or can he be affected with the confusions which finds him prepared to receive them?; or, at best, does he not bear them in a merely natural manner, since he previously knew the end and intention of those who were the instruments of procuring them?   232

Q. 9.—Allowing that one may be at first be surprised by humiliations, does it not seem impossible that in the course of time self-love should not find means of being accustomed to them?   233

Q. 10.—Does it not appear, according to saint John Climacus himself, that mortifications or humiliations were in use only on certain extraordinary occasions, and even then they were enjoined to such persons only as had attained to an eminent virtue?   234

Q. 11.—Is there not reason to think that a superior who assumes the appearance of indignation will become indignant in effect?   235

Q. 12.—Has not a superior reason to fear that in exaggerating the faults and imperfections of his brethren, he should by the same, excite the religious to exaggerate each other's faults, and to judge unfavorably of one another?   237

Q.13.—How can it be known by this practice whether faults are little or great? By what means can those be reprehended which are more important, and in what manner can the merit and the piety of individuals be discerned?   237

Q. 14.—Are not persons who may have even heroic virtue exposed to great temptations of discouragement and revolt by those humiliations?   238

Q. 15.—May it not be said that former practices are not expedient for the present age and that the world is no longer capable of such exercises?   240

Q. 16.—Is there no reason to fear that these mortifications might disgust some novices who without them might in time become good members?   241

Q. 17.—Tell me what your opinion is concerning prostrations because some persons censure and condemn them when enjoined for small faults, saying that they ought to be reserved for such as are more considerable?   242

Q. 18.—Since it is known there are many persons in the world who are not edified by these practices and who consider them so many ridiculous actions, ought we not to conclude that their opposition should be a sufficient motive to forsake them?   244

Q. 19.—What can be replied to the authority of Saint Anselm, who in one of his letters blames a superior, who when any of his religious were proclaimed for negligence or some other faults of levity, reprimanded them as if they had been guilty of something considerable?   246

Q. 20.—Although it may be allowed that those mortifications and sharp humiliations may produce some advantage in favor of such persons that are entirely dead to their passions, yet that does not appear a sufficient reason to

*authorize the practice of them, because it would allow
that the injustices, the persecutions and the outrages
committed against the servants of God might also be
justified on the pretext that all these things were so many
means by which they acquired merits and eternal crowns.
247*

Q. 21.—*Would it not be more proper to lead persons advanced
in virtue by the royal path of love?   248*

Q. 22.—*What can be replied to those who say that to reprehend
in a forcible manner such faults as are light and uncertain
is a sort of fiction or lie, and that whatever good may be
derived from it can never make such a practice lawful?
254*

Q. 23.—*Does it not seem that the authority of Saint John
Climacus is not of much weight on the present subject,
since, being a Greek, he, like other fathers of the East,
approves of fictions and lies?   256*

Q. 24.—*Are there not some passages in the works of the same
saint, which denote that he approved of the practice of
officious lying; and that consequently he was not of the
opinion you attribute to him, as may be seen in the 70th
and 72nd articles of his letter to the pastor?   258*

12

ON PENANCE

Penance is a duty as essentially necessary to the religious life as that of preaching the word of God is to the apostolic, and as that of confessing the faith of Christ is to him who aspires to the crown of martyrdom. And, as the apostle is destined by God to announce His truths, the martyr to defend them by the effusion of his blood, so ought the religious to honor and support them by his voluntary sufferings. But as the penance of a monk owes its birth, strength and merit to the penance of Jesus Christ, so ought it to be a continual retracing, a faithful imitation of that of our suffering Redeemer. And though it be true that all Christians, according to the apostle, ought to follow Him in His sufferings, if they desire to follow Him to glory (Rom 8:17),it is, nevertheless, the advantage and prerogative of monks in a particular manner. It is what they ought to consider most attentively in the life of Jesus Christ. To them, more perfectly than to other men, our divine Savior presents the chalice of His passion. And though it is written that all the sinners of the earth, that is, all men, shall drink of it after Him (Ps 74:9), yet the portion of religious persons, or rather their happiness, is to suffer for Jesus Christ, as Jesus Christ suffered for them.

This it was that made the holy abbot Pynufe say that the renunciation and engagement of a religious is nothing less than a public testimony by which he proves to all men that he is crucified and dead; that he ought to examine what the cross of Christ is, and retrace it in his life, exemplifying in all his actions the state in which his Redeemer was when He hung on the saving tree; that thus, according to the word of the royal prophet, piercing our flesh with the fear of the Lord (Ps. 118:120),[316] as with so many nails,

---

[316] Ps. 118:120 [Vulgate: "horripilavit a timore tuo caro mea et iudicia tua timui"; Douay-Rhiems: "Pierce thou my flesh with thy fear: for I am afraid of thy judgments."]

we may keep our wills and desires subject not to our concupiscence, but fastened to the cross and to mortification.[317]

Therefore, to know what the penance of religious persons ought to be, we must consider what the penance of Jesus Christ was. Among many circumstances that we might adduce, it will sufficiently answer our purpose, to remark one, which is that our Lord being willing to satisfy the extreme ardor which impelled Him to repair the honor of His heavenly Father by His sufferings, was pleased to make His entire humanity contribute to that end.

For that purpose, He gave His body up to the embraces of the most rigorous torments, to the labors of penance, to the austerities of a mortified life, and His soul to every species of reproach and contempt. We are well informed of His fastings, retirement and silence, for the holy scripture tells us that immediately after His baptism He was led by the spirit into the desert where He remained forty days without eating or drinking, and having no society but those of wild beasts, and of the holy angels (Mark 1:13). His watchings are no less evinced than His great fatigues. We learn by the sacred writings that He passed whole nights in prayer (Luke 6:12), and that His weariness was so great that He found it necessary to seek relief in a little rest (John 4:6). Dispossessed of all things, His poverty exposed Him to extreme sufferings and want. So great was the indigence in which He chose to live that He did not enjoy the comforts that nature never refuses to the birds of the air, nor to the beasts of the field (Matt 8:20).

His interior pains and afflictions are equally clear by the same divine oracles, for they tell us that He wept over the misfortunes of the unhappy Jerusalem (Luke 19:41) and also at the death of Lazarus (John 11:33); that He groaned in spirit when He was about to effect the cure of the man (Mark 7:34)who was deaf and dumb from His birth; that being afflicted at seeing the malice and obduracy of the Pharisees (Luke 8:12), He sighed over their insensibility, which was proof against His many and splendid miracles, that only served to make those masters of iniquity seek to behold new ones. In a word, He continually suffered the whole sum of His passion, as evidently appears, from His frequently speaking of it during His life.[318]

The judgments of His heavenly Father were continually before Him, as we may clearly gather from what He Himself exclaimed by the mouth of His prophet: "My God! my God! look on me, why hast thou forsaken me" (Ps 21). And a little before His death, being filled with bitter grief,

---

[317] Cassianus, *Institutiones,* PL 49:194 / *Institutes* 4.34 (NPNF2 /11:230).

[318] Matt 16:21; 17:12,21,22; Luke 9:3.

He Himself cried out in anguish of soul: "Father if it be possible, let this chalice pass from me" (Matt 26:39). His humiliations and debasements were no less exercised. Dwelling in the midst of an ungrateful people, who neither respected the sanctity of His person, the wisdom of His conduct, nor the truth of His doctrine, they treated Him as a fool, as an impostor, and as one possessed of the devil.

Hence we may infer that the penance of a religious ought to be both interior and exterior, that the soul must be afflicted as well as the body, and that he ought to join the mortification of the spirit to that of the senses. That is to say, that he ought to live in a holy sadness, in a profound humility, and in rigorous austerity.

Hence, in brief, you will decide properly on this subject, my brethren, by being persuaded that interior penance consists in humiliation, in meditation on death, on the judgments of God, and in compunction of heart; and that retirement, silence, austere food, manual labor, watching, poverty, patience in sickness and infirmities, are the virtues and exercises of which the essence and reality of exterior penance is composed.

ON HUMILIATIONS

QUESTION 1.—*By what means can a religious live in the practice of humiliations ?*

ANSWER..—By the ministry of a vigilant and charitable superior, who shall diligently exercise him by reproaches, reprehensions, bitter words, public confusions, by low and mean employments, and by everything he may find best calculated to advance his disciple in the way of self-abnegation.

Q. 2.—*If the religious have already acquired a great degree of perfection, how can a superior humble them, without being assisted by such means as are opposite to candour and truth?*

A.—To this I might answer many things, but one of the principal is, that there are very few religious whose actions, even those which are performed in the best manner, are not some way defective and reprehensible in some of their circumstances.

Secondly—The rules of the holy fathers, for example that of Saint Benedict, as it enters into every department, points out the manner of performing the smallest actions, and regulates even our least motions, so that it is difficult to observe it with such exactitude and punctuality, as that at some moment something contrary to its injunctions may not escape the most attentive.

Thirdly—When we have formed a just idea of the monastic state, such as the saints have given us of it; when we consider it as a perpetual crucifixion, as an engagement by which we have promised to imitate the perfection of the Apostles, and to aspire to the purity of angels, then in truth, my brethren, it will not be a matter very difficult to find out means of humbling those who profess it, for, until their mortification be equal to that of a man crucified, their sanctity as sublime as that of the apostles, their purity as perfect as that of angels, their actions must necessarily present more than sufficient occasions for this exercise. Nor shall it be necessary, of course, to call in the assistance of any means which are contrary to candor and truth.

Fourthly—Though we might suppose the life of a religious to be so very circumspect in all its points, as that nothing could be discovered therein sufficient to form the subject of a just reprehension, in that case, it would be easy to lay hold on some exterior action, give it an evil turn of which it might be susceptible without attending in any manner to its real motives, and thus find out abundant reasons to humble him. A religious, for example, shall be deputed to read in the refectory; he may perform that office with more gravity, with more emphatic pronunciation, and with a more elevated voice than his brethren. This he may do with great simplicity, and without the least improper motives.

Nevertheless, a superior may with all propriety reproach a religious in this case, and tell him that his mode of reading has a character of pride and self-sufficiency; that his voice appears more like the vanity of a profane declaimer, than the simplicity of a monk; to which he may add, terms more or less strong, according as he finds them better qualified to promote the spiritual interest not only of him who is the immediate object of the reprimand, but also of those who are there present.

Q. 3.—As the custom of exercising religious persons in this humiliating and sensible way is now so little attended to, so far from being profitable, would there not be danger, in attempting to reduce it to practice?

A.—So long as religious orders maintained an exact discipline, so long as this custom was carefully observed; and as the monastic state, according to the unanimous opinion of the saints, is nothing less than a continual abjection and humiliation, so it cannot be reasonably doubted that the same practice, the same mortifications are as useful and as necessary in the claustral government at present as they had been at any former period.

You know, my brethren, that virtue is acquired and preserved by its acts. Almighty God, who is the source and principle of all virtues, and who produces them in us by His grace, has not herein changed the order of things. Humility is acquired by humiliation, as peace is by patience, and learning by study, as Saint Bernard teaches.[319] In the virtue of humility the entire essence of the monastic state consists. How can it be thought, therefore, that a monk sincerely desires to attain to the perfection of his state if he forsake the practice of humiliations, which is the only way that leads to it, since, moreover, it is written that our Lord purifies all those whom He receives into the number of His children, as gold and silver are purged in the crucible (Ecclesiastic. 2:5)?

Some will say that people who live in the world have other means of becoming humble, independently of those which are found in mortification,

---

[319] Epistola LXXXVII, *Ad Ogerium*, PL 182:217a (1854) / Bernard, *Works*, 313.

and that consequently, these are not necessary. I grant that persons who live in the world have other means to learn humility besides religious mortifications, and that such a virtue is not in them the production of these exercises.

But yet I maintain, and it must be allowed, that when Almighty God is pleased to elevate them to sanctity, and to give them this fundamental virtue of the evangelical life (without which, according to the apostle (Heb 12:14), no person can see God in His heavenly kingdom), He takes particular care to exercise them by other mortifications proportionate to their state, by disagreeable affairs, loss of goods, vicissitudes of fortune, unfaithful friends, by ingratitude on the part of those whom they have favored with many benefits, by injuries, affronts. In a word, those persons with whom they live are so many instruments by which God humbles them, and they have frequently more humiliations and mortifications to endure in the world, in one day, than can happen to a monk in his retirement during the whole course of his life.

Monasteries are sanctuaries and havens of security. Hence, as those privileged souls who dwell in them are entirely sequestered from all communications with the world, so are they placed beyond the power of its misfortunes. The solitary in his retreat is free from the storms which disturb the dangerous ocean of life. He is secure from the vicissitudes and vexations of an unsettled world. Separated even from those with whom he lives, his days flow on without emotion, and he is borne towards his glorious country in an undisturbed peace, tranquility, and repose.

Therefore, the fortunate members of this happy state are emancipated from the tyranny of the world and the passions. Neither are they less exempt from suffering from one another, because, as Saint Basil says, they live in the center of perfect union. In whatever position you consider them, you will find them free from contradiction. Soaring in a region always elevated above the influence of interest or passions, they live in a calm that is never agitated. [320]

But, though their condition seems to be, and is really happy, yet it would lose its principal conservation and would soon become really miserable, if the superior did not studiously apply himself to procure them such occasions of exercising themselves in the practice of humility and mortifications as he shall judge best calculated to promote their spiritual advancement, even as the great master of all, never ceases to assist His elect in every department of life, by the means to which I have alluded above.

---

[320] S. Basilius, *Constitutiones*, PG 31:1582.

The human heart may be compared to a field, astonishing for its evil fecundity. There pride shoots its roots, diffuses its malignant influences in every part, and frequently destroys, though imperceptibly, the good seed which has there been sown. Be not, therefore, too confident, for if the laborer refuse his continual application, the fields shall be quickly over-run with briars and thorns. And the consequence will be that the religious who passes his whole life unexercised in the holy practices of mortification will live in a false security, and will be in his cell, according to the expression of a great saint, a recluse puffed up with pride and presumption, like a dragon in his cave, corrupted with poison and venom.[321]

In fine, my brethren, nothing is more opposite to the spirit of our holy state than pride. And this unhappy tumor is not to be healed without the operation of the lance. As it contains an inexhaustible spring of corruption, so it will form new swellings unless the incisions of humiliations be frequently employed. The reason why this remedy is always necessary is because this evil flows at all times and in every age. It is so far from respecting either age or virtue, that it is never more to be feared than when the one is advanced, and the other is perfect. Hence the spirit of pride rejoices when he beholds our virtues multiplied, [322]hoping thereby to obtain the greater victory over us.

Hence this practice is very holy, very useful, and very necessary. It began to be disesteemed by monks only when they began to blush at the humility and abjection of their holy state. While they lived in simplicity and innocence they sought no reasons to forsake it. Nothing but sin and corruption could ever make them consider it as unprofitable, or induce them to condemn a means so holy, that deserves nothing less than to be rejected and contemned.

In a word, my brethren, it will suffice to say that independently of all other reasons, nothing is more conformable to the rules of the gospel, than to adopt some innocent means of humbling men. Nothing is better calculated to make their lives become like to that of Jesus Christ than humiliations, since the life of that divine Savior was an uninterrupted chain of humiliations. For this reason, there has been nothing more carefully inculcated by His doctrine and example, nor is there anything more authorized by the example of all holy monks, nor better confirmed by monastic tradition.

I think it unnecessary to tell you, my brethren, that in all this discourse I have supposed that superiors in the exercise of humiliations will never violate

---

[321] *Scala*, PG 88:843 (1864) / *Ladder*, 126.13.

[322] *Scala*, PG 88:950 (1864) / *Ladder*, 165.3.

the rules of prudence and charity, that they are attentive to times, persons, and other circumstances, that they are cautious of the choice they make of them, avoiding all vivacity, violence, indecent words, satirical expressions, and every excess that might accompany indiscreet humiliations.

Finally, the condemnation of this practice would become a plea for the immortification of bad monks, and an apology for indifferent superiors. It would encourage the former in their independence, and the latter in their estrangement from the labor necessary to make their government become useful; and thus both would mutually concur in sapping the foundation of the monastic state.

Q. 4.—What can be said of those who allow that though this practice was indeed established amongst the ancient fathers of the east, yet maintain that the spirit which directed it was violent and passionate; that they did not observe the rules of decency and moderation, and suffered themselves to be easily hurried away into excess; that at present these humiliations no longer exist, because the religious of the west being more prudent and reserved, and not being able to conform to such a mode of conduct, have unanimously rejected it?

A.—It is astonishing, my brethren, that the existence of mortifications and humiliations are allowed amongst the holy fathers of the East, and yet they are accused of violence and excess, of which those great saints were incapable. This divests their examples and documents of all authority, and attempts to prove a ridiculous proposition. Allowing them the merit of eminent sanctity, and the demerit of base passions falsely attributed to them, destroys the edification which the Church has always found in the lives of these great men. These were the men under Providence, who supported the Church by their sanctity, mortifications, meekness, patience, prayers, and wisdom, and who enlightened it by their heavenly doctrine.

Hence, the Church on her part considered them as visible angels, raised up by God for her defense and preservation; neither has she anything more holy or sublime than their example, which she continually holds out to the view of her children. Those were the extraordinary men of whom the world was not worthy. To them the west is indebted both for the knowledge of the monastic state, and for all the glory and advantage they derive from it.

All this militates against the unfavorable judgment by which the conduct of those bright lights has been condemned. And indeed I do not understand how, without any formality or scruple, some persons attribute that to the irregular inclinations of nature or character, or to other vitiated dispositions, which in them could be only the effect of divine inspirations, the production of grace, and the operation of the Holy Spirit.

As to my part, I will say that although I had no other reason to prove to myself that the practice of humiliations is good, holy, and even necessary, it would be sufficient for me to be convinced, when I find that it was instituted and preserved with such religious exactitude by those great saints, who, being elevated in charity and purity to an equality with angels, had little more of human nature than its figure, who were raised up by God to become the legislators and guides of the monastic state, and who, consequently, were more eminently adorned with the gifts of its spirit and truth than any other men.

As to what regards that violent and passionate temper of which the character of the Greeks and other people of the East, is said to be composed; I do not think that the least signs or features thereof can be remarked in the lives of Saint Athanasius, Saint Basil, Chrysostom, Anthony, Palemon, Pacomius, Euthymius, Sabas, John Climacus, and of so many others, whose zeal, vigor, and constancy, were no less conspicuous when necessary, than the sanctity of their lives.

Perhaps, some will reply, that these defects were repaired by the grace of Jesus Christ. Well, but the same thing may be said of all the other holy fathers and solitaries of the East, who, being entirely dead to the world, and living in it as if they did not belong to it, had acquired a just right to say with the apostle: "I live now, not I, but Christ lives in me "(Gal 2:20). It is certainly unjust to endeavor to extract such consequences from some extraordinary facts which may be found in monastic history.

It must be acknowledged that the character imputed to the East has been evinced by the factions, violence, and intrigues of Eusebius of Nicomedia, by George, by the Patrophils and Theophils, but to pretend to extend it to those sacred personages and divine men, of whom we have spoken above, is a thing to which all sincere lovers of the cross of Jesus Christ, and all true Christians, will never be induced to subscribe. It would be in effect to eclipse the most resplendent part of their lives, and to furnish the enemies of penance with arms by which they might combat the most illustrious monuments of antiquity. For what could be said or thought of the solitude of a Saint Paul —of the tears and sighs of a Saint Arsenius —of the abstinence of a Saint Macarius —of the penance of a Saint Simeon Stylites, and of remarkable actions of the celebrated monasteries of penitents; surely nothing more than that all these things were the effects of heated imaginations, and the conduct of men, who were hurried into those extravagances by the impetuosity of their nature, and the violence of their peculiar tempers.

How different were the sentiments of our holy legislator, Saint Benedict, whose opinion should be sufficient to decide our notions on the character and practices of the eastern saints. He admires them, he praises them, and finds nothing better calculated to sanctify his disciples than a devout perusal of their lives and actions; and he holds them up as perfect models for our imitation. "Every book of the holy Catholic Fathers," says he:

> Eloquently teaches us how we may advance, by straight ways, to the possession of our Creator. Moreover, the conferences of these fathers, with their instructions and holy lives, particularly the rule of our holy father, Saint Basil, are indeed a collection of most lucid examples of sanctified men, mirrors of obedience, and models of virtue.[323]

In the meantime, the world no longer presents any occasion to monks of accomplishing this precept, because they have no more commerce with it. And as they are separated from their brethren by the law of silence, by which they live together in uninterrupted peace, so neither can they find in their society any particular means to exercise their patience, or to complain of anything. In this manner they shall never find an occasion to exercise that virtue, nor to accomplish the precept. They will be humble in speculation only, but will never produce one single act, unless the superior, with the charity of a father and pastor, employ his zeal for that end.

For this reason Saint Benedict established this duty, as a means well adapted to the acquisition and practice of the virtue of humility, because he was persuaded, with Saint Augustine,[324] that something may be wrong in those who think seriously on the great affair of salvation, that nothing is more easy than to be mistaken in the idea we form of our own actions, and that humility alone is secure from such errors, because it comes purely from the grace of Christ. And in effect, long prayers, Christian instructions, and rules of life are easily found, but nothing is more rare than true and sincere humility.

Although the authority of Saint Benedict is alone sufficient to prove that the monks of the West are not so entirely incapable of those holy practices, as some are willing to imagine, it may be moreover proved by the united suffrages of monastic tradition. If time would permit, we could

---

[323] *RB* 73:4.

[324] In Ps. 31.

adduce a crowd of witnesses, and an innumerable multitude of facts from every age, which form a certitude on the present subject too strong to be resisted. We shall content ourselves with citing a few.

In the last century, Saint Teresa undertook the reformation of the Carmelites: God, who inspired her with that design, assisted her in the enterprise with such powerful graces that the spirit and fervor of the primitive age of the Church have been renewed in these latter times. The monastic state recovered its first vigor and these new solitaries attained to a degree of austerity and mortification almost equal to those of the ancients.[325]

There might be seen amongst them innocent souls—some chained up like criminals, others exercised by the most humiliating actions—lying prostrate in the dust, and in public places severely reprehended for deeds deserving of praise. There might be seen holy women whose virtuous lives seem to afford no cause for these penitential exercises, more particularly if their youth and birth were considered, and yet embracing the same austerities and the same humiliations. They might be seen, I say, placed under the feet of all, shut up in prison, and deprived of the religious habit for some time, and all for nothing more, than faults which seemed inconsiderable.

The order of Saint Francis affords a multitude of similar examples. That great saint judged them so necessary and profitable that he obliged his brethren to make him some injurious reproaches, and to address him in terms offensive and disagreeable.[326] We read that Saint Philip Neri publicly reprehended one of his brethren while preaching, accusing him of pride in the presence of his congregation.[327]

A thousand examples of the same kind may be found in the order of the Jesuits, and in other religious institutions.

We find in the life of Saint Bernard that his uncle and brothers, who were saints, fearing lest by reason of the miracles which he performed he might become proud, spoke to him in very harsh terms, and treated him so severely, that notwithstanding all his patience, he could not avoid weeping—a conduct which the historian attributes to the charity of his brethren.[328]

---

[325] Hist. de la refor. des Carm. D'Esp.

[326] S. Bonaventura, *Vita S. Francici* (Antwerp: Plantiniana, 1597), 39. / Saint Bonaventure, *The Life of Saint Francis* (London: Dent, 1904), 57.

[327] Vita S. Philip. Ner.

[328] Guillemo, abbate Signiacensi (William of St. Thierry), *Sancti Bernardi Abbatis*

I will here relate an example much more ancient, extracted from the life of Saint Odon, Abbot of Cluny. That saint, being yet young, was proclaimed in chapter for an action in which he had not been guilty of any fault. His excuses were not admitted. He was very severely reprehended, and his abbot, Saint Bernon, assuming an angry appearance forbade him, under pain of excommunication, to ask him pardon for it, as is enjoined by the rule when any monk committed a fault. This was done by that wise and charitable superior for the purpose of trying the patience and humility of his disciple.[329]

Behold here, my brethren, what abundantly justifies the western monks from the injurious imputation leveled against their character. They do not blush so easily as some may persuade themselves at the ignominies of the cross, nor recoil at the humiliations and outrages of Jesus Christ with all that pretended disgust and repugnance. Such a thought would indeed be unworthy of Christians, for it would prove dispositions too mean for those who believe the unlimited power of divine grace.

To make it depend upon natural dispositions, subjecting it to the qualities of temper, is an idea infinitely inferior to its dignity, and tends to divest it of what it really and inseparably possesses. I know that grace does not always change the natural dispositions and character of every person, that there are some in whom these dispositions after conversion remain what they were before. But then it is certain that this natural temper does not impede either the effects, or the progress, or the impressions of grace in them. A man who is naturally mild, loses no part of his meekness, no more than another, who is quick and hasty, loses his natural vivacity. And although the zeal of the one be more lively and ardent than that of the other, yet the virtue and sanctity of both may be equal.

But when it is said that the inhabitants of the West cannot endure humiliations, what can be less imagined than that they are fierce and haughty nations, people of proud and arrogant tempers, whose hearts can neither be civilized nor humbled by the power of grace? And to say something more exactly to our purpose—if the people of the West were so incorrigible, they could never produce either true monks or pious solitaries. For the saints of every nation agree in this point, that he who is not disposed to bear outrages and injuries with patience, and even with joy, is unworthy to bear the name or to wear the habit of a monk or solitary.

Clare-vallensis Vita et Res Gestae, PL 185:253(1855) / Ailbe Luddy, *The Life and Teaching of St. Bernard* (Dublin, Gill, 1950) 80-81.

[329] Martin Marrier, *Biblioteca Cluniacensis* (Paris, Cramoisy, 1614), col. 27 et 28.

Moreover, it will be said that the practices of humiliations have been abolished. It is true they have been neglected and interrupted in succeeding ages, but we ought to examine by whom and in what manner the change was effected. It was done, my brethren, when the vigor of the monastic state became enervated, and by children who degenerated from the virtue of their fathers. Thus it was that the corruption of the times destroyed abstinence from flesh, manual labor, and a number of other holy practices, because monks became weary of such pious and strict discipline.

The mutation therefore ought not to be attributed to an extinction of the law; and what deserves to be remarked is that so often as any new monastic state has been founded, or any ancient one reformed by the ministry of the saints who were raised up by God for that purpose, these practices were always introduced or adopted, not because they were considered necessary to form a perfect organization, but because they as naturally spring from the zeal and fervor of such souls as consecrate themselves in good earnest to the service of Jesus Christ as sparks and flames arise from the activity of the fire that produces them. Nor is it possible that a religious can have the spirit of his state, or love our Lord as he ought to love Him, unless he burns with an ardent desire to endure everything that may humble and confound him, as Saint John Climacus observes.

In the same manner the canons and discipline of the Church are mitigated not because there is anything evil in them, but because Christians have become weak and infirm. Now, though this be the case, if our Lord raised up some fervent souls, and commissioned them to labor for the re-establishment of these holy rules by making men capable to observe them, without attending to opposite practices which have been introduced by the spirit of relaxation, would it be reasonable to blame them—would it be just to condemn their efforts?

In fine, as water is never more pure and limpid than in its source, so, he that desires to find truth in its purity, must, of course, ascend to its origin and its principles.

Q. 5.—Have we not sufficient reason to doubt of those humiliations, since it does not appear that the practice of them is founded on the testimony of the holy Scripture, nor on the example of Jesus Christ?

A.—Your difficulty is indeed quite new, my brethren; nor is there anything, in my opinion, that ought to be less admitted, even in thought, if we allow that which is an article of faith, namely that the gospel inculcates nothing more strenuously than the necessity of humbling ourselves.

Our divine Lord, Jesus Christ, came down from heaven to teach men to humble themselves on earth. The prophets did nothing more in fulfilling the duties of their ministry than the teaching of this virtue both by word and example which drew on themselves the contempt of men.

The gospel proposes not only the will and intention, but also provides, at the same time, the means to accomplish the work. For it would not be reasonable to suppose that the Holy Spirit, who dictated that divine book, would have pointed out the virtue itself without showing the practice and means necessary to assist us in the acquisition thereof. Moreover, all the saints agree, that there is no way more certain and more sure to lead us to humility, than that of humiliations and abasements.

This is what we learn from the manner in which our Lord conversed with those with whom He was obliged to treat during His mission here on earth. We read in Saint Matthew, that the Pharisees having said, "We know, Master, that thou art not influenced by any man; that thou dost not consider the person of men" ; He answered, "Why do you tempt me, you hypocrites" (Matt 22:18)? He says to them in another place: "Woe to you, Scribes and Pharisees"(Matt 23:13); and repeats the malediction eight different times. He frequently calls them blind guides of the blind, serpents, generation of vipers, whitened sepulchres. Saint Luke informs us (Luke 11: 37-44 and etc.) that being invited to dinner by one of the Pharisees, and seeing that this Pharisee murmured within himself because our Lord did not wash His hands before sitting down to table, our gracious Redeemer took occasion from this circumstance to declaim forcibly against that sect, giving them His malediction three or four times, calling them fools, and senseless. And a doctor of the law who was present having complained that He dishonored them by such discourse, received the same compliment as his brethren.

You will tell me, perhaps, that our Lord spoke these things to men who were grievous sinners, and that His zeal was strong and animated in proportion to the hardness of their hearts. But what shall you answer to the manner in which He treated the apostles on many occasions, and in particular, Saint Peter, whom He humbled and abased much more than his brethren, because He designed him to be one day the chief pastor of His flock. That apostle, being animated with a false zeal and with an unenlightened piety, opposed the design his Divine Master had formed of dying for the life of the world, and said to him, "Far be it from thee, O Lord: that shall not happen to thee" (Matt. 16:22). Jesus Christ, who might have spoken to him as He afterwards did to Judas (Matt 26:50), Friend, why dost thou oppose my designs; you do not understand their sanctity nor mystery, on the contrary, expels him from His society with this formidable sentence: "Depart from me, Satan: thou art a scandal to me" (Matt. 16:23).

Using the same terms to His beloved apostle, as He had employed to drive the devil from him when he had the boldness to tempt Him in the desert (Matt 4:10), could He have chosen a way of expressing himself in a more humiliating and more affecting manner? I do not at present remember the many other passages of the Holy Scripture where His conduct assumed the austere form, as we find at the ceremony of the washing of the feet, but the citations would be too prolix (John 13:8;Mark 16:14).

It will be said that these mortifications were the consequences of real and considerable faults, and, of course, very different from those which are employed against light and apparent failings, but this defense of self-love meets its condemnation in the manner in which our Lord humbled His holy Mother on several occasions; and I am convinced that no person will presume to say that her sins were the cause of them, for she never committed any, even the least; nor am I less persuaded, that no one will here avail himself of some expressions, which escaped the attention of some of the primitive fathers; since those of more early times have explained the subject in a very different manner.

That holy Virgin Mother, sought her adorable Son for the space of three days. She found Him, after much pain and sorrow, in Jerusalem (Luke 2:48); and having testified to Him how much grief and anguish His absence had made her suffer, He answered her only in harsh and mortifying terms. That which happened at the marriage feast is yet more strange. The Blessed Virgin addressed Him in a public assembly in the midst of her friends and neighbors, and having represented to Him the wants of the new-married couple (John 2:3), He answered in a manner that requires no apology, since He is the saint of saints: "Woman what is that to me and to thee" (John 2:4)? We must allow that there is nothing more mortifying than such an expression, if it be examined in all its circumstances, as it proceeded from the mouth of Him who is charity and wisdom itself. And yet, though so severe, it was not less holy nor less pious. Hence then, we see in the person of the Blessed Virgin, a saint humbled and repulsed, without having deserved such treatment by any sin.

If you say, my brethren, that there are but few examples of this kind to be found in the sacred writings, it is easy to show that, on the contrary, there are many. But though it were certain that the number were few, Saint Basil's assertion would still remain very true, that every word and action of the Son of God ought to be considered as a true and constant rule of life,

because there are truths and mysteries of faith which are founded only on some obscure passages of the Gospel.[330]

Neither can it be objected that these consequences and inductions are peculiar to ourselves, for it is well known that it has been proved long since how the blessed Virgin entered into the glory of her divine Son only by the way of humiliation and abjection. And an eminent person of our times has employed her example to prove the extent of the duty of self abnegation, as it regards all Christians in general, as well as the particular obligation of those who are separated from the world and consecrated to God by the vows of religion, showing how these latter are bound to endure the humiliations they receive from the superiors who are appointed by God to be their guides. "If in the green wood they do these things, what shall be done in the dry" (Luke 23:31)? I leave you my brethren to draw the consequence yourselves.

If anyone should find that I speak too mysteriously of those practices, and that they are not sufficiently important to deserve so many reflections, I have only one thing to reply, that nothing is more precious in the sight of God than the salvation of His elect. For that alone He came down from heaven, He formed them in His bosom from all eternity, and sanctifies them in time by particular ways and dispositions.

We doubt not, my brethren, that a great many objections may be formed. We have even anticipated a great number, but after having attentively considered them, having placed them in the balance and weighed them in the scales of the sanctuary, together with the profit and advantage arising from those holy practices, we find both by reason and experience that there is too much loss in forsaking them, and that the same thing ought to be done on this subject that is done on many others, that is, that we ought not to attend to objections that might injure a truth so clear and so important.

Every truth—as well those of faith as those that are less considerable—have one thing common to them, and that is that reasons are found to oppose them. God, who spoke to men by the mouth of His Son, could have done it so clearly and so intelligibly, that there could have remained no subject on which men could form doubts concerning the verities He taught. Nevertheless as these truths were to sanctify some, and produce a contrary effect on others, according to each one's docility or pride, He delivered them for the most part in an obscure manner. And He permitted by a like disposition that even the saints should not explain their sentiments and

---

[330] "Omnis actio, charissime, omnisque sermo Salvatoris nostri Jesu Christi, pietatis ac virtutis regula est." S. Basilius, *Constitutiones*, PG 31:1326.

opinions by expressions more clear and intelligible. Thus the most holy and well-grounded opinions are surrounded with clouds and darkness, so that those who preserve truth in their maxims must defend it against the difficulties which are employed to combat it, as those who conserve the divine grace in their hearts must still remain firm against the temptations with which the enemy attacks them.

Q. 6.—*Do not we find in the writings of the saints, that a superior ought not to reprehend his brethren with too great severity and violence, that he ought not to employ bitter or sharp words, and that all his corrections ought to be accompanied with exterior moderation and mildness?*

A.—If you said, my brethren, that they ought to be accompanied with prudence, you would have had reason in your remarks, because as Saint Basil takes notice, every action when separated from this virtue deserves blame.[331] But to forbid a superior the use of proper severity, firmness, harsh and mortifying expressions, and even the appearance of anger, is a conduct never taught by the saints.

I allow that the same Saint Basil teaches in many places that a superior ought to reprehend without passion, anger, or rage, lest he himself should fall into the pit out of which he endeavors to draw another, that he ought to have the sentiments of a father for those he reprehends,[332] and apply himself to the cure of his children with much tenderness and compassion.[333]

But that great master of a monastic life clearly evinces that he did not pretend to condemn every kind of severity in the conduct of a superior. He pointed only at that which might be employed without moderation, rule, or measure. He requires that the correction be such as to show irritated dispositions.[334] He says that to become indignant—when reason requires—it is not against meekness; that, although the fire be enkindled, yet the merit and dignity of mildness is not destroyed;[335] that an opposite conduct is rather a vice than a virtue; that murderers and physicians employ the knife, the one with cruelty to destroy life, the other with prudence and charity to preserve it; that sometimes reprehensions ought

[331] S. Basilius, *Constitutiones*, PG 31:1378 (1857).

[332] S.Basilius, *Fusius*, PG 31:1039 (1857).

[333] S. Basilius, *Brevius*, PG 31:1151 (1857).

[334] S. Basilius, *Fusius*, PG 31:1039 (1857).

[335] S. Basilius, *Constitutiones*, PG 31:1375 (1857).

to be cutting and full of bitterness. [336]He requires that superiors should be formed according to the character of Moses (Exodus 32:27), who did not cease to be meek and charitable, though he commanded so many thousands to be put to death with the sword. In brief, he explains himself in so many places, and is so clear and precise on this subject, that we can only conclude that he condemns rage, indiscreet zeal, anger, and excessive severity in reprehending, but not the good use thereof.

There are some, who endeavoring to reprobate this conduct, call to their assistance the authority of Saint Benedict, because he says that a superior ought to infuse a larger portion of mercy than of justice into his mode of correction in order that he himself may be worthy to obtain the same mercy at the judgment seat of God;[337] that he ought to be careful not to destroy the vessel by too earnestly polishing it, nor break the reed already bruised; that he ought to endeavor to be loved rather than feared; that when forced to reprehend, he ought to avoid all imprudence and excess.

Nevertheless, it must be acknowledged, that the sentiments of this great saint agree with those of Saint Basil, for he declares that he who is appointed to be the guide of souls ought to remember that at the terrible judgment-seat of God his doctrine and the obedience of his subjects shall be both strictly examined. [338]He tells him that he shall answer for the least defects that the father of the family shall discover in his sheep, and that he shall only be declared free who shall have proved that he omitted no care nor necessary diligence to lead his refractory and disobedient flock in the ways of piety and justice.[339] He enjoins that the superior must observe in his instruction the form inculcated by the apostle when he says, reprehend, exhort with vigor (2 Tim. 4:1). By this he insinuates that he ought to fulfill these duties in their proper time, sometimes using mild terms, at other times employing more severe and terrifying expressions, now assuming the character of a severe and vigorous master, again exhibiting the sweetness of a charitable and tender father. He requires that the superior should employ his authority in plucking up the roots of sin as soon as they begin to shoot. [340]

He sets before them the example of Heli, the high priest, who, because he reprehended his sons too mildly, was struck by God, became the cause

---

[336] S. Basilius, *Fusius*, PG 31:1043 (1857).

[337] *RB* 64:10.

[338] *RB* 2:6

[339] *RB* 2:7.

[340] *RB* 2:26.

of the army's defeat, of the capture of the ark, and of the violent death of his two sons (1 Kings 2,4). He requires that he punish those amongst his brethren who are proud, disobedient, obdurate, and viciously inclined; that he employ even corporal penalties to correct them so soon as he perceives that such as the latter begin to stray from the path of duty. [341]

This proves clearly that a superior ought to govern with wisdom those who are under him, conduct himself with discretion in the punishments he is obliged to inflict, be severe in proportion to their wants, and regulate his chastisements according as prudence shall show them to be necessary for the sanctification of their souls.[342]

It is in this sense we are to understand Saint Bernard, when he speaks of the mildness which a superior ought to observe in his conduct, for he teaches in his works that severity is necessary, that the strength of wine must be mixed with the mildness of oil; sharp remedies, vigorous reprehensions with mild and charitable remonstrances; and, if they who resist virtue are hard and obstinate, he who governs them must arm himself with a firmness sufficient to overcome their resistance; that we sin as well by not being angry when we ought to be as in being so with excess.[343]

In fine, this was the sentiment of all the Fathers who wrote on this matter. To discuss all they have said would be almost infinite and would prove nothing more than the truth we have already demonstrated. Saint Augustine was of the same opinion when he said that we must not imagine that a man loves his servant when he does not correct him, or that a father loves his son when he neglects to chastise him; that such conduct is adverse to charity;[344] that the surgeon ought to continue his operation so long as the corruption is not entirely extracted from the wound, without attending to the cries of the sick man.[345] Saint Gregory had no other idea of it when

---

[341] *RB* 2:26..

[342] *RB.* 64:14.

[343] Epistola II, Ad Fulconem, PL182:80a (1854) / "For it is Charity which compels me to reprove you; to condole with you, though you do not grieve; to pity you, though you do not think yourself pitiable. Nor shall it be unserviceable to you to hear patiently why you are compassionated. In feeling your pain you may get rid of its cause, and knowing your misery begin to cease to be miserable. O, Charity, good mother who both nourishest the weak, employest the vigorous, and blamest the restless, using various expedients with various people, as loving all her sons!" *Works,*1:120.

[344] In Epistolam Joannis ad Parthos, Tractatus VII. PL 35:2034 (1845) / *St. Augustin: Homilies on the Gospel of John, Homilies on the First Epistle of John, Soliloquies,* (NPNF1/ 7:50).

[345] In Psalmum LXVII, *Enarrationes in Psalmos,* PL 37:808 (1845) / Augustine of

he declared that mildness must be directed by the rigor of discipline, and that the former ought to be the ornament of the latter, that the words of the wise man are to be compared to spurs, which stimulate the animal to run, but do not make him fall to the ground.[346]

Q. 7.—Does not Saint Teresa combat your opinion, when speaking to her spiritual daughters, she says, I would be much pleased, if they would be satisfied when the rule is observed, in which there is sufficient work, and that mildness should be observed in all the rest, but particularly in what regards mortification?

A.—This passage of Saint Teresa condemns only indiscreet mortifications.[347] The most correct translators of her works so understood her, as may be seen by the explanatory notes inserted in the margin. They were convinced that to understand them in that sense was more according to piety and truth, than to imagine that Saint Teresa, whose humility was without bounds, could have been capable of condemning the practice of humiliations. Indeed, the words you have cited, can reasonably bear no other sense, but that which, after those authors, I have just given them, for she positively censures two excesses, which tended to ruin the bodies and minds of those holy virgins of whom she speaks, such as excessive disciplines and long meditations, in which they employed the time destined for necessary repose.

Though the saint seems to speak absolutely, in the sequel of her discourse it is an undoubted truth that all she inculcates is the condemnation of those indiscreet practices, for if we extend her intention beyond that, it will follow that she condemned herself, censured her whole conduct, and annulled a great number of holy actions, which she had not obliged her daughters to perform, but which she performed herself and by which she even attained to such a sublime degree of sanctity.

The authors of her life inform us that she was accustomed to accuse herself of her faults before the whole community in a manner so humble and affecting that she drew tears from the eyes of all who were present. God alone knows what the faults of such a great saint could have been. She came into the refectory one day when the sisters were at dinner, carrying a pannel and a basket full of stones, walking on her hands and knees

---

Hippo, *Saint Augustin: Expositions on the Book of Psalms*, (NPNF1/ 8:284).

[346] S. Gregorius, *Moralium*, PL 76:138 / Saint Gregory the Great, *Morals on the Book of Job*. (Oxford; Parker1845), 2:449.

[347] Teresa of Ávila, *The Book of the Foundations of S. Teresa of Jesus*. (London: Thomas Baker, 1913), 63.

like a beast. Being come to the middle, she stopped, and exaggerated her faults with such sentiments of humility and penance as filled the whole community with astonishment and confusion. We also find that she obliged her sisters to reprimand her, that they frequently corrected things in the conduct of the saint which were nothing more than small natural defects, and that when their reprehensions did not seem sufficiently mortifying and affecting, she entered into a detail of her past life, and declared her imperfections with such compunction and tears as edified all her sisters and gave them so many excellent lessons of profound humility.

The history of the monasteries which were founded by that saint furnish a great many lessons of the same kind.[348] They followed her example, because they were animated with her spirit. There we find prostrations of several hours; sometimes they were so long that some nuns have been known to have passed whole nights in that posture; and public accusations of faults, which those servants of Jesus Christ exaggerated as much as possible, yet without offending against truth.

We read, in like manner, that she reprehended them for pride in the discharge of their duties, and in the practice of virtue itself. This is sufficient, my brethren, to destroy the supposed proof that seemed to be extracted from the conduct of Saint Teresa, and evidently demonstrates that she had no such thing as the repugnance for humiliations that some would make us believe.[349]

From these different passages we may conclude, first, that the saints never absolutely condemned sharp and affecting reprehensions. Secondly, that they censured only indiscretions and excesses in these practices. Thirdly, that those persons are mistaken who make Christian piety consist in a perpetual undisturbed mildness, or rather, in a languid effeminate disposition of soul on the pretext that peace ought not to be troubled.

---

[348] Hist. de la Refor. des Carm. d'Espag.

[349] Editor's note: *The Life of Venerable Anne of Jesus*, close friend and protegé of St. Teresa of Jesus and re-founder of Carmel in France, quotes one of her novices regarding Mother Anne's methods of training: "One day, soon after I had come, she asked me to tell her any faults I had noticed in her. 'Mother,' I replied, 'I certainly do not myself know any fault of which I can tell your Reverence, but since you oblige me, I must tell the truth. I have heard it said that you are very strict, and I think you are, too.' The saint replied: 'Now, my dear daughter, I shall not correct myself of that so long as I have daughters such as I have at present, animated with so good a spirit. For I would have you know that St. Bernard says that it is taking bread out of the mouths of children to deprive any souls of mortifications they are able to bear.'" A Sister of Notre Dame de Namur, *Life of the Venerable Anne of Jesus, Companion of St. Teresa of Avila*. (Mediatrix Press, 2015), 187.

Fourthly, that the mildness so much recommended by the holy Fathers is compatible with the severity of humiliations and mortifications; that Saint Benedict does not authorize that false meekness as some pretend, and that, on the contrary, he requires that the superior should be severe and rigorous when circumstances make their application necessary; though our holy legislator omits not to put him in mind that he should always conduct himself with wisdom and discretion.

The three first consequences are evident and beyond doubt; the fourth, though not so evident, is still certain. I allow that if the superior be considered only as a master, with a scourge in his hand, striking without attention, and indifferently treating those who present themselves before him without any regard to persons, times, or circumstances, allowing himself to be influenced only by humor, passion, or anger, motions so contrary to decency and gravity; his conduct in such a supposition, I say, might justly be censured as adverse to the sentiments of all the saints, and to all the rules they have left us. But, if the superior, like a true pastor, animated with no other desire but that of procuring the spiritual interest of those whom the Lord has committed to his care, apply himself with zeal and assiduity to the sanctification of their souls by means of profound humiliations and sharp reprehensions, you may be assured, my brethren, that nothing is more conformable to all the maxims of the saints than such a method. Neither can it be said—with truth—that a superior who thus performs his duty offends in the least against that precept of Saint Benedict's rule which obliges the superior to be rather mild than severe and always to prefer mercy before justice.[350] "For love," says Saint Ambrose, "has its severities."[351]

Just as the severity of a superior springs from pure charity, as that alone arms him with zeal towards his brethren, so passion or humor have no part in them. Severe in appearance, his heart distills nothing but the sweetness of honey. He terrifies with exterior reprehensions, but in his heart he conceals a secret love, as Saint Augustine says. [352]Those few moments excepted, nothing appears in his conduct but paternal tenderness, and

---

[350] *RB* 64.10.

[351] Sermo XLIV, Post increpatione allectio ad populum. In *Sermones S. Ambrosio Hactenus Ascripti*, PL 17:690 (1845).

[352] Serm. de verb. Domini. / Editor: Margaret Rowe in her biography of Saint Teresa Margaret, O.C.D. (1747-1770) details the plethora of corrections, reprimands and remonstrances with which her novice mistress, Mother Teresa Maria, plagued her. Yet speaking to her other novices she once said, "I am grateful to God for permitting me to know Sister Teresa Margaret, because with her rare innocence she inspires in me the

consequently it is easy to conclude that even his severity is charity, that he is at all times mild and tender. Therefore, he is no way obnoxious as to those things objected to from the holy Fathers, since he is so very far from committing any of them.

As to the fifth inference, it is evident, from the above points of the holy rule, and though Saint Benedict speaks only of the punishments of real faults and considerable irregularities, it may, nevertheless, be said that a superior who employs the same means to exercise the humility of his brethren, though guilty of nothing more than light faults, and even without having anything to accuse them of but mere suspicion, yet he does not offend against the orders of our holy legislator, nor act in any manner contrary to his intentions, provided, that he keep within the bounds of charity and prudence.

You ought not to doubt, my brethren, of the right that superiors possess of exaggerating, or of judging on the mere appearance of things, and of suspecting when the good of those committed to their care is the only motive that influences their conduct. "Suspicions (says Saint Augustine) are evil in those who form them only to calumniate their neighbor; but are good in those who are placed in authority, because they employ them for the advantage of their subjects."[353] It is lawful for a father to suspect evil of his son, says Saint Augustine. And Saint Basil says that the Apostle condemns suspicions which spring from a malignant heart, but not such as charity forms in the mind, either for the spiritual health of men, or to exercise their humility and to make them become perfect.[354]

Saint Benedict, therefore, is very far from condemning an exercise so holy, supported by the authority of all monastic tradition, and so particularly instituted by the Holy Fathers of the East, whom he always considered as his masters in the spiritual life. Thus we find it established in many places of his rule, and particularly in the chapter that regards the manner of receiving novices, in which he orders that their vocation should be tried by every sort of injurious and humiliating means.

This practice ought not to be limited to the time of probation. Neither can it be said that the time of first entering the monastery is that alone to which the rule adverts, since it not only recommends to the master of novices to be chiefly attentive that they perform all their duties with fervor

---

deepest admiration. " *God is Love: Saint Teresa Margaret: Her Life* (Washington, D.C.: ICS, 2003), 130.

[353] Sermo CCCXLIII "De Susanna et Joseph," PL 39:1507 (1845)

[354] *Brevius,* PG 31:1095 (1857).

and that they be always disposed to endure every species of confusion.[355] But also enjoins him strictly to hold out before them nothing but the humiliations and other hard and painful difficulties which they are to endure in the new life they are about to embrace;[356] which cannot be understood of the former trials, for it would be useless to prepare them for the combat, if they were never to be exposed to it during the remainder of their lives.

That the religious should be exercised by humiliations was, therefore, evidently Saint Benedict's intention. But as neither the world, nor even their brethren from whom they are separated by the law of silence, can afford them any means for that purpose, as we have already remarked, it must necessarily follow that the superiors must supply these either by employing them in mean, humiliating occupations, or by contradictions, mortifications, and reproaches.

But as it cannot be denied that Saint Benedict instituted this practice, some persons affect to persuade themselves that he formed it only for a limited time. Yet though the beginning is seen, the end nowhere appears. Of course, it ought to be considered as a thing made to subsist at all times, since the holy rule enjoins that the novices are to be prepared for it as for an affair that they shall have to perform in times to come. Let him be forewarned that he shall be obliged to endure things hard and difficult, and that such is the way to eternal life.[357]

Saint Benedict was too well enlightened to force his novices to a temptation so dangerous as that would be, which the view of a more lazy and less mortified life after profession than that which they had observed during the time of their probation would naturally produce, for he was well convinced, that such a prospect could have no other effect than to sow the seeds of relaxation in their hearts; and in such a case, they would consider the first mortifications as so many transitory austerities. Instead of esteeming their profession as a more solemn and strict obligation to lead a penitential life, they would impatiently desire it as an alleviation; and they would regard the moment of their consecration to God as the instant of their independence, which would certainly be productive of the most dangerous consequences to the monastic state.

But let us see what reasons Saint Benedict could have had to change a practice so holy. If he could have made a mutation of that nature, he should

---

[355] RB 58:7.

[356] RB 58:8.

[357] RB 58:8.

have first thought it useless, or at least of very little advantage, to persons advanced in virtue, or that they became incapable of supporting its severity. Now all this is very improbable, not to say unreasonable, because the saint prescribed it as a means essentially necessary to acquire humility.

And we know that virtues are cultivated and preserved by the same acts by which they are acquired; and those souls who are advanced in the way of perfection—being more in danger of being seduced by the splendor of their good actions—have more need of humiliations than others, because the want of a counterpoise might be the cause of plunging them into the abyss of pride. Nor is there more reason to imagine that those souls who have attained to any degree of perfection should find the practice of humiliations too severe.

Since monasteries being nothing but schools of humility, or spiritual presses, according to the terms of Saint John Climacus;[358] and the monastic state, according to the great Saint Bernard, being a life of humility and abjection,[359] it follows that the more they are advanced in the perfection of their state, the more strength they possess. They are better qualified to perform its principal actions with greater facility, and consequently, must find no difficulty in the practice we are vindicating.

And though some might be found who are not sufficiently disposed for these exercises, they ought not to be permitted to remain in their debility, but should be assisted and gradually formed to more heroic sentiments according to their capacity and the measure of grace they have received. Therefore, as they are not in a state to be exercised and fortified in humility in the same manner as the more advanced, they are to be considered only as beginners, and therefore to be proved by a proportionate measure of prudent mortifications.

It is a thing worthy to be remarked that if Saint Benedict did not intend that all inferiors should be obliged to observe this practice, if he made any distinction, or restrained it on account of the quality of persons, undoubtedly priests would have the preference. Nevertheless, we find him so very adverse to such a disposition that on the contrary he enjoins that priests should take the lead, and precede their brethren in the practice of humiliations, and encourage them by their example. And he requires, that

---

[358] *Scala,* PG 88:834,1071 (1864) / *Ladder,* 123.25; 213.170.

[359] "Ordo noster abjectio est, humilitas est." Epistola CXLII, *Ad monachos alpenses.* PL 182:297c (1854) / "Our order is lowliness, humility." Bernard, *Works,* 1:440–441.

they be more exactly and severely tried than the other members of the community.[360]

Thus, we find the practice of humiliations useful and even necessary in every case. Saint Benedict ordains it— as is evident. It nowhere appears that he ever revoked his orders, therefore it still subsists by his rule, and consequently, it cannot be justly condemned, and chiefly in the conduct of those who have promised and bound themselves to serve God in the observance of that same rule, and who make public profession of literally observing it in every point.

This was Saint Bernard's sentiment, as appears from that part of his writings of which we have already spoken, where speaking to his brethren and demonstrating to them the advantages they enjoyed in being concealed in cloisters and forests, he tells them that if the world saw the lives they lead, it would honor them as saints or angels; but that religion observed a quite opposite conduct, for in it, they were continually reprehended and censured as slothful, negligent members. That is, occasion was taken to humble them from those very actions which, if performed before men, would have attracted their esteem and praise.[361]

That great saint was of no other opinion when he said in another place that charity was indulgent to the weak, and that it exercised those who were strong and more advanced in virtue.[362] Here he speaks of great faults, for by the word *provectos,* he signifies those persons who are not guilty of any such actions. The word to exercise points out something hard and difficult, and cannot be understood as meaning anything like sweetness and condescension. Hence, it necessarily must be that he speaks of severe reprehensions and of the practice of mortifications. Neither is it anything to the purpose that this practice has been abolished by contrary systems, since our manners and practices ought to be regulated by truth, rather than by customs.

But be particularly careful, my brethren, not to give ear to those who may tell you that trials are not proper for those who are perfect. Be convinced that it is folly to think that there are any persons so eminent in virtue that they have no longer any want of mortifications or humiliations,

---

[360] RB 60:5.

[361] "Propter quod etiam corporaliter in claustris et in silvis abscondimur." Sermo IV in *In Psalmum XC, Qui Habitat,* PL 183:194d (1854)

[362] Epistola II, *Ad Fulconem,* PL182:80a (1854). / "O Charity, good mother who both nourishes the weak, employs the vigorous, and blames the restless, using various expedients with various people, as loving all her sons!" Bernard, *Works,* 1:120.

which the greatest saints thought so necessary for themselves. Saint Bernard, though so holy, and such a friend of God, declared that there was no remedy so effectual for the cure of his spiritual wounds as reproaches and humiliations. Yet it is pretended that there are persons so holy, and of a virtue so superior to his, that they no longer want the application of those medicines, and who thus are much more privileged than Saint Bernard was.[363]

Q. 8.—*Ought not the humility of a religious who earnestly seeks to be humbled be considered as doubtful, and as proceeding from affectation? Or can he be affected with the confusions which find him prepared to receive them, or at best, does he not bear them in a merely natural manner, since he previously knew the end and intention of those who are the instruments in procuring them?*

A.—The answer to this question is not difficult, my brethren. First, as there is nothing more opposite to self-love than humiliations, nor less compatible with pride, so there is nothing also less a matter of doubt, nor more certainly the character and mark of true humility, than the desire of being humbled, when it is sincere.

Secondly, to be prepared for humiliations is a disposition so essential to the monastic profession that a man cannot be a monk, nor even a Christian, without it, according to the sentiments of the saints, and particularly of Saint Augustine. A Christian ought to say in his heart, these words of the Royal prophet, "My heart is ready, O God" (Ps 107:2). And as this disposition does not destroy his power of sensibility, he feels the weight of his afflictions, and even frequently cries out with the prophet, "Deliver me, O Lord, from thy scourges "(Ps 38:10). So does he stand in need of all his virtue, in order to make a profitable use of them.

In like manner, though a religious man be humble and faithful, though he be even ready to bow down under the hand of his superior, as if it were the hand of God, whose place the superior holds in his regard, yet he feels the stings of the mortifications no less, though they are to sanctify him. And as his preparation is general, and as the things which happen to him are usually those he least expected, so is he almost always surprised, and of course, his virtue is always exercised by them.

Thirdly, though there is less suffered from those persons whom we love, and with whose charity we are well acquainted, nevertheless, it is

---

[363] Ad Dominum Papam Eugenium Pro Antissiodorensi Negotio, PL 182:485B (1854); "I think there is no medicine better suited to allay the stings of my conscience than insults and revilings." Bernard, *Life*, 2:783.

no less true that the suffering is real. Chastisement is painful to children, though they are convinced of the sincere tenderness of their father's heart. Though the sick man desired the operation, yet he fails not to cry out when the surgeon applies the fire and iron to his disease. Thus, as we have just remarked, true Christians receive the afflictions which Almighty God sends them for their trial. They suffer, though they love, and have reason to believe that they are loved. If such were not the case, there would be no cross for the saints; the same thing may be said of monks with respect to those who exercise them.

Q. 9.—*Allowing that one may be at first surprised by mortifications, does it not seem impossible that in course of time self-love should not find means of being accustomed to them ?*

A.—Experience proves that such a supposition is unfounded. Self-love always finds mortifications new. It does not become so soon familiar as you think with such things as destroy it. The heart may, perhaps, become irritated, and even hardened against reprehensions. These sometimes become less severe and more supportable by means of good habits which the soul contracts. Some persons may even be found whose passions are so destroyed that they no longer feel anything. The first state is that of some ill-born souls who have neither piety nor true religion, but such is never that of those who are governed by the fear and love of God. In the second, there remains sensation enough to procure a real feeling of the difficulties which accompany the practice of humiliations. And as to the last, they are very rare; their state is that of the perfect, who by a sovereign mortification of all their passions, have, as it were, attained to the impassibility of angels.

Humiliations are useful to the two last; and as to the first, it may be said, that there would be neither light, wisdom, nor justice, in governing an entire community according to the dispositions of a few refractory and irregular souls; or, on a principle so weak and particular, to build a system that would deprive the whole body of the help and advantage it might and would receive from the practice of humiliations. We are bound to stoop with the infirm, and to support the weak, but we ought not to fall with them.

Q. 10.—*Does it not appear, according to Saint John Climacus himself, that mortifications or humiliations were in use only on certain extraordinary occasions, and even then they were enjoined to such persons only as had attained to an eminent virtue ?*

A.—Saint John Climacus, my brethren, says quite the contrary in almost every part of his works. He tells us that humiliations were employed as trials for those who began, and as a constant exercise for the more advanced.

"My son," says that great saint, "if you freely embrace the practice of humiliations from the beginning, you will not find it necessary to labor a great number of years in the acquisition of true peace, for you will quickly obtain an entire victory over all your passions."[364]These words are addressed to beginners. We learn from the 29th article of the same degree, that in a certain monastery, the religious were tried during the space of thirty years.[365] In the 124th article, he says, that he who labors earnestly to overcome his passions, and to be united to God, is persuaded that he has suffered a great loss every day of his life that he passes without any humiliations.[366] These words are directed to persons of whatsoever age or virtue they may be. "My dear brethren," says he, in the 126th article,

> Generous warriors who run to victory amidst the difficulties of this holy course, stand for a moment; again I repeat, stop a little in the midst of your glorious career, and lend an ear to what the wise man says of you, when he exclaims: The Lord has tried them (in their monastery) as gold is tried in the furnace; and He has received them as victims, who freely offered themselves to Him, as whole burnt offerings (Wisdom 3:6).[367]

These are general terms. That saint calls monasteries spiritual presses or lavers, as I have already said, in which all the filth and uncleanness of the soul is purged out and washed away. [368]He says that to restrain our tongue, and to love humiliations and contempt is the beginning of the victory over vainglory.[369] He says, again, that the first degree of the happy virtue of patience is quietly to endure humiliations and contempt, however bitter and painful they may be to the soul.

Q. 11.—*Is there not reason to think that a superior who assumes the appearance of indignation, will become indignant in effect?*

A.—Those who hear, says Saint Augustine, are more happy than those

---

[364] Scala, PG 88:710b (1864). / *Ladder*, 86.65.

[365] *Scala*, PG 88:695a (1864). / *Ladder*, 77.29.

[366] *Scala*, PG 88:727c (1864). / *Ladder*, 97.124.

[367] *Scala*, PG 88:727c (1864). / *Ladder*, 97.126.

[368] *Scala*, PG 88:834, 1071(1864). / *Ladder*, 123.25; 213.170.

[369] Scala, PG 88:955b (1864). / *Ladder*, 169.39.

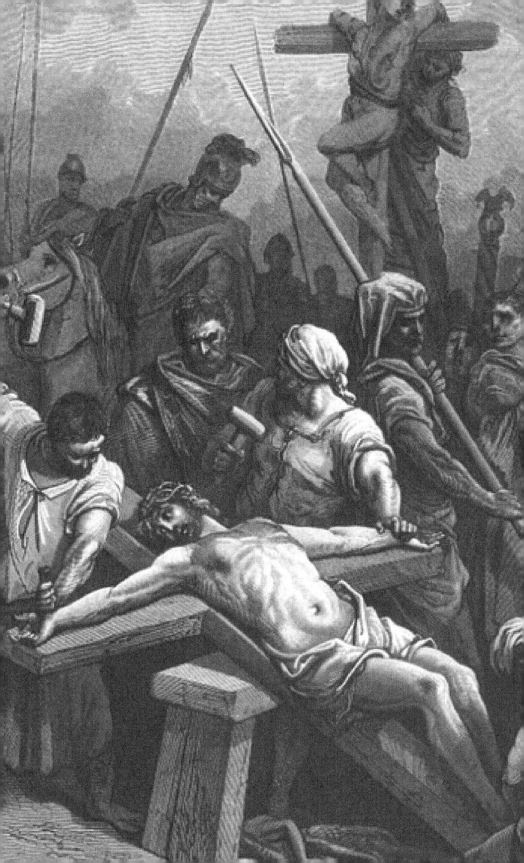

who speak and teach.[370] The former are humble; the latter have much difficulty to keep themselves free from pride. Hence we may conclude, my brethren, that the condition of a man who is placed in authority over others is much to be lamented, but it does not hence follow that because he must humble them, he ought to forsake a means so proper for their spiritual advancement. I allow, it may happen that in repressing the least motions of humor in them, the superior may be hurried away by the impetuosity of his own passions, and that zeal for justice may become irascible, and forsaking its proper sphere, may indulge a real criminal bitterness. These are the dangers of superiority; but you know, that a true pastor ought not to be deterred from his duty by the fear of danger, but should venture his own soul for the preservation of those of his brethren, and expose his salvation for theirs.

Therefore, from this we can infer only that a superior ought to be constantly vigilant; that he should suspect all his actions; humble himself when obliged to reprehend his brethren for light and apparent faults, at the same time that he discovers considerable real ones in himself; that he ought to be confounded at the idea of being obliged to speak with severity to those for whom he would have nothing but words of sweetness had he been in any other capacity; that he ought justly apply to himself what charity alone excites him to say to others; and let him judge himself with so much the more severity as he censures them, being continually fearful lest the great judge should one day reproach him in the following words: "Why have you discovered a mote in your brother's eye, but could not discover a beam in your own" (Matt 7:3)?

Doubt not, my brethren, that these humble dispositions shall obtain of God the graces of which the superior stands in need, by which he shall be preserved from the dangers that you fear; more especially when assisted by the prayers of his brethren, who, being affected by his paternal solicitude, and the zealous assiduity with which, he labors night and day to advance their spiritual interest, will implore the Divine Goodness in his favor, and beseech the Lord to communicate to him the same perfection and purity to which he endeavors to raise them by his great and constant solicitude. After all, it is proper to remark, that there is not much danger in correcting small faults, because being nothing in themselves, they are not qualified to excite ill humor, or to cause any violent emotion.

But, allowing that a superior has reason to fear his own passions when reprimanding with zeal the small faults of his brethren, it cannot be

---

[370] *In Psalmum L Enarratio,* PL 37:594 (1845).

denied at the same time that an opposite mode of conduct would produce as much reason to dread his being seduced by his natural inclinations and propensities. Being influenced with the desire of attracting the esteem of men, he would have reason to fear lest he should act by the spring of such motions, and thus to use weak and timid corrections, or to lay all reprehensions quite aside until awakened from his lethargy by some enormous faults, he should find it indispensably necessary to employ the more severe means and corrections.

How many superiors may be found, who, by a miserable weakness never dare say a word capable of offending any person; or who, by a no less blameable disposition, can never resolve to give themselves the action and motion necessary to form a reprehension however weak; and by thus folding their arms in a kind of lethargic negligence, infuse the same inactivity into the souls of those who are under their charge!

Pride, which is the source of every sin, as I have already said, is more deeply rooted in the heart of man than is usually believed. To purge that evil the strongest remedies and the most active operations are necessary. Is it not better to expose small faults and censure them, such as they really are, that is, to place them in opposition with the sanctity of God before whom none are of small consequence, and thus prevent their growing into great errors?

Can it be doubted that it is a most effectual means to avoid falling into great evils when the most trivial faults are prudently corrected, since such attention imprints a wholesome fear on the mind, destroys those weak ideas which are the cause of all improper conduct and of the criminal familiarity that the soul contracts with sin? Can a superior ever forget the great account he must one day give of the progress those whom the Divine Providence has placed under his charge shall have made in the paths of virtue; and the terrible sentence that the father of the family will pronounce against the pastor who shall have neglected to labor for the perfection of the flock that had been placed under his direction?

Q. 12.—Has not a superior reason to fear that in exaggerating the faults and imperfections of his brethren, he should by the same, excite the religious to exaggerate each other's faults, and to judge unfavorably of one another?

A.—A true religious, whose soul is enlightened with the rays of divine faith, conceives just ideas of the Majesty of God, and of the purity of his state, considers all his faults as great offenses, whether he views them in their principles or in their consequences. He knows perfectly well, however, how to distinguish their inequality and difference. Hence, he does not believe that his superior exaggerates when he represents them in the different points of greater or lesser magnitude of which they are susceptible.

As to the fear that the brethren may take occasion from the practice of humiliations to form unfavorable suspicions of one another, be assured, my brethren, that they who are attentive to their own evils will not feel much inclined to employ their thoughts about those of others. And though it might happen that they may sometimes turn, as it were, and give a passing glance that way, they will form an opinion very different by that which the knowledge of themselves shall have already produced in their minds. The magnitude of their own miseries will diminish the small faults they may discover in their brethren. Besides, they shall find that they commit the same themselves, or that they are inclined at each instant to fall into much greater. On the whole, true religious souls, who are united by the bonds of an inviolable charity, ought to justify the actions of their brethren by persuading themselves that they proceed from a good intention.

Q. 13.—How can it be known by this practice whether faults are little or great? By what means can those be reprehended which are more important, and in what manner can the merit and piety of individuals be discerned?

A.—To this I reply that there are some faults of which no notice is taken, some which are reprehended in mild terms, and others which are frequently reproached with rigor and severity. But all this is done with such distinction of persons and things that it is easy to discern their different quality. It may sometimes happen, though, that the more grievous fault may require a more gentle treatment.

The manner of distinguishing the particular virtues of the brethren is not an affair so difficult as may be supposed. The mode of conduct, the fervor and exactitude with which each individual fulfills his duties sufficiently demonstrate the nature and quality of the virtue he has acquired; this moreover becomes evident by the charity and tenderness that appear in all his conduct; by his modesty and regularity in the chapter and public assemblies; by his holiness of conversation; by his reservedness in point of speaking; by his assiduity in prayer; by his evenness of temper; by his recollection at labor; by his contempt for everything that is not God; and, in a word, by his patience in supporting humiliations.

As to the superior, he decides on the virtues of his brethren without any effort, because the religious having an unlimited confidence in him alone, never approach his person without exposing their hearts and unfolding them to his inspection without reserve.

Q. 14.—Are not persons who may have even heroic virtue exposed to great temptations of discouragement and revolt by those humiliations?

A.—This question, my brethren, supposes a contradiction, for, were that the case, the virtue of those persons, so far from being heroic, would, on the contrary, be very weak. As virtue principally consists in the mortification of the spirit and senses, in a firm and immutable patience, and in a sincere, profound humility, he who has attained to such a degree as might justly deserve the title of heroic is very far from evincing such feeble dispositions. Saint John Climacus was not of this opinion when he said that none but a bad religious can be offended at the reproaches which are leveled against him, and that humiliations are to an obedient man what the bitterness of wormwood is to the body.[371]

The words of the holy abbot are very remarkable: "The soul," says he, speaking on this subject:

> Whom Jesus Christ, has bound to his pastor by the chains of love and a lively faith, would choose rather to pour out the last drop of its blood, than to break that holy union; and in particular, if the Lord had employed the superior as an instrument to heal the soul of its spiritual infirmities, being mindful that it is written, that neither angels, nor principalities, nor powers, can separate from the love of Jesus Christ (Rom 8:39).[372]

Saint Columbanus spoke in the same manner. He says that mortifications are difficult only to proud, obdurate souls, and that they are the consolation of those who are meek and humble. Charity obliges a superior to regulate his conduct according to the capacities of those who are under him; but when a religious shows that he cannot support humiliations, there can be no doubt but that he is far from being qualified to fulfill the obligation that our Lord has enjoined to every Christian, and from which, as from a thing necessary, he never dispenses any person. [373]

Saint Ephrem also reasons very justly on the same subject: "How shall he," says the saint, "who cannot bear a sharp word, support an insult? If an insult be to him insupportable, how shall he endure blows? And, if both

---

[371] *Scala,* PG 88:718b (1864). / *Ladder,* 91.103.

[372] *Scala,* PG 88:694 / *Ladder* 77.28.

[373] S. Columbanus, *De Mortificatione.* In *Regula de Coenobialis,* PL 80:213 (1850)

should be above his strength, alas! how shall he carry his cross, without which no one can be saved ?"[374]

Saint John Climacus says, "We know how much we are attached to what we possess only by the grief we feel when deprived of it." [375] This maxim may be applied to pride; that vice is frequently so concealed and imperceptible that it is discovered only by the haughtiness and resistance which start up within us, at the appearance of some humiliating accident.

Then the mask is taken off, the disguise vanishes, and the man is seen to be what he really is, whether he is truly a sheep, or rather a wolf in sheep's clothing, to use the words of Saint Augustine. [376]How great is the number of those who conceal under a religious habit and exterior marks of sanctity dispositions opposite to both, and, who, as Saint Eucherius says, like vipers and serpents exhibit the external composure of a piety of which they have nothing within.[377] They are easy and mild while nothing displeases them; but if they are touched with the point of the least humiliation, that apparent modesty quickly vanishes, the curtain withdraws, and the hideous monster pride appears with all its deformity. In fine, those who admired the vain outside are disabused; the former expressions are found not to have been the language of the heart; and though they evinced a false humility, their hearts were infected with real pride.

This is an evil so much the more dangerous as it is concealed, and nothing brings it to light better than the practice of humiliations. Now, if you ask me why the enemy makes such destruction in the monastic state, the answer is because he attacks it in its foundations and has succeeded in expelling humility from the cloister—as well as in finding out the secret to destroy the means by which it may be acquired. He has introduced the love of science and learning; monks have substituted the study of other things for that of the holy Scriptures; they preach, they teach, they direct, they make long meditations, they even fast, if you will. As to manual labor, it has been dismissed as an occupation too contemptible.

That poverty of spirit and evangelical simplicity which Jesus Christ so forcibly preached on Mount Calvary, which he produced in the hearts of His elect by the shame and ignominies of His cross, which sanctified deserts,

---

[374] S. Ephraem Syri. *Paraenesis Trigesimaoctava, De Mansuetudine.* In Opera Omnia. Interprete a Gerardo Vossio (Coloniae: Quentelium, 1616), 403.

[375] *Scala,* PG 88:658d (1864) / *Ladder,* 62.11.

[376] S. Augustinus, *De Sermone in Monte,* PL 34:1287 (1845) / *Augustin: Sermon on the Mount, Harmony of the Gospels, Homilies on the Gospels* (NPNF1/6:47).

[377] S. Eucherius. *Admonitio ad Virgines.* PL 50:1209-1212 (1846).

changed the most frightful solitudes into so many terrestrial paradises, and which infused the spirit of the apostles and martyrs into the souls of the primitive monks, is now reduced to such a state of annihilation that the least remnant is scarcely found in the religious houses of our times.[378]

Q. 15.—May it not be said, that former practices are not expedient for the present age, and that the world is no longer capable of such exercises?

A.—If you had said, my brethren, that it is no longer worthy of them, you would have spoken well. We have closed up our hearts, and the divine goodness, after being long offended, is withdrawn. We have forsaken the paths in which our holy Fathers have walked; and because these were the ways of God, so does God refuse us the protection He gave our fathers. But it would not be reasonable to condemn those who after perceiving the greatness of the evil, and discovering the source from which it springs, should employ all possible means to return to the same way in which their fathers advanced, and to retake the same practices and observances by which it is well known they sanctified themselves.

It is vain to say that men are no longer capable of them. We know that God is the sovereign master of men, that His power has received no recent limits, that His arm is not shortened, that our hearts are in His hands at present as well as at any other time, that they are no less susceptible of His grace; that He understands well the art of making Himself beloved, and that according to His own words, He is able to raise up children to Abraham from the hardest rocks and stones (Matt 3:9).

Q. 16.—Is there no reason to fear that these mortifications might disgust some novices, who without them, might in time become good members?

A.—There can be no cause of anxiety, my brethren, when novices fail only in consequence of the means which are employed to try their vocation, chiefly when these means are conformable to the practice of the saints, and to the rule that is professed in the house from which they depart. It is true that the weak and imperfect ought to be considered, and that their weakness and infirmities require sentiments of compassion; but the

---

[378] "These observations are by no means intended to apply to those religious orders and congregations which have been particularly instituted for preaching, serving the sick, and imparting religious education; and who observe an exact religious discipline, according to the approved primitive spirit of each; but only to those religious orders and congregations who have relaxed from and have forsaken their primitive spirit." Editor's note: Evidently these remarks are those of the translator, Vincent Ryan, for they are not found in de Rancé's volume of 1683.

spirit of religion, and the good of monasteries, will not allow them to be admitted, since novitiates have been instituted chiefly for the purpose of discerning them by humiliations and such trials as discover their defects. When these defects are such as militate against the fundamental maxims of the monastic state, the state must, of course, reject such subjects as will not correct those hostile dispositions. Now this is, without doubt, the case of all those who cannot, or will not, support the practice of humiliations. Such dispositions, whatever may be said in their favor, have been at all times, and are in all men, the effect of indocility and pride.

As to what regards us in particular, I do assure you, my brethren, that we never had the least scruple on account of any novices that we may have dismissed. Their departure has been the cause of much grief to us, because we considered that it might injure the great affair of their salvation; but, at the same time we returned thanks to God, that, though we had sometimes particular reasons to desire their perseverance, yet, He fortified us in such a manner as to relax no part of the ordinary discipline, and did not allow any intervening considerations to prevent us from making a disinterested decision on their vocation.

We hold, as an assured maxim, that however virtuous a man may be, he is not sufficiently so to become a religious, if he be not resolved to embrace every kind of humiliation. If any persons present themselves for the purpose of embracing the monastic state, being as yet weak in virtue, they ought to be exercised in this practice in a manner proportionate to their state. And we, by the more severe humiliations which are enjoined as to others who are more advanced in virtue, ought to hold up before their eyes a more perfect degree to which they ought to tend, being persuaded that they are not to consider the common way as worthy the dignity of their state.

All the saints agree on this point. Saint John Climacus says that they who enter the religious state by any other door than by that of humility are thieves and robbers who deprive themselves of life and salvation;[379] and that they ought to remember that they are bound to cast themselves into the fire of mortifications and humiliations lest they should gain nothing by this combat but their own condemnation.

We read that Saint Teresa was about to receive a young woman into one of her convents who had every qualification of wit and health. This person, finding it necessary to return to the world for the purpose of setting some affairs in proper order, remarked to the saint that when she presented

---

[379] *Scala,* PG 88:995b (1864). / *Ladder,* 185.30.

herself again, she would be careful to bring her bible; to which the saint replied,—"My daughter, we neither want you nor your bible, for we are but poor ignorant women, who know nothing more than to spin and obey."[380] That enlightened saint concluded from the above circumstance that the person was not qualified to embrace a state which requires such profound humility and simplicity, and it was evident that the event would have proved her opinion true.

Q. 17.—*Tell us what your opinion is concerning prostrations; because some persons censure and condemn them when enjoined for small faults, saying that they ought to be reserved for such as are considerable?*

A.—Such a thought, my brethren, is never formed by anyone who is acquainted with the practices of the monastic state. Nevertheless, if there be persons who insist that prostrations are a punishment to be inflicted on those only who fall into the more important faults, it may be answered with every degree of certitude that they were never considered in that sense. They were instituted by the saints, and practiced at all times, as appears by religious tradition. Saint Benedict's testimony is sufficient on this subject, for he was at the same time both a monk and a saint, and one filled with the spirit of God. He enjoins that if a religious be reprimanded by a superior—however light his fault may be—if he perceive the least emotion in him who reprehends him, he must prostrate on the ground, and remain at his feet, until the superior being appeased by his humility, permits him to rise. His words are remarkable.[381]

It was expressly commanded in the general assembly held at Aix la Chapelle for the reformation of the monastic order, that when a religious shall be reprimanded by his superior, whoever he may be, the religious must acknowledge his fault and prostrate at his feet.[382]

Saint Columbanus orders in his rule that if a brother, being employed in the kitchen should allow anything to be lost, whether it be dry or liquid,

---

[380] Historia de la Reform. des Carm d'Esp. / Carta de Fray Diego de Yepes in S. Teresa de Jesús, Escritos de Santa Teresa. In Biblioteca Autores Españoles, 53 (Madrid: M. Rivadeneyra, 1861), 1:568.

[381] *RB* 71.7

[382] Ad Conventum Aquisgranensem Pro Monachorum Reformatio. In *Sanctorum Conciliorum et Decretorum Collectio Nova*, a PP. Philippo Labbeo et Gabriele Cossartio (Luca, 1748), 790-799.

he must lie prostrate in the Church during twelve psalms, and remain there without motion.[383]

The book of the usages or customs of the Cistercian order prescribes that if a religious while at dinner lets anything fall, he must rise from his place at the same instant, and lie prostrate until the superior by sign permits him to rise.[384]

Saint Lambert, who had left his bishopric and retired to a monastery, rising one night in the dormitory to pray, happened to let something fall that made some noise. The superior ordered that he who caused such disturbance should go immediately and prostrate at the foot of the cross that stood in the place of burial. The saint obeyed, though it was then excessively cold, and though no one knew who it was, he remained there until the end of the midnight office, and would have stayed there much longer if the superior, who had remarked that he was absent, had not sent to call him in.[385]

Saint Teresa, being on a visit in one of the convents which she herself had founded, happened to cough during the time of prayer. The prioress, not knowing who made the noise, commanded whoever made it to prostrate; the saint obeyed without delay, and it is remarked, that she remained a considerable time in that humiliating posture.[386]

One of Saint Teresa's nuns, being commanded by her superior to prostrate for some insignificant fault, passed the whole night in that position, and was found next morning prostrate on the pavement, although it froze intensely during the night. A thousand examples of the same nature might be adduced, which happened at all times, because there was no practice more generally adopted, nor more exactly observed in the cloister.[387]

Q. 18.—As it is known that there are many persons in the world who are not edified by these practices, and who consider them as

---

[383] S. Columbanus, *Regula Coenobalis* .PL 80:217 (1850).

[384] "76.38-39. If some offense is committed by any of those who are eating, or those who are serving, the offender should ask pardon with a penitential prostration in front of the platform. The prior gives an audible knock with his knife, the offender rises, makes a bow and returns to his place." *Les Ecclesiastica Officia Cisterciens du xiième siècle*, ed. D. Choisselet and P. Vernet (Reiningue, 1989) / *The Ancient Usages of the Cistercian Order [Ecclesiastica Officia]*, (Lafayette, Guadalupe Translations 1998), col 115.

[385] Vita ejus.

[386] Hist. of the Spanish Carmelites.

[387] Hist. of the Spanish nuns.

so many ridiculous actions, ought we not to conclude that their
opposition should be to us a sufficient motive to forsake them?

A.—The opposition of the world does not prove, my brethren, that these practices are not holy, nor that they ought to be forsaken. It merely admonishes superiors that every sort of persons ought not to be admitted into monasteries, nor allowed to be spectators of exercises the necessity and advantages of which they do not understand. Saint Basil's advice ought to be here attended to, where he tells us that we are not to confide in every person who comes to visit us; that they who serve God are continually surrounded with people who lay snares to surprise them; that even those persons who see them more familiarly than others are influenced by views more curious and less favorable to their manner of life.[388] It is an almost unexceptionable fact that the practices of the monastic state are too sublime for the inspection of worldly souls, whose thoughts—according to the expression of a great saint—are not more elevated than their works.[389]

Nevertheless, my brethren, if some laugh at those practices, it is certain there are others on whom they make a quite contrary impression. Some on beholding them cannot restrain their tears; this happens according to the different dispositions of the persons. If from them we were to form a rule of conduct, undoubtedly we ought to consult the latter preferably to the former; at least if we intended to follow the scripture; for you know, that it does not speak in favor of the former, but on the contrary, it pronounces a terrible judgment against them: woe to you who now laugh, for you shall mourn and weep.

But after all, we must let men laugh or weep, approve or condemn what they please. We ought to conduct ourselves according to truth, and not according to these affections. Provided that our actions are approved of by Jesus Christ, we ought to be contented that they are condemned by the world. The reason of which you speak might stand for those who seek glory in this kind of exercise; but can be of no consequence to these who, with an upright will, seek to humble and confound themselves.

Michol laughed at David, when she saw him dancing before the ark, and I doubt not but that there were many who were disposed to favor her opinion; yet she did not persuade that holy king (2 Kings 6:16). It is a thing well known that there are many practices established in the cloister which seem ridiculous to those who have not received the spirit to govern a community in a proper manner.

---

[388] S. Basilius, *Constitutiones*, PG 31:1359

[389] S. Peter de Alcantara.

"That is a most holy game," says Saint Bernard:

Which exposes us to the contempt of worldly people, who lead an easy, proud, and affluent life: for, to speak the truth, what can people of the world think of the life we lead; can they esteem it anything better than a sort of game, or silly amusement, since we make it our duty to despise what they love, and to love what they despise; like those who invert their personal form, placing their head below, and their feet above, and thus support themselves, walking on their hands, contrary to the natural and accustomed manner, to attract the eyes of the multitude. But here it is not children's sport, nor a theatrical entertainment, which by indecent and effeminate gestures excite sentiments of indignation; but it is a spectacle that is truly modest, agreeable, and grave; worthy of being esteemed, and capable of exciting joy in the blessed spirits who are spectators thereto. It is a holy and chaste spectacle, conformable to that of the Apostle, who said; we are become a spectacle to angels and to men (1 Cor 4:9).

Nevertheless, let us take care not to be deterred, nor to interrupt our exhibition, though men may say—proceed, that we, in the mean time, may have an occasion to divert ourselves. Let us continue, though they may deride us so that we may live in shame and contempt until He returns, who will exalt the humble and confound the proud.[390]

If it be objected that there are religious persons who blame this practice, it may be answered, true, but there are many others who approve of it. And, as it appears evident that the opinion of the latter is better founded and more conformable to the manners and practices of the saints, we will pursue the safer path. It is not surprising that they who do not admit this custom should endeavor to excuse themselves and seek reasons to defend their opinion, since it is not a thing very common that men should approve of certain practices, though of their state, when they themselves do not observe them.

Q. 19.—What can be replied to the authority of Saint Anselm, who in one of his letters blames a superior, who, when any of his religious were proclaimed for negligence, or some other faults of levity, reprimanded them as if they had been guilty of something considerable?

A.—That which Saint Anselm blames is very different from what we approve. He writes to a superior whose conduct he reproves because it

---

[390] Epistola LXXXVII, *Ad Ogerium*, PL 182:217 / Bernard, *Works*, 1:314 (1854).

was so improperly regulated that it disturbed the peace of his monastery, and became a subject of murmuring to his brethren. This appears by these words of his letter: "I have heard, that some are murmuring, and this is of a very injurious tendency."[391] From this it appears that the saint supposed that this superior attributed a look, a sign, or some such thing to some evil intention, which was contrary to sincerity and good sense; and proves that, instead of humbling his brethren through charity, and without bitterness of heart, he formed ill suspicions against them, and thus alienated their hearts from him. [392] Now we are convinced that in all such cases humiliations are unprofitable, and that they are not to be employed; and we have already said, that if a religious were not able to support this practice, the superior ought to condescend to his weakness, and stoop, in order to raise him up, by reprehending in his presence those whose virtue is more vigorous and better able to stand an attack.

Essentially, Saint Anselm condemns the proceedings of a superior who, by his imprudence and indiscretion, pulled down instead of raising the structure by wisdom and good conduct; and the saint, I grant, had reason to say that he considered his severe corrections, and unjust suspicions, as so many important infractions of the rule.

To this we may add that though Saint Anselm's opinion were hostile to that which we defend, that would not be sufficient motive to make us abandon our post, since the practice itself is founded on the authority, and defended by the examples of so great a number of saints, and by so many solid reasons. And though we could claim only the suffrage of Saint Climacus, I cannot see why the authority of Saint Anselm ought to be preferred to that of Saint Climacus, who was the most enlightened solitary of his time and one of the most excellent guides that God ever produced in his Church for the government of the monastic state.

Q. 20.—Although it may be allowed that those mortifications and sharp humiliations may produce some advantage in favor of such persons as are entirely dead to their passions, yet that does not appear a sufficient reason to authorize the practice of them, because it would then follow that the injustices, the persecutions, and outrages committed against the servants of God might be also justified on the pretext that all these things were so many means by which they acquired merits and eternal crowns.

A.—The comparison is not just, my brethren. I allow that one of its

---

[391] S. Anselmus, Ep. 91, Anselmi ad Antonium Subpriorem, PL 159:130 (1854).

[392] S. Anselmus, *Antonium,* PL 159:130 (1854).

parts is proper to monks and solitaries, for according to the saints, and in truth, they may be compared to martyrs. However, the same thing cannot be said of the other, nor do I think that any parallel can be formed between a cruel persecutor and a charitable pastor, for the one is the instrument and agent of the devil, the other is the minister and vicar of Jesus Christ. The one is full of hatred against God and his neighbor, the other is actuated by nothing but love and charity for both the one and the other. The one proposes to himself nothing but the destruction of the martyr, the other desires nothing but the salvation of his brother. The one employs every means to expel truth from the heart of him whom he persecutes; the other endeavors to extirpate every appearance of vice from the soul of the religious whom he exercises. The one employs impious and sacrilegious means to accomplish his designs; the other squares his conduct according to the innocent practices of the saints, for the perfection of his work.

It is difficult to understand how a comparison can subsist with so many different oppositions. There is a false and a cruel charity, and there is likewise a holy and charitable cruelty; and, as we learn from Saint Gregory:

> There is a great difference between that which is done from a motive of pride, and that which is performed through zeal for good discipline. Superiors assume the appearance of indignation, but they are not indignant; in effect, they seem to despair of any amendment at the time when they have the greatest hopes; they draw the sword of persecution, but they cease not to love; they exaggerate, because good order compels them; but their charity defends and preserves their spirit in meekness.[393]

Q. 21.—Would it not be more proper to lead persons advanced in virtue by the royal path of love?

A.—You then oppose, my brethren, the way of love to the way of humiliations. Nevertheless, it seems to me that faith teaches something else, since we learn by it that the royal way of love is that of the cross; and that by the cross the sufferings of the spirit are as well signified as those of the flesh; that is to say, that humiliations and pains may be specially called the cross.

By this way Jesus, our King, is gone before us. His whole life was an uninterrupted course of ignominies, humiliations, and contempts. The eternal Father's conduct towards His adorable Son was replete with rigor and humiliations beyond human conception (Rom 8:32). And yet it never

---

[393] Hom. 34. "In Evang."

was asserted that Jesus Christ was led by the mean and servile way of fear, and not by that of love. This royal way, which He pointed out by His actions, as well as by His words, I again repeat, is the way of the cross; it is the only way that He sanctified by His example; the only way known by His true disciples: "The Apostles departed, from the council, rejoicing that they were found worthy to suffer ignominy for the name of Jesus." (Acts 5:41). All their ambition and consolation consisted in embracing it; every other way appeared false and suspicious to them.

The book of the imitation of Christ which—preferably to any other, except the Holy Scriptures—contains the maxims of true piety, begins the chapter of the royal way of the cross by the following words: "This word seems hard to many —renounce thyself, take up thy cross, and follow me." [394] But it proves in every part that there is no way to life, or to interior peace, but that of the cross and continual mortification. This does not agree with the opinion of those who are not of our sentiments. Undoubtedly, they ground their objections on the supposition that no one can love a superior when he is severe and ever disposed to enjoin humiliating exercises; that he cannot love and practice humiliations at the same time; they consider this practice as being a proper means to destroy all sentiments of love.

But what shall they be able to reply to those words of Saint Augustine, who says that it is the part of foolish children only to love or hate their father according as he punishes or caresses them, since he loves them at all times, and that, whether his conduct to them be marked with the one or the other of these qualities, he equally esteems them as his children and heirs. [395] According to the same saint, we ought to love God at all times—in those of affliction, as well as in those of prosperity, His orders and dispositions being equally just and deserving respect. Ought not the same rules be observed with respect to prelates and pastors, who hold His place among men ?

God being invisible, employs their intermediate ministry in the government and direction of His faithful, whom He places under them for that purpose. In a word, my brethren, humiliations, when employed with charity and discretion, so far from producing the effect supposed, on the contrary, become the cause of the one entirely opposite. Let us suppose that they have for immediate objects good Christians who possess some degree of virtue, or at least, who have a sincere desire to acquire it; in such

---

[394] "Durus multis videtur hic sermo, abnega temetipsum, tolle crucem tuam, et sequere me." Lib 2, *de Imit.Christi,* cap 12.

[395] S. Augustinus, *In Psalmum XXXII*, PL 36:275-300 (1845).

as these, humiliations, as they point out the superior's zeal, so do they effectually win their hearts; and in place of destroying love, they give it a more perfect degree of fervor and solidity. This is what Saint Bernard teaches when he says that those among his brethren whom he treated with more severity, were more closely united to him in the bonds of a more strict and tender charity, than others whom he had treated less rigorously.[396]

The reason why there is little or no charity amongst men is because concupiscence has obtained a sovereign power over them; and, as there is nothing so hostile to the reign of that beloved tyrant as humiliations, nor better calculated to place charity, the queen of virtues and peace, on the throne, so, there is nothing to which men are more adverse. Therefore they are deprived of the sweets which they would enjoy under the mild influence of love, and groan under the insupportable yoke of their passions. This is conformable to the words of the Holy Spirit, who tells us, by the mouth of the wise man: "Do not reprehend him who derides, lest he should hate you: reprehend the man of wisdom, and he will love you" (Prov 9:8).

Should anyone say that this practice is only the letter, that serves to very little purpose; I allow that it is only a letter, but then, I beg leave to remark, that, the true Israelites who, in spirit and truth, waited for the accomplishment of the promises, did not observe the law less than the more carnal Jews. The letter alone is of very little use; but we must either combat the entire doctrine of all the saints, or allow that it is no less necessary for the preservation of the spirit than leaves are for that of fruit, or bark for the conservation of trees.

Hence, my brethren, you see, that it is not impossible to answer all the objections that may be formed against this subject by solid and Christian reasons. But, though they were not so numerous and so strong as those we have adduced, still there is one that admits of no reply; and that is, that all reasoning is abortive when employed against certain experience. You may as well endeavor to prove, by solid reason, to a physician, that the regimen he prescribes for his patient is not good, if he be convinced of the contrary by experience; and if it effectually contributes to his patient's recovery, would he not do wrong to follow your arguments, and desist? In like manner, since daily experience proves by sensible facts that the practice of humiliations is a means the most excellent for the health and

---

[396] Sermo XXIX in *Cantica*. PL 183:932b (1854). / "I know not how it is, but it is true nevertheless, that I feel a more tender affection for those whom I have at length restored to spiritual health after and by means of many reprehensions, than for others who have always been strong and able to dispense with such bitter medicine." *Canticles*, 1:345.

sanctification of souls, the best qualified to teach them the spirit of their state, and to inspire them with maxims opposite to those of the world, every objection produced against it is futile, and too weak to convince us.

Be therefore satisfied, my brethren, that this holy practice is as necessary for the preservation of the monastic state as the respiration of the air is for that of the life of our bodies; and that they who are unwilling to admit it, who rise in arms against it, must either have never known, or at least must have forgotten those truths which are so evident and so well recommended by the writings of all the saints. From them we learn,

First, that humility is acquired and preserved by humiliations, as learning is by study.

Second, that the monastic life being nothing less than a school of penance, of humility and abjection, nothing can better coincide with its maxims, spirit, and end than humiliations.

Third, that God is particularly attentive to sanctify His elect whom He has been pleased to establish in the different states of society by a numerous variety of afflictions and humiliations.

Fourth, that monks, being no longer exposed to partake of the humiliations of civil life, have, consequently, need of those which are found in religion; and even of those mortifications which some persons endeavor to banish from the cloister.

Fifth, that to infer that a practice instituted and observed by the saints is no longer good or useful, because things have been changed by length of time, is to condemn the most holy practices of the Church.

Sixth, that it is very difficult to find another cause, or principle, for the repugnance that some persons feel to the practice of humiliations, but self-love; and that all the reasons they employ to combat it are so many colors by which they endeavor to disguise that evil.

Seventh, that in truth, aversion to reprimands springs only from pride, because reprehension is humiliating; and humiliation, according to Saint Gregory, is an insupportable load to a proud mind.[397]

Moreover, the reason why many persons are so hostile to these sentiments is that, for the most part, they form to themselves an idea of regular observances according to the notions they conceive of ecclesiastical communities. They persuade themselves that they ought to be governed by the same rules. There is, however, a great difference between them.

---

[397] "Superbis mentibus pondus grave oneris doctrina humilitatis." Lib. 15, in Job. cap. 35; S. Gregorius, *Moralium*. PL 75:1103(1849) / Saint Gregory the Great, *Morals on the Book of Job*. Vol 2. (Oxford; Parker; 1845), 200.

Although ecclesiastics and monks propose to themselves the same common end, and act by the same principle—that is to say that the glory of God and their own sanctification form the center to which all their actions are directed—and although the spirit of Christ is the spirit that animates them, yet, the ways in which both walk are very different.

Ecclesiastical communities are assemblies, or bodies, composed of persons who having never broken the sacred seal of the holy covenant which they contracted with Jesus Christ, nor defiled the white garment they received at the baptismal font. They have persevered in his love and charity; and preserved unspotted the first innocence with which they were vested by the hands of this heavenly spouse. They are children, who, being always faithful in their love and duty to their father, have no want of the assistance of tears, severe correction, humiliating mortifications or of other such means to appease His anger, because they never provoked Him. Yet it ought not to be forgotten that—from many other considerations— they too are obliged to be more fervent in the practice of humility and penance than other Christians, because, a soft, easy, and undisciplined life is no less unworthy and unbecoming a minister of Jesus Christ than a solitary or a monk.

The Church has, at all times, considered her ministers as a chosen generation, a holy nation, a purchased people, a royal priesthood (1 Pet 2:9). Formerly she would not admit sinners to the employment of her sacred functions. The 11th canon of the Council of Nice, the 33d canon of Saint Basil, [398]the 4th canon of the first Council of Valence, the 9th canon of the first Council of Orleans, and Saint Gregory the Great, in many places demonstrate how exact she was to deprive them of their ministry, when she had sufficient proof that their sins merited such treatment. And though her discipline is now changed in that respect, yet her spirit is still the same, and the Council of Trent expressly declares that those only ought to be invested with the government of churches, and the care of souls, who from their tender years have been exercised in all points of ecclesiastical discipline, and given sufficient proofs of their piety during their whole lives.[399]

---

[398] Epist. 2 ad. Amphil./ The three canonical letters of Basil to Amphilochius, bishop of Iconium, may be found online: https://people.ucalgary.ca/~vandersp/Courses/texts/ cappadoc/basilcep.html#CXCIX (accessed September 8, 2018). They contain several instances of men being deposed from ministry for various sins, for example Canon III of the First Letter: "A deacon who commits fornication after his appointment to the diaconate is to be deposed."

[399] Sess. 6.de reform. Cap. 1. / "Trusting, therefore, that through the mercy of our

Religious congregations, on the contrary, are assemblies of public penitents, who, having been unfaithful to God and provoked Him by their disobedience, presume not to seek any favors from His goodness until by mingling their tears and labors with the blood of their Redeemer, they have satisfied His justice. They are so many prodigal children, who, having forsaken their father's house, have squandered away the goods they had received of Him. That is to say they are Christians, who, having refused to live under the paternal direction of their heavenly Father, and having made a bad use of His graces, find no means to open to themselves the gates of mercy which their ingratitude had closed, but that of placing themselves in the same dispositions as he was, who, considering himself unworthy the rank of a son, requested to be admitted as a hireling (Luke 15:19).

Their hearts deeply penetrated with the enormity of sin, they enter the abodes of penance, there to repair the destructive ruins caused by their insolence and disobedience, and to recover their innocence by the practice of sincere abasements and profound humiliations. According to the expression of Saint Gregory, not being able to take possession of their inheritance by sanctity and innocence like the just, they arm themselves with tears and penance, and endeavor to bear it away by violent conflicts against themselves; the almighty Judge being willing that they should force and do violence to His goodness, and, as it were, compel Him to pardon them.[400]

Some, perhaps, will say, that there are ecclesiastics who are sinners, and monks who are just. I allow it, but as the sinner ceases to be considered as such the moment he is received into the number of the levites, so also, the just man ceases to be considered as a just man so soon as he becomes a monk. As he vests himself with the livery of a sinner, such is he to be esteemed, and no better. He loses his innocence, if I may be allowed the expression, in entering the monastery; like our blessed Lord, who, in some sort, ceased to be considered holy from the moment in which He was pleased to appear under the form and livery of a sinner, not only in

---

Lord and God, and the provident care of His own vicar upon earth, it will surely come to pass that those who are most worthy, and whose previous life and whole career from their early infancy to their riper years, having been laudably passed in the exercises of ecclesiastical discipline, bears testimony in their favour, will be taken unto the government of Churches, according to the venerable ordinances of the Fathers, since it is a burden to be dreaded even by angels . . . ." Buckley, *Trent*, 47.

[400] Gregorius Magnus, *Homiliarum in Evangelia*, Liber I, Homilia XX, PL 76:1169.

the opinion of men, but also before His heavenly Father, who rigorously punished him as such.

The cloister is a prison in which those who have preserved their innocence are leveled with those who have lost it. This was what Saint Bernard taught, when speaking to one of his brethren, he said:

> My son, if you knew how great is the obligation of a monk, you would not eat one morsel of bread without first watering it with your tears; for we shut ourselves up in cloisters for no other purpose but to weep for our own sins, and for those of the people. So that as often as we eat bread, which is the work of their hands, and the fruit of their labors, it may with truth be said, that we eat their sins, in order that we may weep for them, as for our own offenses. [401]

Behold here a portrait of the monastic life; behold the idea that those who embrace it ought to form of it. If they enter it with such dispositions as these, you may be certain, my brethren, that humiliations, so far from seeming a trial too severe, and a chalice too bitter, they will embrace them with ardor; and will esteem those days as lost which shall have passed without finding an occasion to humble themselves. Occupied continually with the view of the eternal confusions prepared for the sinner, they will consider the momentary confusions of this life as so much gain; and holding the portrait of the severe judgments of God before their eyes, they will find nothing but sweetness and mildness in the judgments of men. They will seek no other comfort but those of retracing the outrages and humiliations of an incarnate God in every part of their lives. Thus purifying their hearts from the stains of sin, by the practice of humility, they will be raised to a degree of purity equal to that of angels, according to the language of the saints; and by their humiliations and momentary disgraces, they shall prepare themselves to be one day invited in triumph to the enjoyment of that future glory that shall be revealed in them.

This is what a perfect religious ought to be; this is a true model set before our eyes by the hand of God in the persons of His saints; those are the examples by which we may learn our duties, but which, at the same time, confound our infidelities. For although we are obliged to live in the same perfect abnegation, yet, the last vestige of the sanctity and disengagement of our ancient fathers can be scarcely discovered amidst

---

[401] *Epistola CDXCI*, PL 182:706b (1854).

our multiplied desires and efforts; I should rather say, our slothfulness and degenerate conduct.

Q. 22.—What can be replied to those who say that to reprehend in a forcible manner such faults as are light and uncertain is a sort of fiction, or lie, and that whatever good may be derived from it, can never make such a practice lawful?

A.—We can tell them, my brethren, that our sentiments are the same as those of Saint Augustine, when he said, that he would not tell the smallest untruth, though by so doing he might effect the salvation of all men; but that there is a great difference between considering an action in the ill sense that it may bear, without examining the views and motives of the person who did it; and forcibly reprimanding a religious for an exterior fault, which, though small in itself, yet may be said to be great, when contrasted with the sanctity of God and the perfection of his state; when considered in the effects and consequences of which it may become the cause; and when it is employed as an occasion to discover more concealed offenses.

There is, I say, much difference between this conduct, and that of positively affirming that an action is bad when it is so evidently known to be good that it cannot be disadvantageously explained; when nothing can be found reprehensible in it, whatever way it is viewed; and reprehending a real fault as if it were considerable, though in effect, it is only of small importance. The one would certainly and plainly be to offend against truth and sincerity; a means which a man whose maxims are pure and sound will never adopt: the other is a mode of conduct exempt from any evil; it is useful and even necessary, from which the most extensive advantages may be derived for the direction and government of the cloister, if the superiors know how to employ it with prudence and discretion. This has been recommended by the example of all the ancient monks, and strongly supported by the instructions of Saint Gregory and Saint John Climacus.[402]

The holy doctors, says that great pope, whom we venerate, usually examine the least faults with great exactness so that they may find by these small failings a way to the knowledge of the more interior and considerable. They employ severe reprehensions, in order to pull out the thorns of mortal thought from the hearts of those whom they guide in the paths of perfection; and in this they are influenced by charity. Their severity springs from that pure source, and not from pride and vanity.

In effect, they are ready to die for those whom they seem to afflict even

---

[402] S. Greg. P.1.26.c.5 Moral in Job.,cap. 35.

to death with so much apparent cruelty. Their love and tenderness are preserved in their hearts by the same hand that clothes them with the robe of exterior severity. They are sometimes inflamed when correcting those who are under their care, as if they had expelled every sentiment of peace, while at the same time they possess the lovely virtue of unaltered charity as entire and as perfect as if they had not been moved by the fire of their zeal, and the desire of their inferiors' spiritual interest.

Q. 23.—*Does it not seem that the authority of Saint John Climacus is not of much weight on the present subject, since, being a Greek, he, like the other Fathers of the East, approves of fictions and officious lies?*

A.—It is a fact, my brethren, that many of the Fathers of the East were of that opinion: they taught that it was lawful to employ untruths and fictions, when they were innocent and officious, and when charity was their motive, as Saint Clement of Alexandria says. [403]This opinion prevailed very much in the first ages of the Church. They could not, without difficulty, persuade themselves that to conceal the truth under the veil of fictions and even lies could be evil, when they could by that means procure some good to their neighbor; and there was no doubt concerning an opinion that seemed to be holy in its application, in its effects, and even in its principle.

But Saint Augustine in the West treated that question with so much erudition, diffused so much light on its difficulties, and proved so forcibly that no person can in conscience, in any case, or for the purpose of procuring any good whatsoever employ charitable untruths. His opinion on this subject has been admitted by all those who in succeeding ages were zealous for piety and truth. It may be affirmed, too, that Saint John Climacus, even in the East, was preserved from that error; that though it prevailed very much, yet he may be said to have condemned it; and that God, who had given him to the world as an apostolical doctor, and as a sure guide of souls, would not allow him to be sullied with the least stain, in order that his authority might be more respected, and that the holy rules of an evangelical life might confidently be extracted from his writings, as from pure and wholesome springs.

Amongst the different panegyrics which the eastern Church consecrates to the memory of this great saint concerning the purity of his faith and the excellency of his virtue, one of the principal is that of being favorable to truth. In the prayers which she addresses to him, she sings that his mouth announced the magnificence of the Lord in strains of sincerity and truth;

---

[403] Strom. 1. 7. / Clement of Alexandria, *The Stromata* (Aeterna, 2016)

that he was never found in the darkness of sin; that he served God without blame; that his soul was filled with the unction of truth; that he never was the companion of liars; that by his divine conversation he vanquished all the malice of the spirit of darkness; and that like a man instructed by the Holy Spirit, he was considered as the sure guide and safe leader of solitaries.[404]

But the sentiments of Saint John Climacus himself concerning officious lies will remove every doubt on this subject. Give ear to his own words, by which he both condemns them, and refutes the chief reasons employed by those who endeavor to authorize them, and which they assume from the charity we owe to our neighbor, and from the celebrated example of Rahab. "The liar," says he,

> Alleges as a pretext for his untruth, that he only offends against truth by an officious goodness, and a charitable conduct towards his neighbor. Thus he imagines that to be an act of justice which is the destruction of his own soul. This inventor of fictions and deceits says that in so doing he imitates Rahab, and while he is destroying himself by his lies, he pretends that he is laboring for the salvation of other men.

He adds, in the sequel:

> A soul which is pure, and without malice, knows no more how to lie than a child. As a man whose heart is become gay with wine cannot, though he would, conceal or disguise truth, so, in like manner, he who is divinely inebriated with holy compunction finds it impossible to be guilty of a lie.[405]

Such were his sentiments on this subject; and if he seems on some occasions to approve of some particular fictions, he does it only as the holy scriptures do, where we find Rahab's action praised, not in as much as it was an untruth, but because the motive which she proposed to herself, together with the application and the effects, were holy and charitable. In fine, he could not express himself more clearly on the subject, than by saying, that the love of truth is the source of all virtues.

Q. 24.—Are there not some passages in the works of the same saint, which denote, at least according to appearances, that he

---

[404] Greek menology.

[405] *Scala,* PG 88:855 (1864) / *Ladder,* 132.11.13.14.

approved of the practice of officious lying; and that consequently,
he was not of the opinion which you attribute to him, as may be
seen in the 80th and 82nd articles of his letter to the pastor?

A.—In order to solve your difficulties, my brethren, it is necessary to examine in detail the two passages of which you speak.

In the first, Saint John Climacus writes, that a very wise and judicious superior having a difference to decide between two religious, judged in favor of him who was guilty, because he was weak; and condemned him who was innocent, because he was stronger and more virtuous: the reason why he acted in this manner was lest a great division should take place amongst the brethren if he had observed the rules of strict justice. He took care, however, to inform each, separately, of the motives which regulated his conduct on that occasion; that his object in particular was to apply proper remedies to the wounds of him whom he found really ulcerated, and thus to effect his cure.[406]

To justify Saint Climacus, it will suffice to show some cases in which a superior may, without offending against truth, declare in favor of a religious who is really guilty of some fault. For if that can be done, he will be justified, and you will be obliged to ascribe to his motives the most favorable aspect of which they are susceptible, since it is a principle in the morality of Jesus Christ, and an unalterable rule of charity, that when an action is susceptible of a good interpretation, no person can—without sin—attribute to it an evil one.

Hence, let me suppose, my brethren, that two religious have had some difference or misunderstanding between them; the superior cites them before him; he who has the better cause begins by defending it a little more emphatically than he ought. He even does it with some effervescence and seems to gain some advantage over his brother. At least, he levels his assertions without much reserve. The superior by a wise and charitable discernment judges that this plaintiff wants a little humiliation to smooth his rudeness, and the other being weak, requires a little condescension. Now, let me ask, cannot the superior in such a case assume an air of severity, and, with an irritated voice tell the former that he is less religious, less humble, and less charitable than the other, and even oblige him to withdraw with confusion? Nor do I think, that in such a case, he could be accused either of lies or fictions, since the behavior of him whom he

---

[406] *Ad pastorem*, PG 88:1195a (1864) / *Ladder*, 259..

would have treated in that manner, would have furnished sufficient cause for such a reprehension.

Nevertheless, the whole proceeding would prove that he acted in favor of the one who had been the real offender in the cause. But he commits no injustice, because he says nothing of the principal affair. He does nothing more than remit the decision thereof to another time, which is evident by the manner in which he leaves the essential part of the question. He does not examine the reasons that each party may have to adduce; he enters into no examination of the misunderstanding; nor does he give either the merit he may have deserved; and on the whole, he is not obliged to give his brethren any reasons for his conduct, as is expressly declared in the 80th article of which we are speaking. This is quite sufficient to prove that the doctrine of Saint John Climacus is not a source from whence the supposed evil consequences can be derived. Therefore, by the supposition I proposed, you can only conclude that the saint acted according to the wisdom of the superior of whom we speak, when he decided precisely in the same manner.

In the 82d article he says take notice of those amongst your brethren who are more virtuous and strong; humble them in the presence of the weak, though they may have done nothing that deserves humiliation; that by the remedy you thus seem to apply to the apparent indisposition of those who are in health, you may heal the real infirmities of those who are sick; and by this means, raise them to a state of strength and vigor.[407]

These words, being properly understood, admit of no difficulty. Saint John says nothing more than what Saint Bernard and Saint Teresa say on this subject; nothing more, in a word, than what all those say who have applied themselves as they ought to the good government of the cloister, though they may have expressed themselves in different terms. As they knew that nothing was more useful than good example, nothing more conducive to raise souls that are languid in the paths of virtue than to exercise others who have made progress therein, and to do it before their eyes; so do they require that the strong be mortified and humbled even when they do not deserve it, when their actions are not only good, but holy, in order that the weak may be thus taught by the most convincing lessons. This is what Saint Bernard would insinuate, when he says, speaking to his brethren, that they ought to think themselves happy when they are reprehended for those actions which would procure them glory before

---

[407] *Ad pastorem*, PG 88:1195a (1864) / *Ladder*, 259.80.

men, if they had performed them in the world.[408] This is what Saint Teresa practiced, when she reprehended her spiritual daughters for actions which they performed with great regularity and exactitude, as we read in her life.

If you find it difficult to conceive how that can be done, without offending against sincerity and truth; it is easy to answer, as I have already said, that it can be done by reprehending some defective circumstance which may be found in the good action, or by recollecting some defect of a prior date, or by attributing an unfavorable motive to such actions as are indifferent in themselves, but which are susceptible of such interpretations; or, again, by making some natural failing, some disposition, which, if neglected, might produce disagreeable consequences; in brief, by many other ways which ingenious charity will never fail to suggest when the superior applies himself studiously to promote the spiritual interest of those whom Divine Providence has committed to his care.

In all these cases, humiliations may be employed without danger of sinning against truth, or without any real cause being found in him who is the object of the humiliation. But, at the same time, whatever the fault may be, if it be considered in its principle and in its consequences, nothing will be found excessive in this manner of proceeding. Hence, it appears evident that nothing can be deduced from the above passages that can tarnish the purity of the doctrine attributed to Saint John Climacus, since it can bear an explanation so favorable, so innocent, and so useful to piety; and, moreover, when it is remembered that in such a case no one can attach an unfavorable meaning to it without offending against charity.

If any person should insist on those words of Saint Climacus: "In order that by the remedies you seem to apply to the supposed infirmities, you may effectually heal the real maladies,"[409] it may be answered, according to the principles laid down by Saint Augustine:

A fiction employed only to signify a thing that really exists, and not that which does not exist, is not a fiction, but a sign, and contains neither the malignity nor the falsity of a lie. The patriarchs of the Old Testament, used fictions of this kind, that is to say, actions which seemed fictions; but, as they were only mysterious expressions and figurative words, they neither offended against truth nor sincerity by them (Gen 20, 22 and 27).

---

[408] Sermo IV, in *In Psalmum XC, Qui Habitat*, PL 183:193c (1854).

[409] *Ad pastorem*, PG 88:1195 (1864). / *Ladder*, 259.

It may be prescribed, by way of preservative, to a man in good health not to expose himself to the heat of the sun nor to the cold of the night, for the sole purpose of persuading another, who, though really sick, cannot be induced to use remedies, or to observe any rule of life by reason of the great repugnance he feels to subordination; and thus induce him to conclude that if those who are in good health use remedies, it is quite unreasonable that those who are sick should pretend to be dispensed from them. Now it would be wrong to conclude, that truth would be violated by such a mode of conduct.

This was precisely Saint Augustine's opinion when he said, that a wise mother seeing her child weary, and still persuading himself that he can go without her assistance, sits down, saying, that she is fatigued, in order to persuade the child that he is himself weary, and to invite him to her; and having thus allured him, to seek repose on her bosom, she immediately rises up, taking the child in her arms, and continues to carry him the rest of the way.

Now here the case is just the same. There is question of a spiritual cure. Saint John Climacus attempted nothing more than to demonstrate the method of teaching those souls who are really infirm in what manner their disorders are to be treated, by applying the same remedies which are necessary for the recovery of the weak and infirm, to those who are strong and sound.

This impels them to conclude that if humiliations are necessary for those whom they behold so far advanced in perfection, they must, of course, be still more necessary for themselves, who as yet have acquired no virtue in its perfection. It should be remarked that though the above mode of prescribing remedies, which we have supposed to have no real infirmity for its immediate object—since we suppose that the man to whom it directly applies to be in good health—nevertheless, the prescription may be considered good, and may serve, in effect, either as a means to diminish those humors the redundancy of which might become the cause of sickness; or to fortify health against the return of a malady already past; or, as a relief for some present indisposition; or, in fine, as a preservative against future attacks.

In like manner, humiliations, in all the cases which we have already supposed, can be justified by proper motives, either from the good of him to whom they are directed, as for the correction of some defective circumstance, for past faults, or natural imperfections, or at least, as a preservative against some inconvenience for which there may be sufficient reason to fear, or for the profit of someone present. And if Saint John Climacus be silent as to these circumstances, it must be attributed to their insignificance, or that having in view only the principle which he desired to establish, he took no notice of these details.

It is unnecessary to say that the terms *supposed* and *apparent* infirmities, do not denote fictions; or, that the words persons in good health, destroy the necessity of humiliations. I have been supposing, because Saint John Climacus neither understood, nor wished to express anything more, by apparent infirmities, than small faults, and light improprieties, when compared with the great and considerable evils, the cure of which he proposes as the principal object. By the expression, *persons in good health*, he indeed means perfect souls; but we must allow, that virtue is never pure in this life. It is always accompanied with weakness and imperfections, which, being considered in themselves abstractedly, may lawfully be employed as a sufficient reason to refuse the epithet of innocent to the person in whom they are found.

Besides, if they are considered in their sources, which are concupiscence and pride, or in the consequences of which they may be productive were they not prevented by a particular favor of God, they will be found so considerably deformed, and present such real subjects of fear, that they may be always regarded as proper objects on whom humiliations may be lawfully exercised. These are the evils for which the saints accused themselves as sinners, and were persuaded that they could do so without lies or fictions. This is what forced them to sigh and weep. This is what frequently armed them with a holy indignation against themselves. In a word, this is what they chastised in themselves by such rigorous austerities, and severe penances.

I thought it necessary, my brethren, to unfold to your view the real sentiments of Saint John Climacus, in order that having proved their entire purity, and dispelled every vapor and shadow of suspicion from your minds, you may without the least difficulty embrace the means which are prescribed by the instructions of that perfect servant of God, that second Basil, that solitary, whose mortification was consummate, that incomparable man, one of the greatest and most holy saints that ever flourished in the Church of Christ, that faithful interpreter of the Holy Spirit, whose words may be compared to so many fiery darts, which pierce the soul with heat and light.

13 |ON THE MEDITATION OF DEATH

13

ON THE MEDITATION OF DEATH

QUESTION 1.—*Is the thought of death a thing very useful and necessary for religious persons?*

ANSWER.—The reason why people of the world are not willing to think on death is because they are not satisfied to die. Bound to the earth by so many chains and engagements, they think of everything except that which is most important to think about.

If they enjoy undisturbed the goods of fortune, they find nothing but horror in the thoughts of that moment which is to separate them from what they love, as the word of God declares: "O! death, how bitter is thy remembrance to a man having peace in his possessions!"(Ecclesiastic. 41:1) If their affairs be in a bad state, they desire to live to bring them to a better condition. If they enjoy strong and vigorous health, they imagine they are never to die. If, on the contrary, they are weak and infirm, they flatter themselves with the hopes of a future recovery. In fine, they whose faith is entirely extinct, and consequently, who are concerned only about present things, discover in death nothing but dismal separations and cruel privations.

Even those who preserve some sparks of this faith, yet, by not drawing any consolation from the promises made by Jesus Christ to Christians of a lively faith; and perceiving nothing in their lives but matter of fear and apprehension of death, and of its consequences; I say, even those exert all their faculties and abilities to expel its thoughts and remembrance from their hearts.

But true religious, who are no longer of the world, who have no connection with the transitory affairs of this life, who live by faith and in the hope of the good things to come, such as these not only discover nothing at the close of life that can give them the least anxiety, but, on the contrary, their most delightful consolation consists in the frequent meditation of death. Nothing can be better applied to these men, so disengaged from all sensible things, than that which a father of the primitive age said of Christians in general: that they were a certain race of men, always ready and disposed to die.[410] Because they have this thought imprinted in their minds, and the desire of death deeply engraven in their hearts, they consider it as the end of their sorrows and the beginning of their eternal joys. They are a people who are distinguished by their contempt of life, and are never more satisfied than when they are about to lose it.

That which afflicts others comforts them. These divine men—knowing that by baptism they were separated from the world almost as soon as they came into it—are exceedingly pleased when death takes them by the hand and separates them eternally from it. In effect, if those who fear death are as yet unacquainted with the first principles of Christianity, as Saint Cyprian says, [411]and if that weakness be found only in persons who are engaged in the delights of a worldly life, and bound fast in the chains of false, deceitful, and enchanting pleasures, it must necessarily follow that those who have renounced the world, and who despise all its goods and pleasures, who love nothing but invisible riches and joys which can be obtained only by the loss of the present life, it is, I say, a necessary consequence that such persons should find their chief happiness and principal delight in the frequent meditation of death, which alone will put an end to all their miseries, and introduce them to the enjoyment of eternal felicity.

Saint Chrysostom speaks in the following manner of solitaries:

> When anyone among them is arrived to the final period of life, nothing resounds in the tabernacles of the just but cries of joy and exultation. No mourning nor weeping is heard in the sacred assembly of the saints; no doleful lamentations, nor sad complaints, disturb those happy dwellings. They indeed die because they are not immortal, but they are far from considering their dissolution as a death. They accompany the remains of those who depart from them with the joyful sounds of sacred hymns and canticles. They regard as a solemn pomp and triumph what others esteem as a funeral ceremony. They are informed that some one among them has

---

[410] Tertullianus, De Spectaculis, PL 1:630-631.

[411] S. Cyprianus, *De Mortalitate,* PL 4:581 (1844)./ St. Cyprian. "On Mortality." In *Fathers of the Third Century: Hippolytus, Cyprian, Novatian,* (ANF 5:469).

terminated his combat. They are consoled, and rejoice, and no one presumes to say such a one is dead, but, such a one has finished his course. Thus, all is thanksgiving and jubilation; every one aspiring after the same happy moment; each individual desiring to depart from the field of battle in the same manner, to behold his labors crowned, and at length, to see and enjoy the glorious presence of our amiable Lord and Redeemer, Jesus Christ.[412]

"The children of darkness," says Saint Bernard, "Sleep during the night, but you, my brethren, being children of light, encourage yourselves to watch in expectation of that last day which shall be to you the dawn of eternal light."[413]

"Death will come," says the same saint,

But its aspect will not be terrifying. It will be nothing more than a sweet sleep for the children of love; it will introduce them to the possession of the inheritance prepared for them by God before the foundation of the world; it will be the beginning of their eternal repose—the ladder by which they shall ascend the holy mount, and the entrance of that admirable tabernacle, which has not been erected by the hands of men but by the wisdom of God. Let us animate ourselves with a holy joy so that we may dispel this fatal drowsiness of the world. Let worldlings close their eyes to the good things we hope for, and place all their satisfactions in the enjoyment of momentary pleasures. They have no more to expect, since the end of life will disclose to them a frightful scene of horror. Their exit shall be filled with sadness, and the glory that shall accompany the great God, whom we serve, shall overwhelm them with never-ending confusion on that formidable day. As we have no part in their blindness and insensibility, my brethren, let us raise our eyes to heaven, from whence we expect our help shall come. Let us continually beseech our Lord to break our chains, and quickly call us to the possession of that land whose beauty, riches, and excellence are infinite. Let us sing at the prospect of that happy moment,

---

[412] Joannes Chrysostomus, *Homiliae XVIII in Epistolam primam ad Timotheum*, PG 62:577 (1860) / "On the First Epistle of St. Paul the Apostle to Timothy. " In *Saint Chrysostom: Homilies on Galatians, Ephesians, Philippians, Colossians, Thessalonians, Timothy, Titus, and Philemon. (NPNF1/13:457)

[413] *Sermo XXVIII,* PL 183:619 (1854).

and praise the Lord for having promised us that He will not leave the just in hell, nor suffer His holy one to see corruption (Ps. 15:10).[414]

The saints, my brethren, thought the meditation of death so profitable that they recommended it to religious persons in a most particular manner, as a thing that ought to be their most accustomed employment.

Saint Ephrem exhorts monks to preserve a continual remembrance of death.[415]

Saint Benedict requires, that his disciples should always keep the thoughts of death present to their minds, and never lose sight of that important moment.[416]

Saint Bernard tells us that monks formerly built their monasteries in unwholesome places, in order that being frequently sick, they might be induced to meditate continually on death.[417]

Saint John Climacus says that as bread is the most necessary of all food, so is the meditation of death the most necessary of all spiritual practices.[418] It makes those who live in community embrace penitential exercises and find their chief delight in humiliations and contempt. As to solitaries, who live separated from the noise and tumult of the world, it produces in them an entire disengagement and an exact vigilance over all their thoughts.

Q. 2.—*Tell us more in detail, what are the advantages which are found in the meditation of death.*

A.—The first is, it defends the innocence of the soul, and preserves it from being defiled with the filth of sin. The thought of death excites those who have had the misfortune to fall into that abyss to implore His assistance who alone can deliver them. It animates others to resist courageously the temptations of the flesh, and to disarm the efforts of their spiritual enemies with such strength, that it may be said, that the heart which is penetrated with the thought of death, is, in the strongest and most violent temptations, what a rock is in the midst of a furious tempest. This is what we learn from the Holy Spirit who tells us in the sacred oracles

---

[414] "Manet enim eos horror in exitu, dolor in transitu, pudor in conspectu gloriae magni Dei." Sermo XXVIII, in *Sermones de Diversis,* PL 183:619a (1854).

[415] S. Ephraem Syri, *Opera Omnia* (Antwerp: Keerbergium, 1619), 463.

[416] *RB* 4:47

[417] "Sancti enim patres, majores nostri, valles humidas et declives monasteriis exstruendis indagabant, ut saepe infirmi monachi, et mortem ante oculos habentes, securi non viverent" PL 182:706B (1854).

[418] *Scala,* PG 88:794 (1864) / *Ladder,* 108.4.

that the most effectual means to avoid sin is to be always mindful of our last end. In all thy works remember thy last end, and thou shalt never sin (Ecclesiastic. 7:40).

For it is certain that it is impossible to commit an evil action when a man considers himself on the point of losing its fruit and receiving the punishment due to it. No one can be so bold and decided as to offend His Divine Majesty when he considers that justice has raised His arm, and that He is ready to strike, and that the same moment that beholds the crime completed may be the witness of the pain inflicted. Again, as no man— without being in a state of the most wretched delirium—would labor to amass great treasures were he convinced that he would lose them as soon as collected, so it is no less true that a religious being always mindful that the moment he becomes unfaithful to God by violating the promises by which he has consecrated himself to His love, may be the instant of his chastisement and that while beholding the pleasure which he expected from his crime vanish from his sight, he would have instead the heart-rending view of a glorious crown eternally lost. Certain it is that being impressed with such sentiments as these he will not easily consent to sin, nor expose himself to such imminent danger.

And as he has, according to the essential principles of his state, broken the bonds by which he was formerly bound, and renounced all worldly engagements for the love of Christ, so he ought to fear nothing more than to renew his former connections, or to link himself again in his primitive chains. Frequent meditation on death is of all others the most effectual preservative from such a misfortune, for by it he will be always persuaded that he is bound to maintain his ground against his enemies, and to persevere in this holy separation without having any commerce with the world from which he is divorced, a disposition so necessary in every religious that without it no member of the cloister can pretend to live in innocence, or attain to the perfection of his holy state. It was this consideration that induced a solitary of Mount Corel to answer all the questions which were proposed to him by the brethren at the moment of his death in these few words: "Pardon me, my brethren, if I answer nothing to all your demands, but this, that he who has the thoughts of death deeply engraven in his mind will never sin."

The second effect that the meditation of death produces in a religious is the entire divesture of his heart from all the remnants of his former affection to created things; and a determined resolution of his will against anything new of that nature. Our Divine Redeemer has been pleased to employ this reason to confound the folly of those who place their affections on earthly things, telling them that death is prepared to rob them of all they have collected with so much solicitude; and that in a short time all their pain and labor will be unprofitable (Luke 12:20).

The reason why men are hurried on, with so much ardor, to raise magnificent houses, to seek elevated stations and abundant riches, is no other than their thirst after pleasures and sensual delights. The hope of a long enjoyment of these things influences all their actions and desires; but let them be once persuaded that all their labors will become abortive, that all their diligence will be to no purpose, that death will quickly strip them of all they possess and it is certain that they will cease so to act, or rather that they will begin to labor for those possessions which are beyond the reach of that inexorable deprivation.

Thus, my brethren, a religious who preserves the lively and continual thought of death will view all things present in the same light as if they were already passed. He will consider himself as dead among the living, or rather as living among the dead (Luke 24:5). And so far from contracting any new alliances with creatures, he will view them all with the same eye of indifference: life, death, sickness, health, rest, labor, shame, glory, praise, or contempt, will make no more impression on him, than if he were impassible. He will be like the statue of that ancient solitary, which was neither moved with injuries nor with praises.[419]

And if by the effect of the frailty inseparable from the condition of all men, while in this mortal life, his heart should become heavy, or fix its affection on any of those things which it ought not to love, he will rise immediately with indignation against himself, and level this reproach against his soul: "This night they require thy soul of thee" (Luke 12:20). O my soul, of what are you thinking? Have you forgotten where you are, or what things they are with which you are occupied? You are on the point of being summoned before the tribunal of Him who prohibits you the

---

[419] In actionibus SS. Patrum. / Abba Anoub threw stones at the face of the statue and in the evening he said to it, 'Forgive me.' During the whole week he did this. On Saturday Abraham they came together and Abba Poemen said to Abba Anoub, 'Abba, I have seen you during the whole week throwing stones at the face of the statue and kneeling to ask it to forgive you. Does a believer act thus?' The old man answered him, 'I did this for your sake. When you saw me throwing stones at the face of the statue, did it speak, or did it become angry?' Abba Poemen said, 'No.' 'Or again, when I bent down in penitence, was it moved, and did it say, "I will not forgive you?"' Again Abba Poemen answered 'No.' Then the old man resumed, 'Now we are seven brethren; if you wish us to live together, let us be like this statue, which is not moved whether one beats it or whether one flatters it.'" *Sayings of the Desert Fathers,* trans. Benedicta Ward, S.L.G. (Kalamazoo: Cistercian, 1975), 32.

enjoyment of them. Do you not know that you are no longer allowed to make them your own, and that they are no longer worthy of you; that you must forsake them the moment you imagine that you have them in your hand, and fall for eternity into His hands, whom you shall have so ungratefully forsaken for the love of these?

A third advantage which is found in the meditation of death is that in separating our affections from the things of the earth, it opens a passage to the love of God and to the things of heaven. It makes the heart insensible to the one and tender to the other. And in proportion as it destroys in us the love of the world, it establishes in its place the delightful reign of divine love. The reason why we are so little affected to eternal goods, and so insensible to the felicity which our Lord has promised, is because we consider them as things far distant. The supposed interval which separates us from them diminishes them so much in our minds that we esteem nothing comparable to the labors to be endured for their acquisition. In vain are the goods and evils of a future state unfolded to the consideration of unthinking men, because they are so accustomed to be directed by sense alone that when things are not susceptible of being investigated thereby, they know not how to value them; and at most they only esteem them as doubtful events.

But, my brethren, the serious thought of death destroys the illusion. The true religious, who impresses it deeply on his mind, has the eternity of God continually before his eyes. As he considers his life only as a moment, that this moment alone separates him from that unbounded ocean of all good, he lives in a constant expectation that his Lord will summon him at every instant, and unite him to the glorious society of His saints. His Savior is the only object of his desires, and the principal delight of his soul. He considers Him as the source of all his happiness, and holds himself always ready to be invited to His enjoyments. The gratitude with which he ought to be filled for the innumerable graces he has already received from His heavenly Father, and for those he is to receive, occupy all his thoughts. The infinite majesty of his God, the immortality of His kingdom, the glory of which will be as permanent as the eternity of its duration form the subjects of his uninterrupted meditations, as Saint John Climacus says.[420]

He reflects on the ardent zeal with which the martyrs were inflamed, and on that invisible witness of all his actions, who never turns aside the eyes of His mercy from him, according to these words of the royal prophet: "I have placed the Lord always in my sight, for He is at my right hand lest I

---

[420] *Scala*, PG 88:795 (1864) / *Ladder*, 109.15.

should be troubled, and removed from the term to which I tend"(Ps 15:8). He contemplates those blessed spirits, the holy angels, who surround the throne of God. Let us add, my brethren, that he salutes the moment of his exit from this world, which, according to the hope he has laid up in his bosom, he considers as the beginning of his eternal triumph and exultation.

We may enumerate compunction of heart among the advantages arising from the meditation on death, and as, in effect, the fourth advantage of that salutary exercise. As it unmasks the two faces of eternity, by placing its unchangeable goods and evils before us, it must, consequently, make different impressions on our minds; and the ideas which are thus formed in us, of the mercies of God, must be tempered by the terrific view of His judgments. Thus a religious, who during his life frequents the school of pious meditation on death, reflects on all the circumstances with which it is to be attended.

He beholds himself standing, as it were, before the dread tribunal of Jesus Christ, who is about to decide his lot for ever. He considers the account he must give to this awful Majesty, of His image, which He imprinted on his soul by creation, restored by baptism, and re-impressed by the grace of vocation to a religious state. He considers the excellence of his profession, and the disproportion of his works. He beholds the almost infinite number of his sins, of which he is not sensible in detail, but which, collectively, appear like mountains: that multitude of unprofitable words, those crowds of distractions and idle thoughts—not one of which escapes the knowledge and justice of God.

He views his best actions in the light of the sanctity of the Lord and finds them similar to defiled linen, as the prophet expresses it (Isa 64:6). All that he ever said, did, or thought contrary to the sanctity of his profession, and to the responsibility of his duties, are exposed before his eyes. He represents to himself innumerable troops of devils, who falsely accuse him of crimes and faults that he never committed. He represents to himself those devouring flames, those bottomless abysses, those frightful darknesses, those obscure descents just receiving the unhappy victims of divine vengeance.

Impressed with the idea of such terrifying objects, the reflecting religious enters into a serious examination of his whole life. And if he discover that it is not entirely conformable to the sanctity of his state, he feels penetrated with a fear that fills his whole soul; and God beholding him with an eye of pity, inspires him with the resolution of entering on a more holy and better regulated way.

But if his life has been an exact accomplishment of all his duties, if he has been faithful to his promises, the meditation of death, so far from exciting any confusion in his soul, serves only to console him, and to animate his courage. All the favors he has received from the goodness of his Redeemer present themselves, ready to fortify his mind and to strengthen his faith and hope. He takes refuge under the wings of that paternal Providence, the power of which he has so often experienced.

His heart is inflamed with love for so much goodness, and stung with remorse for having offended Him so often. His sorrow is continual, and his eyes become fountains from whence unceasing tears in abundance flow. His dwelling, the witness of his sighs, becomes his cherished abode; and though he mingles his drink with weeping, night and day, yet he may say with truth that the Lord changes his sorrow and grief into consolation and joy (Ps 29:12); for his soul being refreshed and purified by his abundant tears produces nothing but thoughts of peace, gratitude, and benediction. She exclaims, in ecstatic transports: "Ah! yes, O my sweet Lord! thou alone art my strong protector, thou alone will deliver me from all my enemies, and from those who hate me" (Ps 17:19-21, 48).

In fine, a fifth advantage arising from meditation on death is that a religious soul finds therein the most powerful motives to comfort him, during his long exile, amidst the afflictions which are the portion of all who live piously in this valley of tears. Through this medium he beholds the face of this earth deformed with sin, he beholds men united in a holy society by some exterior bonds, who, by the whole tenor of their conduct disavow what they profess. Concupiscence is the soul of their actions, and instead of exemplifying those marks by which our Lord's disciples are to be known, their works exhibit nothing but the stamp and character of their passions. They seldom act but to promote their own interest, their pleasure, or their ambition. Though the will of Jesus Christ ought to govern all they do, yet His will is not found in anything they perform. It seems that—if we judge of the manner in which they live—to be a Christian it is sufficient to have only the name.

If he turns to the consideration of those places, which, according to the designs of God, and the sanctity of their institution, ought to be so many asylums, where piety, when persecuted by the injustice of men, ought to find refuge, he discovers that disorder has found entrance there, as well as in other states. He discovers moreover that the simplicity, piety, charity, discipline, or maxims of the saints are no longer to be found in them; that the spirit of Jesus Christ, who formed them, has retired from those abodes of disunion; that their inhabitants are walking in ways different from His; and that things have arrived to such a degree of excess, that they who are thus acting, though ashamed of their irregularities, are yet unwilling to forsake them, and even seek reasons to approve and defend them. This view awakens all his zeal; his love for his Lord and Master makes him sigh; beholding His Divine Majesty offended by such an universal conspiracy, his soul plunges into a sea of grief and affliction.

Returning into himself, he not only can find nothing there to

satisfy him, but discovers in every object matter of increased affliction; he beholds in the midst of his soul a living source of every evil, which indeed he does not suffer to flow, but which undoubtedly would exceed all bounds if God did not preserve him with particular care. He discovers a frightful multitude of different passions, which, being only chained up by the bonds of grace, but not destroyed, are like so many roaring lions who continually menace his most holy resolutions. He feels the law of sin in his members continually rebelling against the law of reason; and what most afflicts him is that he never resists with such fidelity, as to escape without doing or permitting something that offends the sanctity of his Creator, against whom he ought not to do anything displeasing. Thus he fears lest his multiplied infidelities should weary the patience of his Redeemer, close the gates of his mercy, and exclude him from the happy effects of his usual protection.

A religious impressed with all these considerations, beholds nothing here below sufficient to console him. Public evils, his own miseries, the injuries done to Jesus Christ, his loving Savior, by an almost universal disobedience, overwhelms and plunges him into an abyss of sorrow. But so soon as he calls in the consideration of death to his assistance, he beholds at the end of life the term of his grief. He learns that in ceasing to live he shall also cease to be unhappy; his sorrow is soothed, his soul is fortified; he is, as Saint Augustine says, like a traveler who beholding himself near the end of his journey, comforts himself in the midst of the inconveniences he finds; or, as a combatant, who supports his labors and wounds, hoping that each moment may terminate the combat, and present him the victorious crown.

In fine, my brethren, the helps and advantages that a religious soul may derive from the frequent meditation of death are so great and numerous, that it is not possible to give you an adequate idea of them; and though I might have told you that it expels all sloth, fixes the inconstancy of the soul, prevents the dissipation of the mind, makes penance become agreeable, destroys the asperity of humiliations and contempts; that it kills intemperance, produces a disengagement from all earthly things, excites more fervor in prayer, inspires pious sentiments, preserves devotion; in a word, that, according to Saint John Climacus, all the virtues are its daughters; I could not express more to you than what the saints have taught us concerning it. But, Oh! how happy are those religious, who have no need of studying those truths in books, but have learned them by their own experience.

14 | *ON THE JUDGMENTS OF GOD*

14

ON THE JUDGMENTS OF GOD

QUESTION 1.— *Ought a religious to make the consideration of the judgments of God, one of his usual subjects of meditation ?*

ANSWER.—It would be difficult to meditate on death so frequently, as I have endeavored to inculcate in the preceding chapter, without being equally attentive in meditating on the judgments of God—this being the inevitable consequence of death. They are events so closely united to one another that we ought not to separate them in our thoughts. Death has nothing so closely attendant at its gate as judgment. To die, and to be judged, may be said to be one and the same thing. The thoughts on death would be unfruitful, if they were not united to those on judgment. Men usually say that the consequences of death, the things of which it is the harbinger, give them much more concern than death itself; that is to say that they are not afraid to die, but that they are terrified at the appalling scrutiny of judgment.

Saint Augustine, speaking to his flock, said that they ought to entertain themselves continually with the judgments of God.[421] That is, that they ought to reflect on that subject, since we speak of a subject, only that they who hear may reflect upon it. Jesus Christ admonishes us to think on this great affair at all times: "Watch ye, therefore, for you know not the day nor the hour" (Matt 25:13); and in effect, that day and hour are so terrible, and the affair that shall be then decided is so important, that we cannot be sufficiently astonished (being convinced that it must assuredly happen) how we can forget it and think of anything else? Let a man be told that his house is ready to fall, that he may thereby lose his life any moment, and

---

[421] In Psalmum CXLVII Enarratio Sermo ad Populum, PL 37:1845-1937 (1845).

he will not hesitate an instant to depart from it. And is it not astonishing, that seeing himself threatened with the greatest of all misfortunes, with a destruction of which the fall of a house is not even a shadow, that he may become the victim of irrecoverable ruin every moment; he yet lives on in security, without making the least reflection on it, as if there were nothing to be feared!

This man beholds so many unfortunate accidents, so many sudden deaths, by which great numbers of persons are hurried out of life. And though he ought to consider all such events as so many effects of the secret judgment issuing from the tribunal of the great Arbiter of life, yet he is insensible. They make no impression on him, his obduracy resists all. So much so, that beholding his conduct, and the security in which he seems to live, one would think that the Apostle excepted him when he said that it is decreed for all men to die, and that we must all appear before the tribunal of Christ in order to receive either the reward of the good, or the punishment of the evil, that we shall have done during life (2 Cor 5:10).

The saints, who were no less careful to preserve them selves from this mortal lethargy, than they were solicitous to deter others from falling into it, were very attentive to keep the remembrance of the last judgment constantly in their minds; they have left us useful instructions on that subject, together with some lively descriptions of its eventful consequences.

Saint Ephrem says, "Judgment ought to be the ordinary subject of the conversation and entertainment of monks. In whatever place you may be," says that great saint,

> Whether on a journey, or at table, or in bed, think continually on the judg-
> ment to come, and the arrival of the just Judge. Preserve the sentiment
> thereof deeply engraved in your hearts. Ask one another, what shall that
> exterior darkness be; that fire, which is never extinguished; that worm,
> which never dies; that gnashing of teeth. In what manner those rivers of
> fire shall inflame, and set the whole world in a blaze, and purge it of its
> crimes! How the heavens shall roll, like the velocity of parchment when
> it folds. The stars shall fall, like the leaves of trees in autumn; the sun
> and the moon shall become dark: how the Judge shall descend, glittering
> in His robes of light; how His coming shall be preceded by an universal
> convulsion of all nature. What shall be the attendants of His dreadful tri-
> bunal; earthquakes, the frightful sound of trumpets, the bursting open of
> graves: in what manner the dead shall awake from their sleep; the reunion
> of souls with their bodies: in brief, how the saints shall be taken up into
> the air, to meet Jesus Christ; and how the wicked, and those who shall

have neglected the care of their salvation, shall be excluded for ever from His heavenly kingdom.[422]

The words spoken by the holy abbot Evagrius to his disciples, are not less worthy of notice:

Recall your thoughts, my brethren, and enter into yourselves. Place your-selves in spirit on the bed of death. It is a proper means to mortify your senses. Think what a dreadful misfortune it is to be damned. Represent to yourselves that insupportable silence, those continual fears, those interior heart-rending combats, those piercing sorrows, that cruel expectation of being still more miserable, and those bitter tears which never diminish, nor cease to flow. Call to mind also the day of the general resurrection; represent to yourselves that terrible and dreadful day of judgment. Think what confusion will overwhelm sinners, when they shall behold Jesus Christ, in the presence of all the angels, and all mankind. Consider, that this confusion will be succeeded by an eternal fire, by remorse of con-science, which, like an immortal worm, shall gnaw them without inter-mission, by the darkness of the infernal abyss, by gnashing of teeth, and by every species of torments, not to be conceived.[423]

I cannot omit uniting to this important lesson the sentiments of a great solitary, who, having heard the different dispositions in which they who spoke before him had passed their retreat, said:

For my part, I consider myself, wherever I am, and to whatever place I go, as entirely surrounded with my sins; for which reason, I consider myself as deserving nothing but hell, and I reproach myself in this manner: Begone, wretch, with those whose company you should have kept long since, and whose number you may soon augment. There I behold, with the interior eyes of my mind, continual weeping, accompanied with sighs, gnashing of teeth, and inconceivable alarms. I behold a fiery sea without bounds, the burning waves of which rise in great swells, and seem to extend their portending fury to the heavens, and reduce to ashes all they meet. I behold an innumerable company of men cast into this sea by the devils, whose united howlings are so terrible, that nothing within the whole sphere of creation can be imagined like them: their crimes forcing the mercy of God

---

[422] S. Ephraem Syri, *Opera Omnia* (Antwerp: Keerbergium, 1619), 463.

[423] Pelag [dR has "Paschase"]. Diac. tit. 3.

to fly from them. I then cast myself on the ground; I cover my head with dust, and beseech the Lord never to suffer me to fall into those horrible torments. I deplore the misfortune of unhappy men, who, without considering those excessive torments which await them in a future life, presume to entertain themselves with any other objects in this. I employ all my faculties in considering them; the punishments and afflictions with which the justice of God threatens to chastise our ingratitude are always before my eyes. I acknowledge myself unworthy to be supported by the earth on which I walk, or that I should appear in the sight of heaven; and I apply to myself these words of the royal prophet: Tears have been my bread day and night (Ps 41:4).

Saint Benedict teaches us in his rule, that a monk ought to keep the fear of the Lord continually before his eyes, and never forget the thoughts of his future judgments; that these words of the humble publican, ought to dwell always in his heart and mouth: "Lord, I am not worthy to raise my eyes to heaven" (Luke 18:13).

Saint Bernard comprises in a few words all that many saints have said on this subject. "I fear," says he,

> To behold the countenance of that Judge, capable to make even the angels tremble; I fear that Almighty God; I fear the effects of His fury; I fear the crash of the world, when about to be overturned; that conflagration of the elements; that frightful tempest; that cry of the archangel; that sharp and terrible word. I tremble when I think on the teeth of that infernal monster, on the gulf of the dreadful abyss, on those hungry lions, ready to devour their prey. I am filled with horror when I consider that never-dying worm that shall gnaw the wicked; that fire that shall burn them; the sulphurous stench and vapor that shall stifle them; those impetuous winds and exterior darknesses! Who will give water to my head and a fountain of tears to my eyes, that I may prevent those eternal weepings, those horrible gnashings of teeth, those cruel fetters, and the weight of those chains, which will crush them, bind them, and burn them, without consuming them.[424]

Moreover, it is not enough to tell you that meditation on the judgments of God is holy, that it is useful and proper for you. You must be persuaded that it is moreover necessary for you, that you ought to rank it in the number of your indispensable occupations, not only because this exercise

---

[424] Sermo XVI, in *Cantica*, PL 183:852a (1879). / *Canticles*, 1:156-57.

is recommended by the saints, but because it is a thing essential to your state. By your condition you are professed penitents, and a penitent is a man who has only one affair in this world, which is to prepare himself to appear before the judgment seat of Jesus Christ, that by purifying his soul in the tears and labors of penance, he may escape the severity due to his sins.

Hence, let the meditation on this terrible, but salutary subject be one of your favorite employments; for, by that means, you will make it favorable to yourselves. Reflect, my brethren, on the justice of God, while you are now in the body; but do it so effectually, that you may find mercy when you are summoned to leave these earthly tabernacles. Think on it in the manner that He prescribes, that is to say, in watching over yourselves with such care that nothing may escape you that may provoke the anger of your Judge rather than appease Him. Pray with such fervor that you may compel Him to deliver you from these dreadful evils which continually threaten all, who, while they live in the flesh, are always in suspense between hope and fear. Watch ye, therefore, praying at all times, that you may be accounted worthy to escape all these things that are to come, and to stand before the Son of Man (Luke 21:36).

Q. 2.—*Is it not to be feared, that the view of the judgments of God would plunge the soul into a state of discouragement and sadness? Would it not be dangerous to make them the subject of our ordinary meditations?*

A.—The consideration of the judgments of God has been esteemed so useful for sinners, both before and after their conversion, that nothing is more recommended by the holy Fathers, as we have already remarked in all we have said on the obligation by which every religious is bound to deplore his sins, and to live in a continual preparation for death. But in order to convince you entirely of a truth so essential, and so well calculated to assist you, and all those who, like you, are obliged to live in the practice of an exact piety, I will, moreover, add the following considerations.

Consider therefore, my brethren, that it is by the fear of the judgments of God that the Holy Spirit severally produces in the hearts of sinners the first thoughts and desires of conversion and salvation, that by it He stems the torrent of their iniquities, by it He prevents them, touches them, moves them, overthrows them; and, having filled them with terror, makes them in the excess of their fear, exclaim in the following words: "0 Lord, who understands the weight of thy indignation? and who can comprehend the extent of thy anger ?" (Ps. 89:11)

By it He leads them to the only means that can deliver them from the state of confusion and terror in which they groan, which is no other but that of hope in the Divine Mercy through the merits of Jesus Christ, by which He inspires them to rise with confidence.[425]

Hence, considering Him as their only refuge, by whom they may escape the dreadful tempest that threatens them, they must, by a necessary and inevitable consequence offer Him the first sentiments of acknowledgment and love, and regard in future all those actions with horror and detestation by which they had the misfortune to offend Him.[426]

Behold here, how much a sinner is indebted to the fear of God, and in what manner he receives the first rays of divine consolation, from the view and consideration of the judgments of the Lord.

But if this fear were so profitable in the beginning of his conversion, it will not be less advantageous, nor less necessary afterwards. It assisted him to recover the innocence he had lost; it will re-assist him to preserve it when found; and so far from disturbing the peace of his heart, as it is supposed, or veiling it under clouds and darkness, nothing will more effectually preserve its security and peace, nor more assuredly prevent him from losing its tranquility, or rather the charity of Jesus Christ, which is the living source of true peace and happiness.

It usually happens that souls who are converted to God from the broad road of the world, fall into discouragement in the progress, as well as in the beginning of their conversion; they find themselves oppressed with sadness and weariness, arising from the fear of not persevering, and from the doubt that the great number of faults of which they are guilty every hour may provoke the Lord to forsake them and draw back the assisting hand He had stretched out to them. This is the cause, more frequently than is imagined, from which the great anxiety springs, which for many days deprives religious souls (who are exempt from all great irregularities and enormous crimes) of their happiness, and of the consolations of the Holy Spirit. By this they are deprived of those ineffable delights, which the same Holy Spirit diffuses in the souls of those who persevere in His love, and carefully avoid everything that might displease Him.

If you inquire of that religious who bears the mournful aspect of

---

[425] "From the fear of divine justice whereby they are profitably agitated to consider the mercy of God, are raised unto hope." Council of Trent, *Session 6 on Justification*, Chapter 6.

[426] "And they begin to love Him as the fountain of all justice; and are therefore moved against sins by a certain hatred and detestation." Trent, *Justification*, Chpt. 6.

pain and discontent from whence his affliction proceeds; if he candidly acknowledge the cause, you will find that he is unhappy because he is unfaithful. He will confess that he is distracted in his prayers, dissipated in his exercises, subject to murmuring against his superior, impatient with his brethren; that he languishes in the service of God; that he is quick and active in such things as please his natural inclinations; immodest, frivolous, unmortified, always curious, ready to laugh at and to censure the conduct of others, and negligent in point of regulating his interior. In a word, he is weighed down with such a multitude of vicious habits, and irregular actions, that he makes bad use of the graces attached to his profession, and thus his soul is continually plunged in a sea of bitterness.

But if you are willing to deliver him from that evil state, to apply a speedy and effectual remedy to his disorders, persuade him to meditate on the justice of God, to live in a continual remembrance of His judgments; and frequently call to mind that nothing escapes His all-seeing eye, that He knows the number of our thoughts, words, and actions, and that every instant may be that in which He has resolved from all eternity to call us to an account.

This is an excellent means to awake his vigilance; to make him become more exact and attentive over his conduct, to excite his zeal and application in the observance of the law of God, and to regulate the smallest circumstances of his life. Nothing can more effectually lead him to a state of sublime purity and innocence, and fix his unsteady will in a just conformity to the holy will of God. Nothing, consequently, can more assuredly procure him liberty of spirit, peace and tranquility of soul. It will expel all that anxiety and affliction, which were the consequences of his negligence, sloth, or infidelity.

Q. 3.—May it not be said that this practice is profitable for those who only begin to walk in the way of perfection, but not for those who are already advanced?

A.—It is easy to show, my brethren, that it is useful for both the one and the other; for those who are advanced, and for those who begin; and that those who lead a solitary life find great advantages in it either to preserve the treasure they have already received by their vocation to religion, or to raise themselves to a more eminent perfection, until they finally attain to the state of consummate charity, wherein that chaste and holy fear—being seated on the throne of their hearts—shall expel the more servile fear of punishment, and establish its never-ending and delightful reign.

The means employed by the enemy to overcome those who give themselves up to God are different. He sometimes attacks them with violent temptations. At other times he endeavors to cast them into a state of insensible weakness and debility. And indeed I may affirm that in both cases the meditation of the judgments of God will furnish considerable strength to resist his attacks. It will animate them, encourage, and essentially contribute to enable them to keep their ground.

A religious is suddenly surprised by the rebellion of some malignant passion, which, like a violent tempest, threatens to overwhelm him. In this state it frequently happens that his love of God is not sufficiently ardent, its roots are not sufficiently deep in his heart. He is moved, the temptation becomes urgent. He begins to yield, for the hand of love is then too weak to sustain him, but that of fear comes into his assistance. It holds him suspended on the brink of the precipice and preserves him from a fall which would otherwise be inevitable. Thus the consideration of the judgments of God effects in those souls who are yet imperfect, what the motives of love cannot perform.

The same thing may be said of temptations which the enemy directs with a more slow and imperceptible effort, when by secret impressions of liberty, relaxation, indevotion, etc., he prepares the soul for the poison by which he intends to effect her ruin. For what more powerful antidote can be found to prevent the fatal consequences of his malice, than the view of that awful tribunal, where justice shall pronounce an irrevocable sentence conformable to the quality of the facts it shall have investigated? No, there is nothing better calculated, as we have already remarked—and as the saints declare—to dispel that lethargic disposition, that interior drowsiness, which sometimes produces enervation and a mortal insensibility in those who have advanced with the greatest vigilance and fervor.

The consideration and fear, therefore, of the judgments of God are means by which religious persons may effectually escape the snares which their enemies lay for them, resist the force of their attacks, and not only preserve the treasure of divine love in their souls, but by a good use of the same may considerably increase it.

The reason why divine love is so inactive in our souls, why its growth advances with so much difficulty, is, because its strength is impeded by the many obstacles with which its action is forced to contend. Our vices and evil habits are like so much filth that stops the conduits and fills the passages in such a manner that this pure celestial water, not finding its course free, is obliged to remain closed up, and thus cannot diffuse itself abundantly.

Now as the peculiar effect of fear is, according to Saint Basil, to maintain the soul, to bind it to an exact observance of the law, deterring it from doing anything it prohibits, so, in like manner—as the same saint teaches—it is impossible that he who keeps the remembrance of the judgments of God present to his mind should ever omit anything that the will of God prescribes.[427] Thus it is certain that fear opens the passages, removes every obstacle, and leads the soul on in the way by which she at last arrives to that state of perfect charity which banishes all fear.[428]

This has been at all times the sentiments and unanimous doctrine of the saints. One of the fathers of the first ages says that no one can love God with all the affection of his heart, unless he has first learned to fear Him with all the powers of his soul;[429] that fear purifies the soul, softens it, makes it become properly disposed for the exercise of charity; and that none but those who are no longer of this world, who have no part in its cares, can possess this fear; that fear united to imperfect love belongs to those who are yet in the purgative way; but that those who are entirely purified, enjoy perfect charity that casts out all fear.

He tells us that those words of the prophet: "Fear the Lord all ye His saints" (Ps 33:10), "Love the Lord all ye His saints" (Ps 30:24), are to be understood of the just; that fear is for those whose charity is weak, and that love is for those whose charity is perfect; that the fear of those whose love is weak is a fire that purifies them; and that it diminishes in proportion as charity increases: so that when love is perfect, fear retires, and the soul inflamed with heavenly ardor, and—stimulated by the operation of the Holy Spirit—is raised to an intimate union with God.

Saint Augustine teaches the same doctrine. He tells us that by the fear which withdraws the soul from offending God, we acquire the habit of justice; that we begin to love what seemed hard and difficult, and that we find sweetness in the service of Jesus Christ; that this fear is good and useful, though it is not that chaste fear that remains for ever and ever.[430]

Nevertheless, as it is perfect charity alone that casts out fear, and as no one suddenly passes from this fear to that perfect charity, but is raised to it by little and little, and as it were by different degrees, it necessarily follows that fear must exist in the same subject together with charity; that the latter must be supported by the former, and that it never forsakes its post

---

[427] Basilius, *Fusius*, PG 31:890 (1857).

[428] "Timore locum praeparat charitati." St. August. tract. 9.4 in epist. 1. Joan. / S. Augustinus, *In Epistolam Joannis ad Parthos*. PL 35:2047 (1845).

[429] Diadedec. de perfec. spirit 16&17. Bibliot. P. Tom 5.

[430] *In Ps 127*; S. Augustinus, PL 37:1680-1683 (1845).

until charity—having attained its full maturity—stands no longer in need of its assistance.

This is also what our holy legislator Saint Benedict teaches, when, having pointed out twelve degrees by which we may ascend to the perfection of our state, the first and last of which oblige us to preserve the fear of the judgments of God continually in our minds, he assures us that when we shall have ascended by those different degrees of mortification and penance, we shall then obtain the possession of that perfect charity that expels all fear; and we shall then begin to perform without difficulty— by a holy habit, and purely for the love of Jesus—what we did before only through the motive of fear.[431]

Saint Bernard was animated with the same sentiments. He tells us that he found nothing more effectual to recover grace, to preserve and increase it, than to walk before God at all times in humility, not in much knowledge, but in fear; and that the man who always fears is blessed: "Fear," says he, "when you possess grace, fear when you have lost it, and fear no less when you have found it again; let these three fears succeed one another continually."[432] Almighty God has inculcated these truths at all times, either by the holy scriptures, or by the example of His servants who were animated with His Holy Spirit. We find the utility and advantages of fear, and even its necessity, pointed out in many places of the Old Testament. We read in Ecclesiasticus (Ecclesiastic.33:1), that God sustains those who fear Him, in all their temptations, and preserves them from the dangers to which they are exposed; that he who fears God is blessed (Ecclesiastic. 34:17); that nothing shall move him, because the Lord is his hope (Ecclesiastic. 34:16).

Jesus Christ, in the new law, commands us to fear His judgments. When speaking to His apostles, He tells them : "I tell you who are my friends, and I will show you whom you ought to fear: Fear Him, who having killed, has power to cast into hell" (Luke 12:5). He calls them His friends, they had therefore His love, and yet He tells them to fear. And Saint Paul exhorts the faithful to work out their salvation with fear and trembling (Phil 2:12).

Were it necessary to add some examples, the sacred writings abound with them; but none are more remarkable than those of holy Job and the holy King David. Job, that man so irreproachable, that prodigy of holiness,

---

[431] RB 7:10 and 7:62

[432] Time ergo cum arriserit gratia, time cum abierit, time cum denuo revertetur. . . . Succedant vicissim sibi in animo tres isti timores ." Sermo LIV in *Cantica*, PL 183:1042d (1854). / *Canticles*, 2:124.

teaches the necessity of this virtue, when he informs us that his fear was so great and so continual that he considered the judgments of God like so many angry waves ready to burst every instant over his head; the idea only of which, was to him insupportable (Job 31:23).

Although the royal prophet was a faithful servant of God, and was a man according to his own heart, he nevertheless declares that he was continually penetrated with fear. He everywhere dreads the anger of God. He always joined the consideration of God's justice with that of His mercy. He prayed to the Lord to pierce his flesh with the fear of His judgment (Ps 118:120); and testifies in a great many places that his fear still subsisted—notwithstanding the greatness of his love—and that the fire of his charity was not as yet so strong as to consume it entirely.

Such were the dispositions of Saint Hilarion at his last moments, when he cried out: "Go forth my soul, why do you fear? You have served God now three score and ten years, and do you still fear to appear in his presence?" [433]

Saint Arsenius at the close of life felt impressed with the same fear, and having poured out many tears, those who were present inquired what might be the cause of his weeping, and whether he yet feared death. He answered that he feared it indeed, and that he always preserved that fear in his soul, since the time he first came into the desert.[434]

Hence, my brethren, never say to yourselves, on pretext of advancing by more noble, more sublime, or more pure ways, that meditation on the judgments of God is not useful or necessary for you; that it is better to walk in the paths of love than in those of fear; to wear the honorable dress of children, rather than the livery of slaves. I do not require that your fear should be dry, barren, and without love, by which you might indeed be deterred from vice and sin, but yet by which you would not efface the love and affection for it in your hearts, nor prevent your will from being inclined to commit it. But I require that while you dread that terrible arm which punishes crimes, that you adore the merciful hand that distributes rewards and crowns; that you keep in mind the remembrance of His goodness and justice; that your charity keep always in company with your

---

[433] "Egredere anima mea, quid times? Septuaginta annis servisti Deo, et adhuc times?" Vita. Pat. Sanct. Hilar. c.. 38. / S. Hieronymus, *Vita Hilarionis*. PL 23:52 (1845) / S..Jerome, Hilarion, 6:314

[434] Rufinus. *De Vitis Patrum*, Liber Tertius. In Vitae patrum. PL 73:794B (1849) / Ida Hahn-Hahn and John Dalgairns, *The Fathers of the Desert,* Vol. 1 (London: Burns, 1907), 231.

fear, as I have already said; that they combat both together; that they both stand out in your defense.

In fine, let your fear lead and excite your love, animate your affections, and fix them purely on Him whose grace alone can preserve you from the evils you behold, and without which your fears should be vain, barren, and unfruitful. Be careful never to imagine that your virtue is so perfect that you have no need of fear, lest you should deceive yourselves by rashly judging of your dispositions, and attributing to yourselves a perfection that you do not possess. Think with Saint Bernard, that if they who are the greatest before God nevertheless fear that judge whose ways are so unsearchable and profound; with how much more terror should not we— who are so miserable— be penetrated when we call to mind that future discussion on which our eternal lot depends.[435]

It is a rare thing to find persons whose piety is so accomplished that we may tell them you ought to fear nothing more. But it is common to behold many who have only a false, superficial, or at least, but a weak virtue, and who, nevertheless, live as securely as if they had nothing to fear and in whom, if their conduct were strictly examined, the marks of charity could no more be discovered, than those of fear.

Be assured, my brethren, that when you perceive that your passions are still alive, when you find the law of the senses revolting against the law of the spirit, you cannot be too powerfully assisted; neither will you deceive yourselves, if you arm your souls with fear, as well as with love, by considering both aspects of the judgments of God; that is to say, the severity of His justice as well as the sweetness of His mercy and love.

---

[435] Sermo XV, in *In Psalmum XC, Qui Habitat*, PL 183:246 (1854).

15

ON COMPUNCTION

QUESTION—Compunction is the last disposition by which, as you have already taught, a religious may attain the perfection of his state; but as you have spoken of it in so many places, does it not seem that you have anticipated all the questions we may propose relative to it ?

ANSWER.—Although I have said much concerning compunction, yet I will tell you besides, my brethren, that meditation on death and judgment produces compunction of heart, as fire produces heat and light. The consideration of these two important events is never dry or unfruitful; and it seems difficult how men can restrain their tears, if they duly consider such terrifying truths. A great saint once said, that if souls were mortal, they would die of fear at the view of the judgments of Christ. Indeed it is not possible that such a dreadful scene can be brought to mind by meditation without exciting all the powers of the soul, and making the most profound impression on the heart.

Saint Gregory Nazianzen tells us that the fear of judgment tormented him day and night, and almost deprived him of life,[436] and Saint Ephrem found no subject so well qualified to excite his contrition, and so efficacious in producing in his heart a sincere sorrow for his sins.[437]

I have told you many times that monks ought to pass their lives in mourning; that they are obliged to weep, not only for their own sins in

---

[436] S. Gregorius Theologus, Opera Omnia. PG 35:786 (1857) / S.Gregory Nazianzen. Select Orations of Saint Gregory Nazianzen. In S. Cyril of Jerusalem, S. Gregory Nazianzen, (NPNF2/7:237).

[437] S. Ephraem Syri, Sermo Asceticus et exhortatius ad Fratres, *Opera Omnia*, (Colonia: Quentelium, 1616), 487.

particular, but for the iniquities of the world in general; that their state is a profession of sorrow and compunction. I repeat that if monks knew how great their obligation is on this point, if they duly reflected on the account they must give to God, and on the advantages flowing from this holy disposition, they would continually beseech the Divine Goodness to bestow it on them abundantly. Their greatest grief would be that of not having sufficient sorrow to pour out torrents of tears every day of their lives.

Saint John Climacus says, that a religious will learn only at the end of life what advantages he shall have derived from his tears;[438] and we may be assured, that he shall then discover, but too late, the misfortune of not having sufficiently wept for his sins while he had time. Then he shall behold the greatness of his evils, but will be no longer in a state to remove them. His too late repentance will be unprofitable. Alas! if he have lived in a manner unworthy of his state, the worm of conscience will then prey upon him, and shall never cease to torment his unrelenting heart. Moreover, the anger which shall arise from the views of his misfortune will produce in his soul nothing but rage and despair, according to the words of the prophet: "The sinner shall see and be angry, he shall gnash with his teeth and be silent"(Ps. 111:10).

These were the sentiments of all holy monks who understood perfectly the responsibilities attached to their state. They considered religious as persons who were obliged to live in a holy affliction, either because they were bound to meditate continually on death, or because being by their condition public penitents, nothing seemed to be more proper to their character than compunction of heart.

Saint Anthony speaking to his brethren said,

Afflict yourselves night and day for your sins; fold yourselves up, and cover yourselves day and night in your robes and tunics. Never elevate yourselves, never laugh; and let the weeping for your sins be like the lamentation of those who bewail the dead . Let your countenance be always stamped with the mark of your interior sorrow, unless when you are visited by some one of your brethren.[439]

We read, that Saint Macarius being come from Skete to the mountain

---

[438] *Scala*, PG 88:810 (1864) / *Ladder*, 115.

[439] In sua regula, 25.30.47 / S. Antonius Abbas, Regula Monachorum, XXV, XXX, XLVII. PL 103:426, 427 (1851).

of Nitria, at the request of the solitaries who desired to receive some instruction from his mouth before his death, would say nothing more to them than these few words:

> Let us weep, my brethren, and let our eyes pour out abundance of tears, before the time comes in which we may find ourselves in that place, where our tears, so far from being a refreshment to our bodies, (being all of fire) shall serve only to afflict and torment them.[440]

A solitary seeing another laugh, said to him: "Why do you laugh, brother, seeing that we are to give an account of our whole lives to the Lord of heaven and earth?"

Saint Isaias exhorted his disciples to a continual sadness, but at the same time told them to assume a more serene countenance when any of the brethren came to visit them, in order, said he, to show that you fear the Lord. Never allow yourselves to laugh, said the same saint, for that would prove that your souls are divested of the fear of God.[441]

The holy abbot Pastor, having found a woman on his way who wept over a grave, made this reflection :— "Were all the pleasures of the world offered to this woman, she would not interrupt the course of her tears. In like manner, a solitary ought never to interrupt his weeping and tears."[442]

Saint Ammon being requested by a solitary to give him some instruction, answered him as follows:

> Be always like those criminals who are in prison, who weep continually, and who inquire of all those who visit them, Where is the judge? When shall he come? In like manner, a solitary ought to live in a state of continual expectation, loading himself with accusations and reproaches, until our Lord Jesus Christ comes to judge him.[443]

---

[440] "Vidit senex quemdam ridentem, et dicit ei: Coram coeli et terrae Domino rationem totius vitam nostrae reddituri sumus, et tu rides? " PL 73:864 (1849)..

[441] St. Isaias Abbas, *Regula ad Monachos.* In S. Benedicti Aniani Opera Omnia. PL 103:429D,430b (1851).

[442] De Vitis Patrum, Liber V, auctore Graeco incerto, interprete Pelagio Diacono, Libellus III, v. 11. PG 73:862 (1849) / online: http://www.vitae-patrum.org.uk/page80.html

[443] Heriberti Rosweyde, S.J. *De Vitis Patris,* PL 73:860C (1849) / Owen Chadwick, The Sayings of the Fathers, in Western Asceticism, (Philadelphia, Westminster, 1958), 43.

Saint Ephrem was so convinced of this that he says that the ruin of a solitary begins with laughing with impunity; that laughter and licentiousness destroy the good works of a religious; that laughter destroys the beatitude of mourning and affliction; that laughter scandalizes, that it overturns the spiritual edifice, grieves the Holy Spirit, injures the soul, corrupts the heart, and expels virtue from it. "O Lord! " cries out that great saint, "take from me laughter, and give me sighs and mourning."[444]

Saint Basil says:

Since Jesus Christ in His gospel condemns those who now laugh (Luke 6:25), it is evident that a true Christian can never find a moment in his whole life, in which he may give himself the liberty to laugh, and more particularly, when he reflects on the great number of persons who continually offend the Divine Majesty by violating His holy law. [445]

He says in another place, with Saint Gregory Nazianzen:

A religious ought to banish from his conversation all raillery and facetiousness . It is impossible to preserve the vigilance of the soul when we allow ourselves the liberty of being diffuse in pleasant discourse and facetious words. If we are sometimes obliged to relax a little this austere gravity, our conversation ought to be replete with grace and spiritual cheerfulness. It must be seasoned with the salt of evangelical wisdom, so that our conduct may thereby diffuse the good odor of virtue and holiness.[446]

"Do you laugh," says Saint John Chrysostom,

You who profess the monastic state? You who are crucified: you laugh, who are obliged to weep! Tell me where have you read, that Jesus Christ ever laughed? Have you even heard it? Undoubtedly not, but on the contrary you may have read that He was sad and wept.[447]

---

[444] S. Ephraem Syri, Non Esse Ridendum sed Lugendum Potius atque Plorandum, in Opera Omnia (Cologne, Quentel, 1603), 104-106.

[445] S. Basilius, Brevius, PG 31:1103 (1857).

[446] S. Basilius, Constitutiones,PG 31:1375 (1857).

[447] "Qui monachum profiteris, qui crucifixus es, qui deves lugere, rides? Dic mihi ubi Christus hoc fecit?" Hom. 15 in Epist. ad Heb. / S. Joannes Chrysostomus. Homiliae XXXIV in *Epistolam ad Hebraeos,* PG 63:339-340 (1860).

"Rejoice not, O Israel," says Saint Nilus, "give yourselves not to joy, like the nations who know not God; for, being separated from God, you ought to weep."[448]

Saint Jerome says, that the state of a monk is a state of tears; that he ought to weep continually for himself or for the world, and await the coming of Jesus Christ in fear and trembling.[449]

Saint John Climacus says:

> A true religious, being profoundly afflicted in his soul with the salutary sadness of penance, is always occupied with the thoughts of death. He never stems the cause of his tears, nor ceases to send forth profound and secret moans, until, like another Lazarus, he beholds the face of his Redeemer who comes to him, removes from his heart the stain of obduracy, and delivers him from the bonds of his sins.[450]

He says:

> Religious ought not to imitate those, who after having buried the dead, sometimes weep over their tombs, and sometimes rejoice.[451] We have not, says he, been called to the religious solitary life as to a feast or a wedding; but we are called by Jesus Christ to weep for ourselves.[452] Criminals have no days of mirth in prison; nor have true solitaries any days of festivity or human consolation on earth.[453]

We read that Arsenius wept so constantly that he held a pocket-handkerchief always near him to wipe his eyes.[454]

Saint Benedict enjoins that his disciples should always keep their eyes cast down and their heads inclined, reflecting that they have offended God by their sins, considering themselves always as criminals ready to be

---

[448] Vit. Pat

[449] Hieronymis, Contra Vigilantium, PL 23:367; "But, indeed, a monk's function is not to teach, but to lament; to mourn either for himself or for the world, and with terror to anticipate our Lord's advent." Jerome, Letters, 6:423.

[450] Scala, PG 88:644 (1864). / Ladder, 54.4.6.

[451] Scala, PG 88:806a (1864). / Ladder 112.13.

[452] Scala, PG 88:806b (1864). / Ladder, 113.16.

[453] Scala, PG 88:810c (1864). / Ladder, 115.38.

[454] Vitae Patrum, PL 73:807 (1849); Richard Challoner, The Wonders of God in the Wilderness, (London: Needham, 1755), 173.

presented before the awful tribunal of Christ, and with tears confessing the multitude and variety of their crimes. The same saint condemns and specially prohibits the use of all words which might excite jesting, laughter, or dissipation, and which would, in time, completely destroy interior recollection and holy compunction.[455]

"Fly laughter, my dear sister, as an error," says Saint Leander in his rule,

> And separate yourself from all transitory joys; change them into mourning, that you may rejoice in heaven, after having wept in this world like a stranger, since they who weep, according to God, shall be comforted. He wept over himself like a stranger, who said in the bitterness of his grief: Woe to me that my exile is prolonged (Ps 119:5). Your heavenly spouse will receive you into the arms of His mercy, and comfort you with His presence if He perceive that you ardently desire to behold Him, and that with tears you lament His absence.[456]

Saint Fastredus teaches that a religious is charged with his own sins, and with those of the people, and that this two-fold obligation binds him to a continual weeping.[457]

Pope Eugenius says that the word monk signifies both alone and sad. Let him therefore, he adds, remain in sadness and repose, that he may fulfill his duty.[458]

Hence, let monks say what they please in order to conceal the true idea of their state from themselves as well as from others, the true portrait of a solitary religious will never be any other but that which is verified by those words of the prophet:

> He whose soul is afflicted and dejected, and who bends under the weight of his sins, the light of whose eyes is almost extinct with his abundant weeping, and who continually sighs after thy mercy; he only, O Lord, can give glory to thy holy name, and satisfy thy divine justice (Baruch 2:18).

---

[455] *RB* 7.62, 7.60.

[456] Cap 1, Reg / S. Leandrus, *Regula sive Libellus de institutione virginum et de contemptu mundi ad Florentinam sororem*, PL 72:886 (1849)

[457] In Epist. Fast. Inter oper. S. Bernard / Epistola CDXCI Fastredi Abbatis Clarae-vallensis Tertii Ad Quemdam Ordinis Sui Abbatem. PL 182:706B (1854).

[458] "Sedeat tristis, ex officio vacet." Decret. P. 2, Causa XVI, Q. 1.; *Decretum Gratiani*, PL 187:993A.(1861)

Shall we not therefore conclude from such convincing proofs of the uninterrupted tradition and unanimous consent of so many saints on this subject, that the joys of this world are no longer the inheritance of monks; that its sports, laughter, facetious expressions, and everything that savors of human mirth is not lawful for them;[459] that their daily food ought to be seasoned with holy compunction; that their lives must be a continual mourning; and if they cannot at all times exhibit exterior marks of this holy sadness, they ought to preserve it constantly in the interior sentiments of their hearts, demonstrate it in all their actions, and never give anyone occasion to believe that they have forgotten an obligation so essential to their state.

Therefore, my brethren, let me exhort you, to attend to these instructions in a profitable manner. Weep now for a few moments so that you may deserve hereafter to live in eternal joys. Bathe your faces continually in the bitter waters of penance. Be solicitous only to pour out tears abundantly, and leave to God the care of drying them up. The time will come when He will calm your sighs, wipe away all your tears, and change your sorrow into never-ending consolation and joy. "God shall wipe away all tears from their eyes, and death shall be no more, nor mourning, nor weeping, nor shall sorrow be any more, because the former things are passed away" (Apoc 21:4). Carefully avoid everything that might dry up the source of your tears; let no dissipation enter into your employments, or affairs that might destroy your sorrow and compunction; but, on the contrary, call in to your assistance everything that may nourish and preserve it.

"Let the position of your body, when you are extended on your couch remind you, " says Saint John Climacus,

> Of the form it will take when laid in the grave. When you are sitting at table, let the food you are eating help to put you in mind of that dismal table where your own bodies shall be served up as food for worms; and let the water you drink assist you to think on the cruel thirst that shall eternally torment the damned, in the midst of unquenchable flames.

---

[459] Editor: From Geoffrey of Auxerre's biography of St. Bernard: "But as for laughter, we can only repeat what we often heard him say in puzzled response to outbursts of it from those professing religion. As best he could recall, from his earliest conversion onward, it had always cost him more effort to laugh than to avoid it, for his laughter needed less a bridle than a spur." In *Bernard of Clairvaux: Early Biographies by William of St. Thierry, Geoffrey of Auxerre and Others* (Carlton, Oregon: Guadalupe Translations, 2012), 91.

Let the severe humiliations and reprehensions by which your superior proves your virtue recall to your thoughts the terrible sentence that the sovereign judge will one day pronounce over the wicked, and which shall be followed with dreadful and eternal execution. Let even the habit of religion that you wear excite you to weep. Being a penitential habit, it ought at every moment remind you of your sins. In fine, say to the Lord, with the same sincerity as His prophet did: "O Lord, my God, my sighs issue from my breast with such violence, that they may be compared to the roarings of a lion (Ps. 37:9)."

Cry out to yourselves, like Saint Ephrem:

Be pierced with grief, O my soul, for the unprofitable use you have made of all the favors you have received from the divine goodness, for all the evil you have committed, and for the many occasions to which you exposed yourself, and in which His amiable providence watched over you and supported your ingratitude with such astonishing patience.

If, after all this, your insensibility is so great that you are not yet moved; if it can resist such powerful motives and such piercing considerations; weep because you cannot weep, and press your heart so effectually, that you may at last force from it, as from a rock, those tears of compunction, which you cannot draw forth from a more tender spring.

Index of Images

Page 21. Saint Benedict, ca. 1640–45 by Francisco de Zurbarán.

Page 28, St. Isidore de Peluse. M. Ceroni in Marin, *Les Vies,* Tome III, frontispiece.

Page 34. Religieuses de Syria. 44. Marin, *Les vies,* Tome V (Paris, L. Vives, 1864), 44.

Page 44. S. Romaine Anacorete by Math. Elyas with inscription, "Je suis attache a la croix avec Jesus-Christ. Gal. 2:19." Villefore, in *Plates from Villefore's Vies des SS. Pères des déserts, (a book so designated by a curator at Hathitrust as it has no publication information),* 209.

Page 52. Monks working at La Trappe, Villefore, *Plates*, 514 .

Page 59. S. Macaire d' Alexandrie. Villefore, *Les vies,* Tome I, 126

Page 63. S. Hilarion. Villefore, *Les vies,* Tome I, 30.

Page 69. Monks in choir, Villefore, *Les vies,* Tome IV (Amsterdam, P. Brunel, 1719), 416.

Page 74. Monks talking at Sept Fons, Villefore, *Plates,* 522.

Page 80. S. Euloge Pretre, Villefore, *Les vies,* Tome I, 98.

Page 82. Saint Bruno, 1764 by Jean Bernard Restout.

Page 85. The Virgin Appearing at Mass, Agostino Masucci 1692–1758.

Page 87. St. Theresa Kneeling in Prayer, 1661. Claude Mellan.

Page 89. The Virgin Adoring the Host, 1852 by Jean Auguste Dominique Ingres.

Page 98. Draconce, Eveque et Solitaire by M. Ceroni. Marin, *Les vies.* Tome II, 370.

Page 221. S. Pierre de Galatie. M. Ceroni in Marin, *Les vies,* Tome IV, 381

Page 234. Saint Teresa.

Page 241. S. Antoine in Villefore, *Les vies,* Tome I, 22.

Page 250. Crucifixion of Jesus 1866 by Gustave Doré. Wood engraving drawn by Gustave Doré, engraved by J. Gauchard Brunier. Printed in: Heilige Schrift 1867 by Stuttgarter Druck- und Verlagshaus Eduard Hallberger.

Page 261. Saint Macedoine, Marin, Michel-Ange, 1697-1767. *Les vies des pères des déserts d'orient : leur doctrine spirituelle et leur discipline monastique.* Tome IV, (Paris, L. Vivès, 1869),

Page 279. Saint Siméon l'ancien by M. Ceroni. Marin, Les vies, Tome IV, 402.

Page 283. Monks in the Desert, 1797. Jean Jacques de Boissieu.

Page 287. The Abbot, from The Dance of Death, ca. 1526, published 1538. Designed by Hans Holbein the Younger.

Page 291. The Death of Saint Anthony, surrounded by saints on his deathbed,1649. Peeter Clouwet.

Page 294. Saint Hilary Dying, M. Elyas in Villefore, *Les Vies,,* Tome Premier, (Paris: Marriette, 1715), 42.

Page 307. Christ on the Cross with the Virgin and Saints Longinus, Mary Magdalen and John, 1505, Hans Baldung (called Hans Baldung Grien).

Page 316. The Last Communion of St. Mary Magdalen, after Benedetto Lutti, ca. 1761–64. Louis Jean Jacques Durameau.

Page 325. Assumption of the Virgin, Merry Joseph Blondel 1822.

Index of Scriptural Citations

Image Credits:

The frontispiece and the images on pages XXVII, 13, 59, 63, 69, 80, 118, 155, 190, 212, are from Joseph François Bourgoin de Villefore, 1652-1737, *Les vies des ss. Peres de déserts, et des saintes solitaires d'Orient et d 'occident,* Tomes 1-4 (Amsterdam, P. Brunel, 1714). The image at page 293 is found Villefore, *Les vies,* Tome I, (Paris: Marriette, 1715), page 42. The images on pages 44, 514 and 74 are from *Plates from Villefore's Vies des SS. Pères des déserts,* Per Hathitrust all this material is in the public domain and Google-digitized.

Images on pages 18, 28, 34, 98, 178, 199, 219, 260, 278 are found in the public domain and Google-digitized at https://catalog.hathitrust.org/Record/008976292 from Michel-Ange Marin, 1697-1767, *Les vies des pères des déserts d'orient:leur doctrine spirituelle et leur discipline monastique,* Tomes 1-6 (Paris, L. Vivès, 1869).

Images on pages 2, 9, 21, 82, 85, 87, 89, 111, 172, 188, 283, 287, 291, 306, 315 and 324 are found on the open access page on the Metropolitan Museum of Art site, https://www.metmuseum.org. The image on page III is the frontispiece of F. Vacandard, *Vie de Saint Bernard, abbé de Clairvaux,* (Paris, V. Lecoffre, 1910); the image on page VIII is from fom the fronstispiece of *Dom Vincent of Mount Melleray* (Dublin, M.H. Gill and Son Limited, 1962) and per correspondence with that company is in the public domain; the image on page 107 is in the public domain in the United States and Google digitized; the image on page 136 is a 17th c. portrait from Wikimedia Commons (https://commons.wikimedia.org/wiki/Category:Ana_de_Jes%C3%BAs?uselang=fr); the image on page 233 is from https://commons.wikimedia.org/wiki/Teresa_of_%C3%81vila; the image on page 266 is from Wikicommons: https://commons.wikimedia.org/wiki/File:Gustave_Dor%C3%A9_-_Crucifixion_of_Jesus.jpg. The image on page 249 is found at https://commons.wikimediaorg/wiki/File:Gustave_Dor%C3%A9_-_Crucifixion_of_Jesus.jpg.

In religious life a man lives more purely, falls more rarely, rises more quickly, walks more cautiously, receives more graces , rests more securely, dies more confidently, is purified more quickly and in Heaven receives a greater reward.

Saint Bernard of Clairvaux

Made in the USA
Monee, IL
07 February 2021